EYEWITNESS
THE
WHO

This is a Carlton Book

This edition published by Carlton Books Limited 2001
20 Mortimer Street
London W1N 3JW

ISBN 1 84222 307 0

Design: Adam Wright
Picture research: Faye Parish
Production: Alastair Gourlay

THE DAY-BY-DAY STORY

Told through eyewitness accounts by friends, family and fellow musicians

Contents

PICTURE CREDITS

The publishers would like to thank the following sources for their kind permission to reproduce the pictures in this book.

London Features International/1, 2, 3, 5, 6, 8, 9, 11
Pictorial Press: 4, 10/ Jeffrey Mayer 16
Ronald Grant Archive/12
Topham Picture Point/13
Corbis/Neal Preston 14

Every effort has been made to acknowledge correctly and contact the source and copyright holder of each picture, and Carlton Books Limited apologizes for any unintentional errors or omissions which will be corrected in future editions of this book.

Introduction

This is a unique telling of the story of The Who – unique because every word is spoken by someone who was there as the story was unfolding. There is no journalistic intrusion into the story. It's also a complete chronicle of The Who's lives and career – as near as possible to a day-by-day log of every significant event from the births of the original band members through to the tragic death of drummer Keith Moon.

This is genuine eyewitness recollection – the story of The Who in the words of those who watched it unfold. Virtually every word in this book was spoken or written by someone who was in the presence of The Who as it happened.

As well as library research, numerous interviews with band members, friends and associates have benn specially conducted for the book. The quotes have been edited to ensure the story runs smoothly, resulting in a compelling read, with quotes frequently taken from more than one source interview, then combined to create a more coherent and complete account.

This unique method of telling the story vividly brings to life the excitement, creativity and unpredictability that surrounded the diverse characters who lived, loved and fought together as The Who.

AUTHOR

Johnny Black writes every month in the UK's most highly regarded rock publications, *Q* and *Mojo*. He has also written for *The Times, Sunday Times, Observer*, and other publications as diverse as *Smash Hits* and *Radio Times*. As a broadcaster, he has worked for BBC Radio 4 and Classic FM. He contributed to the *Guinness Encyclopaedia of Popular Music* and wrote the popular music section of the *Oxford Children's Encyclopaedia*. Having worked for CBS and Polygram as a press officer, he has insight into both the creative and business aspects of the music industry. His first rock book, *Eyewitness Hendrix*, is rapidly turning into an ongoing series.

This book is dedicated to Jonathon Green and Danny Kelly, who between them put me on the path to writing books like this.

1925

July 1925

10. Indian mystic Meher Baba begins 43 years of total silence. In due course, Baba's teaching will profoundly influence the life and work of Pete Townshend.

1934

June 1934

11. Christopher Sebastian Lambert is born. As UK rock entrepreneur Kit Lambert, he will manage The Who, found Track Records and much more.

Roger Daltrey: Kit's father was a very famous English composer and he started the Covent Garden opera house. His name is Constant Lambert, so Kit was educated in classical music. He was an incredibly intellectual man. He loved pop music! He loved pop singles, he loved rock'n'roll.

1944

March 1944

1. Birth of Roger Harry Daltrey, vocalist with The Who, in Hammersmith, London.

October 1944

9. John Entwistle, bassist with The Who, is born in Chiswick, London.

Pete Townshend: John was a great friend to me in the very early days. John and I always knew we would be famous, even at 13 years old, and made careful plans to marry cute girls and buy lots of guitars.

1945

May 1945

19. Peter Dennis Blanford Townshend, guitarist with The Who, born in Chiswick Hospital, London.

Pete Townshend: I grew up with parents who came out of the end of the war with a great resilience, excitement, and big ideas, and I got a bit left behind for a while.

I never had any lessons as such. My mother and father were both in the music business. My father had a dance band called The Squadronaires that used to be an Air Force band like The Glenn Miller Band. And I used to travel with them a lot before I went to school, and in fact I travelled with the band until I was about seven and so I got an early taste of the road.

There wasn't much music at home except for my dad practising his clarinet in the back room. We didn't have a very good record player and we had a shitty radio and there was no piano in the house. And the only music I enjoyed until I was 11 was mouth organ.

I had a very strange relationship with my mother. She was very beautiful and married a good-looking man, then had this very ordinary kid. She was loving, but I could sense her confusion and disappointment. I somehow failed to interest her once I stopped being a baby.

My parents split when I was very young, and I was sent to live with my grandmother, who had just been dumped by a very wealthy lover. She was in mid-life crisis. She was my age today, and I identify very much with this woman who had to look after me. She ran naked in the streets and stuff like that. She was completely nuts. She was a very strict woman and I hated her. I wanted my mum and dad back. I had two years with her before my parents realized they'd left me with somebody that was insane.

1946

August 1946

23. Birth of Keith John Moon, drummer for The Who, in Central Middlesex Hospital, Wembley, Middlesex.

1951

September 1951

Keith Moon starts school at Barham Primary School, London.

Linda Moon (sister of Keith Moon): The teachers all loved Keith, because he was a loveable kid.

Keith Cleverdon (school friend): He was always getting in trouble, laughing and joking and farting. Even then he couldn't give a shit. He just had that attitude – "I go to school and if I don't learn anything, who gives a toss anyway?"

1955

Pete Townshend: I was in the Sea Scouts – sort of the nautical equivalent of the Boy Scouts. One day, when I was about 10 years old, we went out for a ride in a boat with an old, rusty outboard motor on the back. As we bobbed along in the water, the engine made these funny *noises*. By the time we had gone up the river and back again, I had to be carried off. I was in a trance of ecstasy. When they turned the outboard motor off, I broke down – I actually physically broke down. At some point in the journey I had gone off into a trance. I began hearing the most incredible sounds – angelic choirs and celestial voices. What I heard was unbelievably beautiful. I've never heard music in my imagination like it since. But I've always realized the potential for sounds to ignite my imagination like that. To this day, I'm a bit scared to let a sound take me that far.

October 1955

10. When the movie *Blackboard Jungle*, featuring "Rock Around The Clock" by Bill Haley & The Comets, opens in the UK, Pete Townshend is taken to see it by his father.

Pete Townshend: We had seats in the gallery at the very back of the old Odeon Marble Arch, and the walls rumbled and the floor moved.

A chill ran up my spine as I heard the native rhythms. I looked round at my father and I said, "What is this amazing music?" He said, "Hmm, not bad." And that was really all.

My grounding in music was trad jazz and a bit of classical thrown in after listening to my dad's orchestra, and then suddenly the miracle of rock'n'roll, in the shape of Bill Haley, Cliff, and Elvis. Rock'n'roll got to my blood as a new form.

1956

Pete Townshend: I met John Entwistle the first year of high school.

John Entwistle: He [Townshend] was much smaller then. I guess when I met Pete we were about 12. I think he actually grew another six inches when he left school. I just remember him having a good sense of humour. So he joined the comedy clique that we had together. Basically, the same people who used to sit and make up jokes all day – or stand and make up jokes – became our first band, The Scorpions. But we had no sting in our tail.

May 1956

11. "Heartbreak Hotel" by Elvis Presley enters the UK singles chart, where it will peak at No. 2.

Pete Townshend: Actually, it was the church that led me to rock'n'roll. I used to visit what was called the Congo Club – the Congregational Church Youth Club – which was very much like the bit in *Tommy*: The minister comes into the clubhouse where all the kids are going wild. He looks around and asks, "What's happening here, boys and girls? Good. Carry on." What was actually going on was that lots of 15-year-old girls were getting their brains fucked out on the pool table in the back room. And in the dark room we were playing the pop records of the day, pre-rock'n'roll Bobby Darin, Paul Anka, Neil Sedaka. Then suddenly it wasn't Bobby Darin any more, it was Elvis Presley. I went cold. I remember hearing "Heartbreak Hotel" and thinking, What the fuck is that? Then my father took me to a Bill Haley concert. I was hooked.

December 1956

25. For Christmas, Pete Townshend is given his first guitar by his grandmother.

Pete Townshend: My father was going to buy me a guitar for Christmas, and he would have bought me a fabulous instrument. But what happened is that she bought it! She bought me one like you see on the wall of a Spanish restaurant, a phony guitar. I was excited for a while, standing in front of the mirror, but I realized very quickly that I was never going to be able to play anything on it. My father said, "Well, let's see what happens." So I struggled with this fucking instrument for two years.

I realized the only way I was ever going to fit into society and have a role was via the guitar. I really did think this. I thought I'll go and shut myself in my room and I'll learn the guitar. And when I come out they'll want me.

1957

Pete Townshend: When we were 13, I met Roger. He was threatening me with a belt buckle because he'd beaten up a friend of mine on the playground and I shouted that he was a dirty fighter because he kicked the guy when he was on the ground. Roger came over to me and said, "Who called me a dirty fighter?" And I said, "I didn't." And he said, "Yes, you did." And he got his belt off and went to whip it across my face. I should have taken it as a sign.

"Mack" McMahon (caretaker, Acton County Grammar School): Townshend was a good kid, quiet like. He and that Entwistle lad used to go around together. Friends, you might say. They all wore their school uniforms. But Daltrey, he had to be different, didn't he? He rolls up to have his school photo taken in his teddy boy suit. The headmaster didn't think much of that, I can tell you.

1958

Townshend smashes his first guitar.

Pete Townshend: John Entwistle and I were rehearsing together in the front room of my house. My grandmother came in shouting, "Turn that bloody racket down!" I said, "I'll do better than that," and I got my guitar – this was a good guitar that I had paid for myself with money I earned from a paper route – and smashed it to smithereens. I said, "Now will you fucking get out of my life?" and she stomped out.

I looked at John and said, "What now?" And he said, "Another paper route, I think." Once I had done it, it was always there as a possibility. If ever I wanted to deal with any kind of hidden rage, I could always take it out on the guitar. I could always trigger the same little bit of psychotherapy.

1959

At Acton County Grammar School, Pete and John form The Confederates.

Pete Townshend: We formed a traditional jazz band, which grew out of a marching band. We used to take it around the pubs during holidays to make money. At the same time we also had a kind of Shadows or Ventures type of band with another guy from school, with John on bass, me on rhythm guitar, a lead guitar player and a drummer.

1960

Townshend develops his guitar-playing skills.

Pete Townshend: I could learn records in a couple of days, and I was playing the same licks as the guy on the LP. That gave me satisfaction for a little while, and then I thought, "Why am I bothering to copy this guy who can only really play as well as I can?" Then I started going beyond that.

I'd become aware that there were little girls giggling and pointing at me nose. And I'd think, "Sod 'em, they're not gonna laugh at me." I'd get angrier still. . . most pop singers were pretty, but I wanted people to look at my body and not bother looking at my head if they didn't like the look of it. So I used to think, "I'll bloody well show them. I'll push me huge hooter out at them from every newspaper in England. Then they won't laugh at me."

1961

Pete's brother Simon Townshend is born.

Pete Townshend: My parents split up briefly, and I went to live with my grandmother. Then they got back together and I was back with them, and it was a very pleasant time. Finally, when I was 12 they had my first brother, Paul, then soon after that, Simon. I loved them and doted on them, but I always looked for older boys to hang around. If not older boys, certainly boys who were more emotionally equipped than I was.

November 1961

5. Keith Moon and his friend Gerry Evans attend a Guy Fawkes Night bonfire in Queensbury, London.

Gerry Evans: Of course, he was the guy who ran through the bonfire. And he was the guy who let off all the bangers behind the girls. And the next week, all my neighbours said, "Who's that little bloke? He's a complete nutcase, did you see what he did?" So I was always going round apologizing for him.

1962

Mid-1962

Pete Townshend joins West London band The Detours, led by Roger Daltrey.

Pete Townshend: He came up to me in the corridor at school and I thought, "Oh, my God, what is he going to do to me this time?" He was a horrible, horrible boy. A real kind of spiv, you know? But he said, "I hear you play the guitar." I nodded, and he said, "My house. Tonight. Seven-thirty." I was secretly quite delighted.

Roger Daltrey: Contrary to what some people seem to think, I was never a bully. I was just a hard man. I seem to have read somewhere recently where Pete suggested that the first time he met me I punched him in the nose at school. Well, that quite honestly is not true. I met Pete first when he came to one of our rehearsals with a guitar. I saw him at school, he was a character. You could hardly miss him. But he loves to make those kinds of stories up and we have had a lot of fights in the past and I did used to rule the band with an iron fist.

Pete Townshend: On my way to my first rehearsal, I saw a beautiful blonde girl running towards me. She was weeping and my adolescent heart went out to her. For a second, I faltered because she was approaching me. "Are you going to Roger Daltrey's house?" she demanded. I proudly confirmed her suspicions. "Well then," she sputtered, "you can tell him it's either me or that guitar of his." She then burst into tears again and flounced off into the night. As far as I could project, it was quite clear that The Detours were finished, and I popped along to Roger's to let him know I didn't mind, and would probably be quite happy to be back at Sea Scouts. But Roger chose his guitar, and the first rehearsal went well, with no mention of the pretty girl, whom I never saw again.

July 1962

The Detours play three gigs at The Paradise Club, Peckham, South London.

Pete Townshend: Roger was really the balls of the band, and ran things the way he wanted. If you argued with him you usually got a bunch of fives. It was good in a way because every band needs someone in that strong, pushy role.

Roger Daltrey: When the group started, I was a shit singer. They didn't need a singer in those days anyway. They needed somebody who could fight, and that was me.

Betty Townshend (Pete's mother): I used to ride them around in a little yellow van and cart all their gear about. I helped as much as I could because I could see the potential. I used to hear them upstairs making all that noise. I told Cliff, "I'm going to try to help them because the only way of gettin' rid of them is to help them." Seeing that they don't live here forever.

I didn't hang around and wait for them, though. Mainly I used to deliver the goods, come home, and then go back and pick them and the gear up. Very seldom did I want to stay with the noise.

I got in touch with all the people I knew in the business, and practically all of them gave them jobs.

September 1962

1. The Detours play at Acton Town Hall, West London.

Roger Daltrey: We went on to play blues, but when we first started, it was pure chart music. And then it was Del Shannon, the Everly Brothers, and Johnny Kidd & The Pirates, Johnny Cash. Johnny Cash was kind of a stepping stone to the blues. Again, Johnny Cash spoke to us. This was a guy who understood us.

Late 1962

Keith Moon plays his first gig with The Beachcombers, as support to Cliff Bennett & The Rebel Rousers, at the Fender Club, Kenton.

Norman Mitchener (guitarist, Beachcombers): He was good, he was loud. He had something in his playing. His snare work was heavy and it was drivey.

He strived to be the centre. He was flamboyant, he was extrovert. You had to give him credit, he worked really hard at being a showman. People used to come just to see him.

November 1962

23. The Detours play their first engagement for influential West London promoters Bob Druce and Barry Foran of Commercial Entertainments Ltd, at the Grand Ballroom, Broadstairs, Kent.

Pete Townshend: We used to supplement our regular money from the Druce gigs by doing weddings and things. At the end of the evening, you'd get some bloke come up pissed as a rat, determined to spend as much money as possible on his daughter's wedding. "You were great, lads," he'd say. "Here's fifty quid."

30. The Detours play at the Grand Ballroom, Broadstairs, Kent.

Roger Daltrey: It used to be a bloody nightmare. John, Pete and I used to go with Betty. Pete would sit in front with her, and we used to lie on top of the gear in the back of a five-hundredweight van with the roof about three inches from our heads all the way to Broadstairs.

December 1962

27. The Beatles' first single, "Love Me Do", peaks at No. 17 in the UK charts.

John Entwistle: When The Beatles came along, Roger switched to singer because the other singer had left ,'cause he and Roger were always fighting and Pete, who had been on rhythm, was switched to lead. But he was still basically a rhythm guitarist, always has been.

We played Beatles stuff and so on until we discovered rhythm and blues. Pete was going to art school and got to know about John Lee Hooker and so on. We knew we wouldn't get anywhere playing the other stuff, so we switched to this until all the other groups, The Yardbirds and The Downliners Sect, got hold of it.

Pete Townshend: I had a natural artistic bent, which was why I ended up at art school. I should have done something with writing, I suppose, but if I had I probably wouldn't have ended up so open-endedly creative as I later became.

1963

January 1963

4. The Detours play at the Grand Ballroom, Broadstairs, Kent.

Pete Townshend: The group was doing okay. We were doing five gigs a week in pubs and getting twelve quid a night split four or five ways. It would be blasphemous to say it was tough. We were young and enthusiastic. Actually, I think it's tougher now I'm a so-called millionaire. I find it troublesome leaping 20 feet across the stage getting housemaid's knees. No, I don't remember it being tough at all. I hated the long journeys, but one gets used to that.

11. The Detours play at the Fox & Goose Hotel, Ealing, West London.

John Entwistle: We played five nights a week after work. We'd play everything. We'd open with a few guitar numbers, then Pete would play the one-finger organ and we'd do a few Tornadoes numbers, and then we'd got a singer who'd do country and western. Then we'd do some John Barry Seven numbers and I'd change to trumpet, and then we'd do a couple of Dixieland numbers with Roger on trombone.

18. The Detours play at the Grand Ballroom, Broadstairs, Kent.

19. The Detours play at the CAV Sports Ground, Northolt.

20. The Detours play at Douglas House, Lancaster Gate, London.

Pete Townshend: It was a USAF club, and they would have country bands on. Because of my parents' connections, though, we got the date and eventually the band we replaced was my father's!

I remember the day my father handed over to me the function he felt he had been carrying out until the sixties. He said, "Things have changed, Pete, and now it's your turn." He knew that the war was finally over, and he never complained when rock'n'roll usurped his audiences; few of the real musicians of the old big-band order complained.

February 1963

22. The Detours play at the Grand Ballroom, Broadstairs, Kent.

26. The Detours play at the Oldfield Hotel, Greenford, West London.

March 1963

22. The Detours play at the Grand Ballroom, Broadstairs, Kent.

29. The Detours play at the Grand Ballroom, Broadstairs, Kent.

May 1963

17. The Detours play at the Carnival Ballroom, Park Hotel, Hanwell, West London.

24. The Detours play at the Grand Ballroom, Broadstairs, Kent.

June 1963

1. The Detours play at the Oldfield Hotel, Greenford, West London.

28. The Detours play at the Club Druane, Notre Dame Church Hall, Leicester Place, Central London.

July 1963

26. The Detours play at the Club Druane, Notre Dame Church Hall, Leicester Place, Central London.

August 1963

30. The Detours play at the Club Druane, Notre Dame Church Hall, Leicester Place, Central London.

September 1963

7. *Melody Maker* runs an ad for Marshall speakers, listing The Detours as Marshall users.

13. The Detours play at the Club Druane, Notre Dame Church Hall, Leicester Place, Central London.

20. The Detours play at the Club Druane, Notre Dame Church Hall, Leicester Place, Central London.

November 1963

15. The Detours play at the Feathers Hotel, Ealing, West London.

22. The Detours play at the Goldhawk Social Club, Shepherd's Bush, West London.

Roger Daltrey: All of us were like three loonies – Entwistle, Townshend and me. Always changing. We had quite a good following for a small local group. We were the first group to get fed up with playing the Top Twenty stuff, and move on to really hard R&B . . . like Howling Wolf and those sort of people. We were the sort of group that would always take chances on losing all the fans.

The drummer we had was just like a . . .he didn't really fit in, in that sense . . .

30. The Detours begin a residency at the Railway Hotel, Greenford, West London, secured by their new manager Helmut Gordon.

Roger Daltrey: We got discovered by a Jewish door handle manufacturer. He decided he wanted to waste some money on a pop group, so we thought, "Well, we'll waste your money for you," which we did with the greatest of pleasure. His name was Helmut Gordon. It was at the time everybody was exploiting every group . . . only The Who were a bit rougher than most.

December 1963

7. The Detours play at the California Ballroom, Dunstable, supporting Wayne Fontana & The Mindbenders.

22. The Detours support The Rolling Stones at St Mary's Ballroom, Putney.

Pete Townshend: I was just blown away by them. Blown away by everything about them. How wild they looked but how friendly they were and how erotically charged everything around them was. You know, it was really between Jagger and Brian Jones at the time. Brian Jones was very beautiful-looking for the time, and Jagger was just kind of this kind of gawky, you know, body, really.

They used to fight one another for the attention of the audience and I suppose it was my male response to that eroticism that actually surprised me. You know, it wasn't me looking at a bunch of screaming girls. It was thinking, "How the fuck do they do it?" I didn't realize that it was just because girls liked to scream.

Roger Daltrey: Keith Richards was backstage before they went on, stretching his right arm high above his head. He never did that on the stage, although he did play with these little wrist-windmills sometimes, but he was just stretching his arm, and we were all standing there, watching . . .

Pete Townshend: He swung his arm up in a swirling motion before the curtain [then] as the curtain opened, he sort of brushed it away and they went into "Come On".

I was amazed . . . they were so scruffy, so organic, and yet they were stars.

Jagger was very polite and so was Brian, who was extremely complimentary about The Detours. . . . It was like God touching me on the head.

Roger Daltrey: . . .and the next night, there's fucking Townshend going whoooo! Hahaha! So thank you, Keith.

1964

January 1964

3. The Detours support The Rolling Stones at Glenlyn Ballroom, Forest Hill, London.

Pete Townshend: The first time I swung my arm was after seeing Keith the night before . . . I thought I was copying him, so when we did a gig with them later, I didn't do it all night, and I watched him and he didn't do it all night either. "Swing me what?" he said. He must have just gotten into it as a warming-up thing that night, but he didn't remember, and it developed into my sort of trademark.

24. The Detours support The Hollies at Glenlyn Ballroom, Forest Hill, London.

30. The Detours play at the Oldfield Hotel, Greenford, West London.

Pete Townshend: I used to try to make up visually for what I couldn't play. I'd get into very incredible visual things where, in order to make one chord more dramatic, I'd make it a really lethal-looking thing, whereas really it's just going to be picked normally . . .

In fact, I soon forgot all about the guitar because my visual thing was more my music than the actual guitar. I got to jumping about so much, the guitar became unimportant. I banged it and I let it feed back, scraped it, rubbed it against the microphone, it wasn't even part of my act. It didn't deserve any credit or respect.

February 1964

1. Seeing a group called Johnny Devlin & The Detours on UK TV show "Thank Your Lucky Stars", The Detours decide to change their name to The Who.

Keith Moon: I don't really know whose name The Who was. I think it was a guy named Barney [Richard Barnes], who was a friend of Pete's. And he said, "Well, as you know, there's The Searchers, The Seekers, The Lookers, The Watchers, but let's have something abstract – Who! Yeah!"

Richard Barnes: It made people think twice, and it worked well on posters because it was so short and therefore would print up big.
6. The Detours play at the Oldfield Hotel, Greenford, West London.
13. The Detours play at the Oldfield Hotel, Greenford, West London.
20. The Who play at the Oldfield Hotel, Greenford, West London.

John Entwistle: The Who sound came from us playing as a three-piece band and trying to sound like more. I certainly played standard bass, but I combined it with long runs where I took over lead while Pete bashed out the chords.

Pete Townshend: What's interesting in our group is, of course, that the roles are reversed. John is the lead guitar player and although I'm not the bass player he does produce a hell of a lot of the lead work. It's really funny to this day where you get a song like "Dreaming From The Waist" when John is doing this blinding bass solo and making Alvin Lee look like he plays in slow motion and I'm just standing there strumming a chord. And the audience looks at me and goes, "How does he do it? How does he produce that noise?" And of course John won't demand attention, not like the guy in Earth, Wind & Fire. You see, for years nobody even knew John was there. He used to wear all black and nobody ever put a lamp on him: if we appeared on TV you never saw him unless the camera was whipping from Roger to Keith.

March 1964

The Who audition for A&R man Chris Parmeinter at the Zanzibar, Edgware Road, London.

Pete Townshend: I took the band over when they asked me to write for them in 1964 in order to pass the Decca audition and used them as a mouthpiece, hitting out at anyone who tried to have a say (mainly Roger) and then grumbling when they didn't appreciate my dictatorship.
7. The Who play a wedding reception at Old Oak Common Institute, Shepherd's Bush, London.
13. The Who are mentioned in a *Melody Maker* article headlined "Massive Swing to R&B".
29. The Who play at the Florida Rooms, Brighton.

John Francis (audience): I went down in my MG with my mate Christopher Robbins. It was freezing cold and snowing, but we camped out on the outskirts of Brighton in an inflatable tent, which unfortunately deflated at regular intervals in the night. It was the first time I'd seen loads of mods together with their Vespas and parkas, because a lot of them were staying on the site. The gig was pretty grotty, but absolutely packed out.

April 1964

4. The Who (wrongly billed as The Detours) support The Tony Meehan Combo at the California Ballroom, Dunstable.

9. The Who are auditioned for BBC radio at Maida Vale Studios, London. They fail.

John Entwistle: Everyone was called Simon or Clive. They all had white shirts and red ties. It was horrible. It was like going back to high school; you had to behave yourself and everything's got to be prim and proper.

Roger Daltrey: In those days it was all very, very British proper. And God knows what they thought of the sound we were making. We just used to say, "Well, 'ere we are; take us or leave us," and we did our thing and left. That really was it.

John Entwistle: The whole thing about the BBC is back then, it didn't matter how many No. 1 hits you had; if you couldn't play live and you didn't pass their audition, you didn't get to play.

13. The Who support The Mike Cotton Sound at the 100 Club, Oxford Street, London.

John Entwistle: Fights used to start from all sorts of things, usually after we came off stage. They didn't last long. Roger only has to punch you once and that's it. I usually ended up holding Roger away from whoever he wanted to punch out.

We'd fight over stolen girlfriends. Usurping somebody else's authority. Tiny little things sometimes. Us being on drugs and Roger not being on drugs. Roger couldn't do the pills because of his voice. He would have loved to. He couldn't drink much either because he drove the van and we wouldn't let him drink and drive. So he'd be stone cold sober driving this bunch of drunken, pilled-up louts in the back of the van. He hated it.

27. Drummer Doug Sandom quits The Who after a gig at the 100 Club, supporting The Mike Cotton Sound.

Pete Townshend: We were struggling to get a record deal. We had a very good drummer, but he was much older, about 36. We were about to get a record deal with Philips, and the record-company guy told us, "Listen, we'll give you a deal, but you have to get rid of the drummer." We said we weren't sure, and the guy goes, "Listen, you have to get rid of him now. You have to tell him now." So John, Roger and I had a meeting. It was a big question of loyalty because this guy was somebody we loved very much. And at that moment my heart turned to stone and I said, "I'll go tell him." And I went out and said, "He said he would give us a record deal but not if you're in the group, so you're out." And this guy Doug didn't talk to me for 30 years. Quite rightly.

Doug Sandom: I wasn't so ambitious as the rest of them. I'd done it longer than what they had. Of course, I loved it. It was very nice to be part of a band that people followed, it was great. But I didn't get on well with Peter Townshend. I was a few years older than him, and he thought I should pack it in, more or less because of that.

May 1964

Pop publicist Pete Meaden takes over as manager.

Pete Meaden: The Detours were an R&B group but I was introduced to them as The Who. I had this dream of getting a group together that would be the focus, the entertainers for the mods; a group that would actually be the same people on stage as the guys in the audience.

Instead of just listening to R&B records, I thought how great it would be to have an actual representation of the people. Although they were separated by the stage, they had all the necessary factors for audience identification. Townshend identified with the mod scene immediately.

Roger Daltrey: We'd been playing for a while as The Detours when Pete Meaden came upon us. He obviously recognized that within this music, basically an American blues derivative, but which had the Shepherd's Bush anger and frustration running through it, was something that had a particular potential.

In addition to that, here were four of the most odd-looking guys that you could ever come across, who looked pretty much like the kids on the street.

He also recognized that there was this mass of young people with, for the first time, real amounts of money in their pockets and real freedom to be mobile. Brighton and back in a day wasn't a sore arse on a push-bike any more, you know?

But he also saw that these kids were clutching on to things that they really didn't know anything about. Mods' music was very diverse. They liked Motown, blue beat, James Brown, the blues – all black music; they didn't like anything English. There was a huge hole there to be filled, so Pete Meaden took us over.

With our long hair and scruffy clothes, our beatnik, Rolling Stones-type look, no one would bat an eyelid when they saw us together. But Pete was an image maker. He dragged us into the barber's, then put us into white jeans and Ivy League stuff, and the effects were immediate. People started to stare at us, like we were off another planet. So he was totally right.

Pete Townshend: Pete Meaden taught me that mod wasn't just a fad; it could be something sublime or even celestial. I spent the next two years mixing and matching things I noticed in our audience with an exaggerated pop look I thought might suit the colour magazines of the day.

7. The Who play at the Oldfield Hotel, Greenford, London.

14. The Who play at the Oldfield Hotel, Greenford, London.

Roger Daltrey: Word had gotten round to all the local groups that we were looking for a new drummer . . .

Keith Moon: When I heard their drummer had left, I laid plans to insinuate myself into the group. I went down, and they had a session drummer sitting in with them. I got up on stage and said, "I can do better than him." They said, "Go ahead," and I got behind this other guy's drums and I did one song, "Road Runner". I'd had several drinks to get my courage up and when I got on stage I went "arggGGHHHH" on the drums, broke the bass-drum pedal and two skins and got off.

Louis Hunt (manager, Oldfield Hotel): That's not true. Didn't happen. No fear . . . Keith came in on his own. I think he came down expecting to see The Who but it wasn't their night. They used to practise in a drill hall in Acton and, this particular evening, I told him where they were and that he should go down and see them. I asked Keith if he knew where it was. He said, "Yeah, I know." He was all excited. I asked if he was keen, and he jumped for joy. I said, "Go down, tell 'em I sent you and see how you get on."

John Entwistle: We were interested because we had a session drummer that we'd hired who worked for Marshall's music store in the drum department and he was working out extremely expensive, making half the total that we were making. Keith comes over, a lovely little gingerbread man, and we said, "Do you know 'Road Runner'?" He said, "Yeah." In playing it, he smashed the hi-hat and put a hole in the skin. The other drummer wasn't very pleased. He got the gig basically because he could play "Road Runner".

Keith Moon: When I met the other fellows and they were pissed off too with the way everything is, with the alternatives, I knew then The Who would make it. Because of the sheer power of the personalities involved in The Who, and the way we worked together, it really smelled successful.

Tony Brind (bassist, Beachcombers): Keith wasn't devious about it. He came to me, he said he was thinking of joining them, and he'd keep playing with us until we found someone. I was sorry, but I wasn't upset at all. Everyone has the right to leave.

Pete Townshend: From the time we found him it was a complete turning point. He was so assertive and confident. Before that we had just been fooling around.

John Entwistle: After Keith Moon joined, it all came together. We became incredibly arrogant, 'cause we all knew how good we were. We realized we were way ahead of other bands.

Roger Daltrey: When Moon joined it went completely on to another planet. It just gelled. He just instinctively put drum rolls in places that other people would never have thought of putting them.

Pete Townshend: Keith was a very powerful, driving person. He was also unbelievably funny. He was witty the way Groucho Marx and Dorothy Parker were witty. He was a fucking fast-thinking guy.

21. The Who play at the Oldfield Hotel, Greenford, London.

28. The Who play at the Oldfield Hotel, Greenford, London.

Mid-1964

The High Numbers record their first single, "I'm The Face"/"Zoot Suit".

Pete Meaden: The name was perfect. I dreamt of it one night. High – being a little high – and numbers was the name for the general crowd. There was a hierarchy situation with the mods and The High Numbers gave them a step up the hierarchy.

Pete Townshend: We had (previously) done a thing with Barry Gray, who is an electronic film music composer, and he used to do music for a lot of space programmes for kids where they used to use models. He did a lot of popular film music and he had his own studio and we did a demo there once. It was the first song I ever wrote, called "It Was You".

Roger Daltrey: Having been rechristened The High Numbers, we went into the studio to make a single. We were going to record a blues song, 'cause that's what we did, songs about sex and women and feeling down and frustration, but when he heard it, Meaden said, "Hang on, we can't sing these lyrics. They won't mean anything to a kid on the street in England." So he wrote his own lyrics. But the only trouble was that we found we couldn't sing his bloody lyrics either. They were just diabolical.

Pete Meaden: "I'm The Face" was written for Roger to sing, to say he was the leader for the people of that movement. The identification factor had to be total. Roger was the leader of the group then, the spokesman. That was before Peter got his confidence together and had a theme to write his songs on.

Keith Moon: This chap from Philips, Chris Parmeinter, turns up with another drummer. He set up his kit and I set up mine and nobody was saying anything. The rest of the band just didn't care. They were tuning up in one corner and it was dead embarrassing. Then they asked me to play in the first number, but the man from Philips wanted to play. I can't remember if he played or not, but the group said they didn't want him. So I just stayed with them.

June 1964

Chris Downing (guitarist, The Macabre): We played support to The High Numbers maybe fifteen or twenty times that summer. I'd got into The Macabre because I worked in a tax office beside John Entwistle's mother, and she put me on to it because one of the guys in the band was a friend of John's.

16. The Who play at the Kinky Ball, Granby Halls, Leicester.

26. The Who play at Golder's Green Refectory, London.

30. The Who begin a 12-week Tuesday residency at the Railway Hotel, Harrow & Wealdstone.

July 1964

3. The High Numbers release their debut single, "I'm The Face"/"Zoot Suit", in the UK.

Pete Townshend: We were very excited. It was very self-consciously mod. It talked about fashion, faces and tickets. That record was a clear indication of how the mod movement as a fashion was really self-contained.

Chris Downing: By that time, we were hanging out with them quite a bit. I used to go round to Moon's house and Entwistle's, and shortly after they did that single I remember learning that the reason the harmonica solo on "I'm The Face" is so all over the place is that Roger had picked it up upside down in the studio and started the solo with the harmonica the wrong way round. Of course, they wouldn't have had the opportunity to do another take in those days.

Roger Daltrey: We were confused. But that's always the way when someone's honing someone else's talent. And the idea of music specifically tailored for a certain audience of young British mods, played by people who looked and sounded just like them, was, as it turned out, spot-on.

Pete Townshend: We brought out that very self-conscious record, "I'm The Face", you know, I wear white buckskin shoes and side jackets with five-inch vents. The kids out in the street didn't need that kind of leader. They knew that information before you even thought of the lyric.

David Bowie (early Who fan): They wore stuff that was five months out of date as far as we were concerned, but we liked them because they were kind of like us. They were our band.

Pete Townshend: Though we were on stage, we were still Tickets – watchers rather than leaders. We could look down from the stage and instantly see who the Faces were. We could see what they were wearing and what their dances were, and instantly copy them.

7. The High Numbers play at the Railway Hotel, Harrow & Wealdstone.

Chris Downing (guitarist, The Macabre): This was the first time I actually saw them. Pete had the 360 Rickenbacker then, which cost £169 out of Jim Marshall's shop. It was one of the first five that came into the UK, and I had one of them as well. He liked it because it had a very mod look, and it was great for playing chords. That big power-chord sound he got wasn't just his amps, it was partly that he used really thick strings.

Roger was still singing in quite a low register, a kind of Howlin' Wolf voice, but The High Numbers was the start of them changing from R&B and blues to a more soul-oriented kind of music.

Quite soon after we met them the word went round that Pete had somehow acquired this new drug called cannabis which none of us had ever heard of. Purple hearts was the thing up until then.

We went to see them that week, and the next week we started playing support gigs with them.

12. The High Numbers play at the Florida Rooms, Brighton.
14. Ambitious young film-maker Kit Lambert comes to see The High Numbers at the Railway Hotel, Harrow & Wealdstone.

Chris Stamp (co-manager, Who): Kit had a lot of sophistication, because he came from that whole West End bohemian artistic family, he'd been to Oxford, he had a lot of worldly sophistication, he spoke languages.

Richard Barnes (friend of Pete Townshend): Kit turned up at the Railway Hotel in Harrow & Wealdstone, where I was promoting The High Numbers. I was shit scared of him, because he looked so straight. He was around 30 years old and was wearing a really expensive Savile Row suit. He looked trouble.

Kit Lambert: On a stage made entirely of beer crates and with a ceiling so low you could stick a guitar through it without even trying, lit by a single red light bulb, were The High Numbers. Roger Daltrey with his teeth crossed at the front, moving from foot to foot like a zombie. John Entwistle, immobile, looking like a stationary blob. Pete Townshend like a lanky beanpole. Behind them, Keith Moon sitting on a bicycle saddle with his ridiculous eyes in his round moon face, bashing away for dear life, sending them all up and ogling the audience. They were all quarrelling among themselves between numbers, yet there was an evil excitement about it all.

Roger Daltrey: He [Lambert] seemed completely out of place, really flamboyant. He had this upper-class accent that was so out of kilter with everyone else's. He said, "Hi, I'm a film producer." He wanted to make a film about the West London mods. He was sharp, he had ideas. You couldn't help being impressed.

Kit Lambert: I knew they could become world superstars.

Simon Napier-Bell (rock manager and friend of Lambert): When Kit met The Who, he found in Peter Townshend an undirected intelligence that fed hungrily on his own anarchistic, self-destructive ideas. Most critics saw this as an incitement to violence, but they were wrong. It was symbolic suicide – Kit Lambert's glamorized version of his father's drunken self-destruction.
18. Kit Lambert's film-making partner Chris Stamp comes to see The Who play at the Trade Union Hall, Watford, supported by Chris Farlowe & The Thunderbirds.

Chris Stamp: We had seen a number of films about the music business and people in pop music and thought they were terrible trash. We thought we could do better, but we couldn't afford to pay a top pop group ourselves. Our only way was to start from scratch with an unknown group. That was how we came to stumble across The Who.

Keith Moon: We didn't like each other at first, really. They were as incongruous a team as we were. You got Chris, on the one hand, who's yer typical East Ender, and Kit with his Oxford accent. These people were perfect for us, because there's me, bouncing about, full of pills, full of everything I could get my hands on . . . and there's Pete, very serious, never laughed, always cool, a grasshead. I was working at about ten times the speed Pete was. And Kit and Chris were like the epitome of what we were.

19. The High Numbers do a special audition for Chris Stamp at a school hall in Holland Park, London, then play at the Florida Rooms, Brighton.

Chris Stamp: Although he [Moon] had only been in the band three months this thing that was happening, it was like the missing part. He made all the others work to their capacity. The great thing about The Who is that they were this incredible, distorted, dysfunctional energy. All of their bad parts and wrong parts worked in this four-man thing, and when Keith sat on the drum kit he was like the earth part of it, he was the fucking soul part of it. He was this incredible, emotional human being. The other guys – Pete was cerebral, John was very isolated and shut down. And Roger was Roger – his anger came through in his voice. It moved because of Keith. His energy energized them.

Kit Lambert: We offered to manage them. They liked our ideas, and that was that.

21. The High Numbers play at the Railway Hotel, Harrow & Wealdstone.

Elton John: I used to go see them when they were The High Numbers at the Railway Tavern near where I grew up. They were astounding when they started out, they were so loud . . . Nobody knew what was going to happen. That wasn't the point. It was just sheer excitement.

24. The High Numbers sign a management contract with Kit Lambert and Chris Stamp.

Pete Meaden: Lambert and Stamp offered them more material things, mostly wages and cars. The Who were friends. The only reason I started it was because I wanted to have four mates who were stronger than anyone else.

Pete Townshend: The importance of people like Kit Lambert is what he said to me from day one . . . He said all great art was crap. And now I've found that out. We read that Mozart was doing commissions on motifs, numbered motifs, and selling his copyrights. "Oh, the bloody prince of Denmark wants another piece of music, and I'm so busy. Give him fifteen of number twenty-two, six of number four, nine of number fifty-eight . . ." It was very much like computer music. And, of course, Bach was a mathematician. And these have all been elevated to some kind of artistic gods.

Kit used to be extraordinarily funny on the subject. He said, "You've got to be pretentious, you've got to go for gold, you've got to be over the top." So as a kind of agitator in the music business, he was wonderful, because instead of devaluing the whole thing, he was actually making it more real.

Pete Meaden: When they went with Kit and Chris I wasn't going to stand in their way. The Who were becoming important. When they played a place like The Aquarium, Brighton, and the whole town came alive at once, it was amazing . . .

26. The High Numbers play at the White Hart, Acton, London.

28. The High Numbers play at the Railway Hotel, Harrow & Wealdstone, supported by The Macabre.

Chris Downing: Immediately after they signed their management contract with Lambert and Stamp, we played with them again at the Railway Hotel. Their former manager turned up in the middle of the set and repossessed their Commer van. They were left with all their gear and no way to get it home, so we let them use our old butcher's van.

31. The High Numbers support The Kinks at the Goldhawk Social Club, Shepherd's Bush, London.

"Irish" Jack Lyons (audience): The Goldhawk was not 100 per cent mods. Perhaps it was only 50 per cent. But there was a hardcore of Goldhawk people who, because they knew the band well, didn't really care whether Dougie Sandom was a good drummer or a bad drummer. He was Dougie Sandom from Acton, and a lot of the people who came to the Goldhawk were from Acton.

So when Keith came along, everyone remembered Keith as being from The Beachcombers, who were regarded as a capable band, though not a mod band. But he had replaced Dougie, and Dougie had been an indigenous member. So there was this suspicion, despite his acknowledged ability, because he wasn't one of "us". He wasn't from West London. He was from Wembley.

Chris Downing: Keith in those days wasn't the wild man of rock at all. He was a very mild-mannered middle-class boy, exactly as I was, which is why I got along with him so well. His drumming, however, was very energetic and it did eventually develop into being one long drum solo through the whole song, but it wasn't like that at the start.

He was always very energetic though. I remember him at the end of one gig wringing the sweat out of a white T-shirt he'd been wearing, and it half-filled a pint glass.

August 1964

1. The High Numbers play at the Trade Union Hall, Watford, supported by The Macabre.

Chris Downing: We were anything but sophisticated in those days. None of The Who owned a car, and none of our band did either. The only musician I knew who had a car was Mitch Mitchell, who later became the drummer for Jimi Hendrix, and that was because he was also an actor and earned decent money doing that.

The night we played in Watford, for example, the gig ended about midnight and we were all starving, so Townshend said, "Let's go and have a Chinese meal." Well, none of us had ever had a Chinese meal before, so this was a real event. We couldn't even understand the menu, so Townshend ordered the food for all of us.

2. The High Numbers play the All Night Rave in the Florida Rooms, Brighton.

Pete Townshend: I used to say to the band, "Listen, we should look right, we should have an image, we should walk in a particular way. We should look different from other people. And, after a concert is over, if we talk to people we should maintain the facade."

4. The High Numbers play at the Railway Hotel, Harrow & Wealdstone, supported by The Macabre.

Chris Downing: Both our bands had only three instruments in them, so we both based our style on Johnny Kidd & The Pirates, which also had that line-up of one guitar, bass and drums.

The High Numbers played all kinds of stuff, including Buddy Holly songs, and I particularly remember them doing Dion's "Runaround Sue", in A, which allowed Townshend to use a lot of open chords that really ring out, and that became an important element in his style.

5. The High Numbers begin a five-week residency at The Scene, Ham Yard, Soho, Central London.

Pete Townshend: The Scene was really where it was at, but there were only about 15 people down there every night. It was a focal point for the mod movement. I don't think anyone who was a mod outside Soho realized the fashions and dances all began there. We were lucky enough to be involved in the movement at that particular time.

John Steel (drummer, Animals): There'd be a whole roomful of these kids, all out of their brains, getting off on R&B. It was a great atmosphere.

The club was raided quite often. In fact, I remember one night, the police walked in and made us stop playing. There was a sound like a hailstorm when everyone emptied the pills out of their pockets on to the dance floor. When the cops walked round frisking people, it was like they were walking on gravel – crunch, crunch, crunch. We were pissing ourselves.

6. The High Numbers play at the White Hart, Southall, London.

8. The High Numbers play at All Saints Hall, Whetstone.

9. The High Numbers support Gerry & The Pacemakers at The Hippodrome, Brighton.

11. The High Numbers play at the Railway Hotel, Harrow & Wealdstone, supported by The Macabre.

Chris Downing: One night at the Railway Hotel, Roger's father-in-law suddenly appeared just as they were about to go on, and dragged Roger outside and hit him. You see, Roger was the only one that was married, but I got the feeling that it wasn't a very happy marriage. I think he was trying to get out of it.

Roger Daltrey: I was the original pop star, knocking off as many birds as you could get in one night. Pete's got a bit of a chip, because I used to get all the girls.

Chris Downing: We had to go back on stage and fill in until the fight was over. Roger finally reappeared, but he was a tough little guy, and he just got up on stage and went into the act.

12. The High Numbers play at the Labour Hall, South Oxley.

13. "You Really Got Me" by The Kinks enters the UK singles chart.

John Entwistle: When Pete first started writing, his songs were kind of other people's songs badly remembered. We were at Keith's house one night and we were playing "You Really Got Me" by The Kinks, and Pete went home and tried to remember it but couldn't – he had such a bad memory – and so he came up with "I Can't Explain".

Chris Downing: Round at John's house one day, he played me the demo for a new song they'd just written. It was called "I Think It's Spring" – a very light-hearted Doris Day-type lyric. Somebody must have realized it wasn't quite right because the next time I heard that song it had become "I Can't Explain".

Pete Townshend: The Kinks had filled the hole we wanted to fill. That sort of music always came from over the water. I thought that if you want the heavy stuff you could write it yourself. I wrote "I Can't Explain" just for The Who and it remains one of the best things I've ever done. It was based on "You Really Got Me". It just didn't have the modulations.

15. The High Numbers play on the Riverboat Shuffle, on theThames.

16. The High Numbers support The Beatles at the Opera House, Blackpool.

John Entwistle: We were bottom of the bill and they were top of the bill. They couldn't understand why we were setting up this huge amount of equipment for ourselves. When our stuff was taken off, they brought out The Beatles' stuff, and it was half the size, and they were using the theatre's PA system, which was diabolical. The little microphones looked like electric shavers. We couldn't understand why they put themselves through such rubbish.

18. The High Numbers play at the Railway Hotel, Harrow & Wealdstone.

Richard Barnes: We had this kid called Pill Brian who used to come down on his scooter. He'd come down and say, "I've got these today," and we'd take all of them. "This one's for rheumatism," he'd say. Keith would say, "Yeah, I'll have that."

19. The High Numbers play at The Scene, Soho, London.

Pete Meaden: When The High Numbers played at The Scene club, Roger would be up on stage. Pete would be wanging into the speakers with his guitar getting feedback. This was before smashing guitars, just smashing the speakers. The whole essence of the mod thing was on that stage.

It's a wired-up group full of electricity. There is a danger. The response is picked up by the audience because there is a definite tension, lots of tension, loads with a group like The Who. That's what is communicated to the audience, an audience who like getting wired up by The Who. That's the turn-on.

20. The High Numbers play at the Majestic Ballroom, Luton.

22. The High Numbers play at the Trade Union Hall, Watford.

23. The High Numbers support Dusty Springfield and Eden Kane at The Hippodrome, Brighton.

25. The High Numbers play at the Railway Hotel, Harrow & Wealdstone.
26. The High Numbers play at The Scene, Soho, London.
30. The High Numbers support The Searchers and The Kinks at the Queen's Theatre, Blackpool.

Pete Townshend: Some of our earliest shows happened to be with very distinguished people. We played with the Stones several times, The Beatles once, The Kinks twice – this was when we were learning the ropes, right at the formative period. By looking at what they were doing at the time, we were able to grab at things. I remember Kit Lambert saying, "You should run on stage as though it's the most sacred place on earth, as though it's the only place you want to be – however you feel, always run on." And The Who always ran on to the stage. We were Pavlovian in that respect – the bell rang and we ran on.

September 1964

Townshend moves in with Kit Lambert, and later in the month Lambert and Stamp make a promo film at the Railway Hotel.

Pete Townshend: I lived with Kit Lambert for six months in 1964 after leaving art college, and he was open about his sexuality with me, and – unlike the wonderfully vulnerable Robert Stigwood – never attempted to seduce me. I sometimes met Kit's rent boys the morning after, and we swapped little purple pills. I generally liked the gays I knew. They seemed to have a conviction about their entire identity that – at the time – I lacked.

Richard Barnes: Kit thought that he would sophisticate these working-class boys. He would introduce them to the world of restaurants and other things that, in those days, you didn't go to. He only tried it with Pete and Keith.

Pete Townshend: I was a King's Road swan, unsure whether to be gay or not. It was not about fashion. It was about the fact that all the men I admired seemed to be gay, bisexual or just not to give a shit.

Chris Stamp: With a projector in a suitcase, I toured all the promoters offering them free showings. The result was that within weeks we were able to get bigger and better bookings for the group. Their price went up from £10 to £25 a night and then, within a year, we had lifted it to nearly £250 a night.

2. The High Numbers play at The Scene, Soho, London.
4. The High Numbers play with Lulu and Dave Berry at The Big Beat Show, Kelvin Hall Arena, Glasgow.

Lulu: They were at the Kelvin Hall, and they were still called The High Numbers. I took them back to my mum and dad's wee flat in Meadowpark Street. They were top of the bill and I was just supporting them because "Shout" had only just come out. We all went in their van, and we sat in the flat drinking beer.

6. The High Numbers support The Swinging Blue Jeans and The Nashville Teens at the Queen's Theatre, Blackpool.

8. The High Numbers play at the Railway Hotel, Harrow & Wealdstone.

Roger Daltrey: We were in a very small club one night, and the ceiling was quite low. Pete put his guitar up to play a chord, broke the neck off and got absolutely no reaction.

Pete Townshend: I was expecting everybody to go, "Wow, he's broken his guitar, he's broken his guitar," but nobody did anything, which made me kind of angry in a way. And determined to get this precious event noticed by the audience. I proceeded to make a big thing of breaking the guitar. I bounced all over the stage with it and I threw the bits on the stage and I picked up my spare guitar and carried on as though I really had meant to do it.

Keith Moon: When Pete smashed his guitar, it was because he was pissed off. When I smashed me drums, it was because I was pissed off. We were frustrated. You're working as hard as you can to get that fucking song across, to grab that audience by the balls, to make it an event.

Pete Townshend: To me it wasn't violence. It wasn't random destruction. At the time, I considered it to be art. The German movement of auto-destructive art. They used to build sculptures which would collapse. They would paint pictures with acid so they self-destructed. They built buildings that would explode. So I used to go out on stage thinking this was high art.

15. The High Numbers play at the Railway Hotel, Harrow & Wealdstone.

19. The High Numbers play at the Trade Union Hall, Watford.

21. The High Numbers audition for EMI at Studio 2, Abbey Road, London.

Pete Townshend: That was an amazing session. We recorded it in the same room that The Beatles did their first album in. We were overawed by it and incredibly nervous. We did a tape which was bloody dynamite. Dop pop a doo, stuff like that – incredible fucking stuff. "Smokestack Lightning".

22. The High Numbers play the last night of their residency at the Railway Hotel, Harrow & Wealdstone.

October 1964

7. The High Numbers play at the Town Hall, Greenwich.

Chris Downing: None of us had roadies in those days, and we were all acquiring big Marshall cabinets. Luckily, they were very sturdy because I remember watching Pete Townshend get pissed off with humping his gear at Greenwich Town Hall and just tipping the cabinet up at the top of the stairs and letting it go, so it bumped and crashed all the way down to the bottom.

10. The High Numbers play at the Olympia Ballroom, Reading.

11. The High Numbers play at Wolsey Hall, Cheshunt.

14. The High Numbers play at the Town Hall, Greenwich.

22. EMI Records reject The High Numbers' audition.

John Burgess (EMI): I have listened again and again to The High Numbers' white labels taken from our test session and still cannot decide whether they have anything to offer.

28. The High Numbers play at the Town Hall, Greenwich.

November 1964

7. Lambert and Stamp place an advert in *Melody Maker*, advertising the band once more as The Who alongside the phrase "Maximum R&B".

Chris Stamp: The High Numbers was a nothing name. It implied the Top 20 but . . . The Who seemed perfect for them. It was impersonal. It couldn't be dated.

Kit Lambert: It was a gimmick name. Journalists could write articles called "The Why of The Who" and people had to go through a boring ritual of question and answer, "Have you heard The Who?" "The who?" "Yes, The Who." It was an invitation to corniness and we were in a corny world.

18. Having reverted to the name The Who, the band plays at Wolsey Hall, Cheshunt.

24. The Who begin a residency at London's Marquee Club, supported by The Action.

Chris Stamp: Being a keen artist, and a former student, Pete helped us to choose the poster. And we used the same design after that to advertise all their club dates. It was produced by a friend of his, a designer called Brian Pike, and there had never been a pop poster like it.

Keith Moon: Playing the Marquee was the biggest thing ever for The Who when we started. Sure we used to get friends down to see us, but that was because Tuesday was a dead night, and we had to set the ball rolling. We gave free tickets for the Marquee to fans who came down to see us at the Goldhawk . . .

Roger Daltrey: We played there every Tuesday night. When we first did the job, Tuesday was a slow night. That's why they let us in there. God, they didn't know what hit them. We were just a pub band. We were big in our own little area. But the great thing about the Marquee was the West End of London, it was like the whole of England goes out from the West End of London. So it expanded our audience potential by literally a million. And that in itself was very useful. I have to tell you, and I don't mean this as sour grapes or anything, but it is hard to play for fans who see you all the time; makes it much harder.

Pearce Marchbank (audience): There were hardly any people in the Marquee and this guy, who I later discovered was either Chris Stamp or Kit Lambert, was walking round giving people whisky. This was to gee up the audience, since they were all there from the Railway Hotel or whatever. What they did on stage then was completely different to their records. Their show-stopper was "Heatwave", they never played their singles on stage . . . I gathered they were an art-school band by the look of them.

Keith Moon: We were playing a lot of Bo Diddley, Chuck Berry, Elmore James, B.B. King, and they are maximum R&B. You can't get any better. Most of the songs we played were their songs. Pete really got into his writing stride after "Can't Explain". Of course any song we did get 'old of, we weren't playing straight from the record. We "Who'd" it, so that what came out was The Who, not a copy.

Roger Powell (drummer, Action): They were absolutely sensational. Even though they were still raw, they were amazing – a total audio-visual experience, a wall of sound and energy. Keith Moon was taking drumming in this totally new direction. John Entwistle just stood there doing this incredible bass playing, while Townshend and Daltrey were giving everything up front. They were brilliant, mind-blowing.

Roger Daltrey: It all escalated from there. It happened so fast, it was amazing. You had the feeling anything could happen. We were the kids' group.

25. The Who play at the Florida Rooms, Brighton.

December 1964

1. The Who play at the Marquee Club, London.

Dave Goodman (audience): The first time I came out of my shell was when I saw The Who at the Marquee. I'd never seen anything like it. I couldn't imagine that people could do such things. I went straight out and broke a window, I was that impressed. It broke down so many barriers for me, just that one evening of seeing The Who. The set was so fucking violent and the music so heady it hit you in the head as well as the guts. It did things to you. You'd never heard anything like it. "Maximum R&B" said the poster and, fuck me, that was it.

2. The Who play at the Florida Rooms, Brighton.

8. Marquee, Soho, London.

Nick Jones (audience): I was hanging around with some mods in Mornington Crescent. We would cut school and go to the West End and places like Ravel [Carnaby Street] to look at boots. I was walking along Wardour Street and saw that famous poster outside the Marquee, and I was really struck by the image. I was like, "What's this? I've never heard of them. Tuesdays? I wonder if I'd be allowed out on a Tuesday."

I got down there on a Tuesday, took a girl from the comprehensive school next to ours, and there were only 60 people there. It was only about the second or third week. I remember connecting. The hair stood up on the back of my neck. I remember instrumentals – "Green Onions" – the power and the volume. People like The T-Bones, and Clapton in The Yardbirds, only had little Vox AC30s, so this stack . . . it was immediately visual.

And Keith Moon was completely out there. All these mad fills. I was a drummer, and probably my first thought was that "This guy is not doing the same number." And maybe after 15 minutes, I realized that he was there but he had already left the backbeat behind and he was filling it, there was another ensemble going on. It was kind of out of control, so you're sitting there going, "This is rubbish," until you realize that it was another lead instrument. They were trashing numbers most people were doing quite faithfully. I'd never heard "Heatwave" before but I was completely struck by their repertoire. They were absolutely post-modernist deconstruction.

9. Florida Rooms, Brighton.

12. Harrow Technical College, London.

14. Red Lion, Leytonstone.

15. Marquee, Soho, London.

Keith Moon: The only place that had any influence, where the managers and promoters and press could see us, was at the Marquee. They had a very discerning audience there, and it helped us develop our musical ideas. We were finding our feet, and the Marquee put us on our feet.

16. Florida Rooms, Brighton.

21. Red Lion, Leytonstone.

22. Marquee, Soho, London.

Keith Altham (journalist, *NME*): I first saw them at the Marquee on one of the Maximum R&B nights. I walked in and heard this absolute cacophony that sounded like somebody chainsawing a dustbin in half. I didn't really like them at first but I could see even then that the audience did.

Moon was obviously the friendliest. He was also the one with the girl-appeal – this lovely little button face. His first words were, "You haven't seen our singer, have you? Only he's going to kill me." I said. "Why?" He said, "Oh, I've just told him his singing is shit."

23. Florida Room, Brighton.

28. Red Lion, Leytonstone.

29. Marquee, Soho, London.

Roger Daltrey: We were getting 50 quid a night and Pete was smashing guitars worth £200 and amps worth twice that, every night. None of us had a car, and one of our managers had to get a job in a film to help pay off the debts.

Nick Jones (reviewer, *Melody Maker*):

> These four young musicians present their own brand of powerful, stinging rhythm-and-blues which quickly stimulated an enthusiastic audience. "Heatwave" – the Martha and the Vandellas hit number – is given typical fiery "Who" treatment. Another of their outstanding numbers was an instrumental, "You Can't Sit Down". This performance demonstrated the weird and effective techniques of guitarist Paul [sic] Townshend, who expertly uses speaker feedback to accompany many of his solos.

The Who, spurred by a most exhilarating drummer and a tireless vocalist, must surely be one of the most trendsetting groups of 1965.

Pete Townshend: Keith used to get through a lot of drum kits. He used to get a lot of stuff free, but you could never know. I mean, just a set of skins for a drum kit is about $300 and, after every show, he'd just go bang bang bang through all the skins and then kick the whole thing over.

Chris Stamp: It was costing hundreds of pounds a week in equipment to keep The Who on the move. But this was an investment. It made the group known.

1965

January 1965

The Who record a version of "I Can't Explain" at Pye Studios, London with producer Shel Talmy.

Pete Townshend: We were part of a machine. Pop-record churning-out machine, a big package . . . Shel came along at the front of the new wave of recording and of writing and said he was working with The Kinks, whom we admired very much – we didn't like their image but we liked their sound and their music.

We went to Shel and Kit Lambert made the first deal he'd made in show business, a deal which was really pathetic, like one-half per cent or something

John Entwistle: Because we signed the piece of paper, we're still paying him. We got two and a half per cent and he got two and a half per cent, like a 50-50 deal. When we had a chance to get more, we did.

Shel Talmy: The Who sound was something I was greatly responsible for. When I heard "I Can't Explain" on tape, it lasted about a minute and 30 seconds. I rearranged the whole thing and added a couple of choruses, and I think I brought in Perry Ford to play piano on it . . .

And I don't think that's an ego trip. All you have to do is listen to the record they did before I was with them, the High Numbers record, and compare the difference. And I certainly felt that after I stopped recording them, they weren't being recorded nearly as well. But I'm probably prejudiced.

Pete Townshend: He [Talmy] had a specific sound which he would impose on the group and it became very inflexible. I do think he was very talented and, in a sense, if it wasn't for him I don't think The Who would have got off the ground because I think perhaps his best production was "I Can't Explain".

Shel Talmy: My problems with the Who were with Kit Lambert, who was out of his fucking mind – I think he was certifiably insane, if he hadn't been in the music business, he would have been locked up.

The problem with him was his giant-sized ego plus paranoia. He felt I was usurping his authority because I was producing these recordings. His partner,

Chris Stamp, was hardly ever around. I always got along with Chris, I thought. But Chris never said a word.

Keith Moon meets his future wife, Kim Kerrigan, when The Who play at Disc A Go Go, Bournemouth.

Keith Moon: I met her in Bournemouth when I was playing a show. She was 16 and she hung out at the club where we worked, the Disc.

Kim Kerrigan: I thought he was lovely, big wide eyes, very sweet . . . He was funny, he was lovely, but it wasn't something I was looking for.

Keith Moon: Sometime later when I went down to see her, I was on a train and Rod Stewart was on the train. We got chatting and we went to the bar car. It was Rod "The Mod" Stewart in those glorious days and he'd just been working with Long John Baldry. He was playing a lot of small discotheques and pubs, doing the sort of work we were doing. I said to Rod, "Where are you going?" He said, "Bournemouth." "So'm I." So I showed Rod a picture of Kim and he said, "Yeah . . . that's 'er."

4. Red Lion, Leytonstone.

5. Marquee, Soho, London.

9. Club Noriek, Tottenham, London.

11. The Who's first TV appearance is a promotional film used on the UK TV show, "That's For Me".

12. Marquee, Soho, London.

13. Wolsey Hall, Cheshunt.

15. The Who's first single, "I Can't Explain", is released in the UK.

Pete Townshend: Shel Talmy signed us and it was then I really got into writing. I felt I was intimidating the group by writing for them.

Roger Daltrey: We already knew Pete could write songs, but it never seemed a necessity in those days to have your own stuff, because there was this wealth of untapped music that we could get hold of from America. But then bands like The Kinks started to make it, and they were probably the biggest influence on us . . .

Chris Stamp: Pete wanted to record his stuff, of course, but he couldn't push it, so it was down to me and Kit. The only block was Roger. The group was moving out of his grasp, and he wanted to do this heavy R&B thing, so that songs like "I Can't Explain" and later, "Substitute", were like pop to him.

Roger Daltrey: Shel Talmy didn't think that Pete's lead guitar playing was up to it and he didn't think our backing vocals were up to it. He was right about the backing vocals. And obviously in those days, you weren't in overdub facilities. You made the record and that was it. So if you wanted to put a solo on, you had to do it when you were doing the record.

Shel Talmy: It was my first session with The Who. Jimmy [Page] was there in case Pete couldn't cut it, but Pete was just fine.

I had the [guitar] amp off in a corner. I had both amps, guitar and bass, with rugs and baffles round them.

Pete Townshend: I think Shel Talmy didn't have much money and didn't have much understanding of what the band was about. As far as he was concerned, we were a phenomenon that would come and go and be finished in a month.

John Entwistle: He got Jimmy Page in, reputedly because he was the only guy in England with a fuzz box and Talmy wanted that sound.

Pete Townshend: Jimmy was there at the session to play lead guitar but, no, he didn't do the solo.

Jimmy was a friend of mine . . . I said to him "What are you doing here?" He said, "I'm here to give some weight to the guitar. I'm going to double the rhythm guitar on the overdubs. And I said, "Oh, great." And he said, "What are you going to play?" "A Rick twelve," I told him. And he said, "Oh, OK, I'll play a . . ." whatever it was. It was all very congenial.

Jimmy Page: I wasn't really needed on The Who's "Can't Explain" session, but I was there, and all I managed to do was sneak in a couple of phrases on the B-side.

Pete Townshend: Meanwhile, Keith was over in the corner, telling the [session] drummer, "Get out of the fucking studio or I'll kill ya. On a Who record, only Keith Moon plays the drums."

Roger Daltrey: I felt a bit uncomfortable when I had to sing it, because it wasn't like anything we'd ever done before – that kind of rhythm. But I was malleable – ha ha ha! And I think, later on, that added a lot of strength to Pete's writing. It became far easier for him to write for this . . . well, in some ways, almost a fictitious character, someone who was and wasn't him.

It's a bigger canvas to paint on when you're writing for someone else. By writing for a third person, having the words come out of someone else's mouth, even though he was writing personal songs, Pete could be that much more honest in what he was saying.

John Entwistle: Shel Talmy got The Ivy League in to do the vocal backing. It's a little bit too Beverley Sisters, but it probably saved money. He tried to replace me.

Shel Talmy: I talked to them about it beforehand, and memory's terribly selective when you want to do these kind of things – their backing vocals sucked. That's why I got The Ivy League doing them. Perry Ford was the pianist, who was in The Ivy League, on that session. So I didn't arbitrarily bring guys in without telling anybody what was happening.

17. New Theatre, Oxford.

18. As "I Can't Explain" enters the UK singles chart at No. 47, The Who appear on BBC TV show "The Beat Room", at BBC Television Theatre, Lime Grove, Shepherd's Bush, London.

19. Marquee, Soho, London.

23. Corn Exchange, Chelmsford.

26. Marquee, Soho, London.

29. The Who make their first appearance on UK TV show "Ready Steady Go!", along with The Hollies and Donovan.

Pete Townshend: "Ready Steady Go!" was what was really going on. They actually used to send people out to clubs in the provinces and pick out potential trend-setters. Fights used to start in the studio. People would appear on screen with sawed-off shotguns. They were so careful in picking people that were the faces they often got too close to the mark. They got people who really cared about their image.

Roger Daltrey: What happened at that show is that we basically took the show over by blocking anybody who wanted to get in and had a ticket to see the show. We nicked their tickets and filled it with our audience – who were all mods.

Chris Stamp: Really, it was an amazingly successful first television. Sure, the boys were nervous – they knew nothing about cameras or television technique. They didn't know what to expect . . . they went into a hand-clapping, gum-chewing sort of routine and they just about had the audience exploding. This was nationally networked, so it gave them a sort of instant impact.

Roger Daltrey: The director had the great idea of putting Keith on a rostrum with wheels on it, and he was just kinda pushed through the crowd.

The ultimate thing for Moon was . . . his whole thing was that he should have been on the front of the stage and I should have been singing behind him. And that's why he hated me so much, 'cause I stood in front of him. And it was just a stroke of genius. Because there it was, all of a sudden on "Ready Steady Go!". There were all these geeky people doing this weirdo dancing. All that step-dancing. And all these cool mods looking really like people from another planet! And this band, with this drummer who was playing like a complete raving lunatic – the way only Moon could, being pushed around by the crowd.

Chris Stamp: The show went out from Holborn and the audience was almost entirely mod. They all wore these old college scarves and at the end of The Who's spot, they all hurled them all on stage. The boys just stood there, kinda festooned.

Roger Daltrey: You know, it was extraordinary. I think everything just took off from there.

31. Marquee, Soho, London.

February 1965

2. Marquee, Soho, London.

5. Town Hall, Bath.

9. Marquee, Soho, London.

11. Ealing Club, West London.

Speedy Keene (musician): In the early days I used to play in a band out in the west, in Ealing, and there were a few bands who could come in and really break things up, and they were the Stones and The Who . . . Townshend would go into the local music store and buy 10 Rickenbackers. In those days a Rickenbacker guitar meant real class; they cost about 300 quid and anyone who owned one stood apart – and he would bust them all up in a week, then take 'em back without paying for 'em. This caused quite a stir at the time, for a guy to get three grand worth of guitars and bust them up.

Roger Daltrey: We had lots of shops that would give us credit. And thank God for Jim Marshall. We used to just run and say, "Hi Jim," and two of us would keep him talking at the counter while someone else would take a guitar off the wall and run out. He got paid in full in the end, though.

Pete Townshend: Jim Marshall started manufacturing amplifiers and somebody in his store came up with the idea of building a 4 x 12 cabinet for bass. And John Entwistle bought one and I looked at it and suddenly John

Entwistle doubled in volume. And so I bought one and then later on I bought another one and I stacked it on top of the other one.

John Entwistle: I didn't buy the very first one. It was a guy in a band called The Flintstones who got that. I bought the second one . . . and the fourth, and the seventh, and the eighth. Pete bought the ones in between. It was great, I'd buy one, he'd buy one, I'd buy one, then he'd buy another. As I went, "Is it loud enough? Fuck, I'll buy two more." And I started using the two-amp system – bi-amping. Then we had a period where we switched to Vox equipment because we figured it would be louder. But it wasn't. It just blew up. So we'd always been trying to persuade Marshall to make us a 100-watt amp. They told us it would be impossible: the amp would be too heavy to carry around. We said, "Put a handle on each end."

Pete Townshend: I was using a Rickenbacker at the time and because the pickup was right in line with the speakers I was instantly troubled by feedback. But I really used to like to hear the sound in my ears. I didn't like it coming out down there (below ear level) because I felt it was coming in my ear I could get it louder for me but it wasn't necessarily going to be louder out front. And I started to get quite interested in feedback, but I was very frustrated at first. There were a lot of brilliant young players around – Beck was around. I think Roger first saw him when he was in a band called The Triads or The Tridents or something and he came back and said there was this incredible young guitar player. And Clapton was around and various other people who could really play and I was very frustrated because I couldn't do all that flash stuff. So I just started getting into feedback and expressed myself physically.

12. The Who audition for BBC radio in London. They pass, by a narrow margin, and are booked to appear on "The Joe Loss Pop Show".

13. "I Can't Explain" is released in the US on Decca Records, where it will peak at No. 93.

Shel Talmy: The Who was funny, because I brought them to Decca America, who were a very nice bunch of guys, older men who had no idea what rock'n'roll was. They didn't understand what the hell I was doing, but they said if that's what's supposedly selling, then we'll go out and try to sell it, which of course they did.

The second record we did, "Anyway, Anyhow, Anywhere", had a bunch of feedback on it, which I believe was the first record which had that kind of stuff on it. I got a cable from them, after we sent it in, saying, "We think we got a bad tape, it seems to have feedback all over it." So I assured them that was the way it was. Of course, "My Generation" followed that, which had as much or more feedback on it. They didn't really understand, but they stuck to what they knew best, which was selling a record.

16. Marquee, Soho, London.

18. Ealing Club, West London.

22. "I Can't Explain" reaches No. 40 in the UK singles chart.

23. Marquee, Soho, London.

24. First "Top Of The Pops" performance, at Studio A, BBC Television, Manchester.

25. The Ealing Club, West London.

26. Lynx Club, Borehamwood.

March 1965

1. "I Can't Explain" rises to No. 33 in the UK singles chart.

2. Marquee, Soho, London.

8. "I Can't Explain" rises to No. 26 in the UK singles chart.

9. Marquee, Soho, London.

11. Recording sessions for their debut album at IBC Studios, Portland Place, London. ("I Don't Mind", "Please Please Please", "I'm A Man", "Louie (Come Back Home)", "Heatwave", "Motoring", "You're Going To Know Me", "Leaving Here".)

Pete Townshend: We made our first album in, I think, six hours. Shel's attitude was, "You're just a load of punks and I made you; you should be happy you've got where you have because if it wasn't for me you'd be nowhere."

On the first album we had [pianist] Nicky Hopkins in there with us. There's something about recording that diminishes the power of a three-man group and you have to have the extra harmonic element.

12. Nancy Lewis of *Fabulous* magazine interviews The Who during a gig at Goldhawk Social Club, Shepherd's Bush, London.

Nancy Lewis: Being very low on the staff of *Fabulous*, I didn't get to interview The Rolling Stones or The Beatles. I had to go out for the one-hit wonders, so they sent me to interview The Who. I had heard that Townshend was supposed to be strange but not much had been written about them so I didn't know enough to be scared.

Chris Stamp sorta came up and said, "Hi, I'm Kit's partner." He was very boring and talked about this film he had just finished doing in Norway with Kirk Douglas. I just wanted to go home. Then the group came off and I did a very stimulating interview with them, asking, "What are your likes and dislikes?" They were very nice and very young and did the interview totally straight.

They didn't seem to like each other very much and they were such different people, I just could never see them lasting. I didn't do it maliciously.

13. Club Noriek, Tottenham, London.

14. Starlite Ballroom, Wembley.

John Burgoyne (audience): The Starlite was the local dance hall where I'd go with my mates at the weekend. It was up these narrow stairs. The Who started to play there regularly. More than the music, I particularly remember that as they finished Keith kicked his drum kit over and walked off, leaving the drums all over the stage.

15. Recording UK TV show "Gadzooks, It's All Happening" at Shepherd's Bush Television Theatre, London.

16. Marquee, Soho, London.

18. Civic Hall, Crawley.

19. Public Baths, Royston.

20. Goldhawk Social Club, Shepherd's Bush, London.

Pete Townshend: Having written "I Can't Explain", which was a love song of frustration, I was informed by various members of the Goldhawk Club audience, me being informed by them, these uneducated, inarticulate kids, that what it actually was was a song about their inability to communicate their inability to communicate. Now that's a pretty high concept.

They got it, and I didn't. When they came to me with that idea, telling me, "You have to write more songs like that," sort of nailing the nail into my skull for me to get it – "What? Songs about the fact that you can't explain what you want to explain?" – like they're idiots, and they're going, "Yes, that's what we mean. We want you, because you're articulate and you can speak and you can write songs . . ." So I was charged with this job.

21. Trade Union Hall, Watford.

22. Parr Hall, Warrington.

23. Marquee, Soho, London.

24. Ealing Club, West London.
25. "Top Of The Pops", Studio A, BBC Television, Manchester, performing "I Can't Explain". Followed by the Blue Opera Club, Edmonton.

Keith Moon: When I started showing off a bit, the directors would notice. There were two great directors, Mike Lindsey-Hogg and Mike Mansfield, and they started getting the camera on the drums. "Ready Steady Go!" and "Top Of The Pops" really treated the band as a whole and, up until then, it was just Billy Fury and his group or Adam Faith and his group. Most of the TV in those days was only a couple of cameras, one trained on the front of the singer and the other getting a side shot of the singer and they never bothered with the rest of the group.

They were always there as part of the furniture. It wasn't until Townshend started smashing guitars and I started smashing up the drums that the producers of the shows began to realize that there was more than the singer in the band. They'd actually line up a camera for the drums, which was a first. People started to actually notice the drummer.

26. Railway Hotel, Harrow & Wealdstone.
27. Rhodes Centre, Bishop's Stortford.
28. Ritz and Kavern Clubs, Birmingham.
30. Marquee, Soho, London.
31. Bromel Club, Bromley Court Hotel, Bromley.

April 1965

1. "Top Of The Pops", BBC Television, Manchester, followed by a gig supporting Donovan at the Town Hall, Wembley. Rod Stewart is bottom of the bill.
2. At lunchtime, The Who play their first BBC radio session on "The Joe Loss Show" at the Paris Theatre, London, followed by an evening gig at the Youth Centre, Loughton.

Roger Daltrey: We usually had to do them [BBC radio sessions] very early in the morning. Those days we were gigging every night, sometimes two gigs a night, and the morning is something we never used to see in those days, unless it was a BBC session. In that sense they weren't very enjoyable.

John Entwistle: I always hated them.

Roger Daltrey: Some of them were live in front of audiences, kind of a variety show where there'd be a live band, a big band that would play current hits, versions of whatever was in the charts, and usually very badly. One of those bands, incidentally, had Elvis Costello's dad as the singer.

3. London College of Printing, Elephant & Castle, London.

Brian May (later guitarist for Queen): I remember they played at one of the colleges in London, and they were an hour and a half late. No one was sure if they were gonna show up, and the place was seething with about a thousand kids. When they finally came on, they didn't give a shit. Townshend waved his arms and started making airplane noises for about twenty minutes before they even played a song. They didn't have any regard for anything, and it was wonderful and real.

4. Plaza, Newbury.

5. Lakeside Club, Hendon.

6. Marquee, Soho, London.

7. Dacorum College, Hemel Hempstead.

8. Olympia Ballroom, Reading.

Richard Barnes: Reading, 1965, was the first time I realized they were big. But Keith wasn't flash then. He was quite in awe of the band and realized he was the new boy and was a bit polite. He came up to me after the Reading gig and said, "Have you got anything in the upward direction, dear boy?" I had about 24 purple hearts to last me the next three weeks. I expected him to take one or two but in this one amazing movement [Moon gulped them all down]. I was pissed off, but also incredibly impressed at the same time.

9. Stamford Hall, Altrincham.

10. Cavern Club, Leicester Square, London.

12. "I Can't Explain" peaks at No. 8 in the UK singles chart.

Ray Davies (Kinks): I think we should have done something about The Who's "I Can't Explain". Not the song so much, but the whole style. The High Numbers supported us many times, and their music was nothing like "I Can't Explain". We came back from a world tour, heard this record on the radio, and Dave thought it was us. Shel Talmy produced it, like he did us. They used the same session singers and pianist we did. I felt a bit appalled by that. The only reason I let it go was I'd seen Keith Moon play, and he was such a funny, nice, original guy. I think that was worse than actually stealing a song – stealing a whole style.

13. Marquee, Soho, London.

Roger Daltrey: When we got our first hit, "I Can't Explain", we started earning what was then pretty good money, say £300 a night. But after the first year, we were £60,000 in debt. The next year, after working our balls off, we were still £40,000 down. And the biggest choke of all came the year after that when we found we were back up to £60,000 again. Every accountants' meeting was ridiculous. We always owed so much money that we ended up rolling around the office laughing ourselves silly.

14. Il Rondo, Leicester.

16. Goldhawk Social Club, Shepherd's Bush, London.

17. Florida Rooms, Brighton

18. Civic Hall, Crawley.

19. Botwell House, Hayes.

20. Marquee, Soho, London.

22. Waterfront Club, Southampton.

23. Oasis Club, Manchester.

24. Lynx Club, Borehamwood, followed by an all-nighter at Club Noriek, Tottenham, London.

John Entwistle: We used to play up north and dash back in the furniture van to play Tottenham. We were complete pill-heads, and we'd often still be playing when the other group went on. Then we got to playing drunk, and I'd often forget I'd done a gig. Moon would pass out before a gig, sober up just before we went on, play like a maniac, and go back on the bottle as soon as we finished.

25. Trade Union Hall, Watford.

26. Town Hall, Bridgwater.

27. Marquee, Soho, London.

28. Bromel Club, Bromley Court Hotel, Bromley.

30. Town Hall, Trowbridge.

May 1965

1. College of Art and Technology, Leicester.

2. Dungeon Club, Nottingham.

Richard Evans (audience): I was a fashion student at Nottingham Art School in 1965 and had got myself on the Social Committee because it meant you could get into the college dances for nothing. We booked The Who for this gig at the

Dungeon. I'd just bought "I Can't Explain" and I loved it.

The Who turned up about two hours late to a very disgruntled crowd of pissed-off and drunken arts students. Once they started playing, though, they were forgiven. It was worth the wait. I particularly remember Townshend and Moon, but especially Townshend. We thought he was the coolest looking bloke we'd ever seen. I think it was the shoes.

3. Majestic, Newcastle.

Chris Stamp: Early on we had a series of disasters. We were the great group for things going wrong. When we first ventured up north, the people there didn't know what we were trying to do. Most nights ended with a violent punch-up.

Kit Lambert: The clubs, more than the ballrooms, didn't catch on. It seemed a bit beyond them. This affected the boys very much. They're not a group who play for themselves, but rely completely on audience reaction, and if they are not appreciated, they are tremendously brought down about the whole thing.

4. Palladium, Greenock, Scotland.

5. City Hall, Perth, Scotland.

6. Elgin, Scotland.

7. Raith Ballroom, Kirkcaldy, Scotland.

9. De Montfort Hall, Leicester.

11. Marquee, Soho, London.

12. Palais, Bury.

13. Public Hall, Barrow-in-Furness.

14. Civic Hall, Dunstable.

15. Top Twenty Club, Neeld Hall, Chippenham.

16. Town Hall, Stratford, East London.

17. Pavilion, Bath.

18. Recording the TV show "Scene At 6.30", Granada TV Playhouse, Manchester, followed by a gig at the Railway Hotel, Harrow & Wealdstone.

19. It is believed that Townshend wrote "My Generation" on the journey to Southern Television Studios, Southampton, where The Who were recording the TV show "Three Go Round". Later that evening, they play a gig at the Corn Exchange, Bristol.

Pete Townshend: "My Generation" came straight out of the consciousness that I felt I'd landed with. It was the beginning of me taking on some of Roger's attributes and trying to empower myself with some of his attributes. He had

more traditional and acceptable good looks, was very tough, and didn't take shit from anybody. So I took that and kind of combined it with my kind of social sensibility. I think that's what was so successful and why it was an extraordinary moment. There was a whole group of people who realized, "We don't have to be weak because we don't have wars to fight. We don't have to be powerless. We don't have to be shit because they say we're shit. We can be shit because we say we're shit." I don't think it's a healthy song and I don't think it comes from a healthy period, but I think it's led to a healthy place. "My Generation" was one of the songs that helped draw a line right across life and say, "Everything up to this point does not relate to this group of people who are growing older." I think there's a tremendous desire in young Western kids to draw that line again and they're trying, but are finding it much harder than we found it.
20. Town Hall, Kidderminster.
21. The Who release "Anyway, Anyhow, Anywhere" in the UK. On the same day, Keith Moon takes Kim to The Who's recording date for "Ready Steady Goes Live!" at Wembley Studios, Wembley. Later, The Who play at the Ricky Tick Club, Guildford.

Roger Daltrey: We were a bit stuck for a second single. Then, one afternoon, we were rehearsing at the Marquee, and Pete came in with an idea, which we developed into a song. He had the line "Anyway, Anyhow, Anywhere", and a few other bits, but we basically structured it right there on the stage.

Pete Townshend: I wrote the first verse of "Anyway, Anyhow, Anywhere" – "I can go anywhere, I can do anything, anyway I choose . . ." – and Roger helped me with the rest of the verses.

Roger Daltrey: He would do this bit and I would say, "What about that bit?" and we put this bit and that bit and the song came together like that . . . I think I wrote the bridge, toughened it up a bit, and some of the chorus.

Pete Townshend: I was inspired by listening to Charlie Parker, feeling that this was really a free spirit, you know? And whatever he'd done with drugs and booze and everything else, that his playing released him and freed his spirit, and I wanted us to be like that. And I wanted to write a song about that, a spiritual song, "We can go anywhere, we can do anything, we are free . . ." And then Roger started to add lyrics like, "I can get through locked doors . . ."

Roger Daltrey: And we recorded it the next day. That's why there's no demo of it.

Shel Talmy (producer): To my knowledge, it was the first ever record with feedback recorded on it. Pete was playing around with it as an idea and we had to work out some technique in the studio to get it down on tape.

Everybody said that feedback shouldn't be part of a record, and it's impossible to pick up anyway, but I used three different microphones at different points in the room to capture all the overtones of the feedback. It was a very different set-up than "I Can't Explain". I had Pete really cranking it to the max. The combination of those three microphones was the only way to get that sound.

John Entwistle: The funny thing was that the record company sent it back complaining that there was a lot of noise and feedback at the end. We never did get that right.

Roger Daltrey: By this time, the mod thing was really developing. Everything was so fast. Every week there'd be a new fashion, a new shirt style, a new jumper, a new jacket, new shoes would be in.

One night we put flags on our speakers and then Kit came up with the idea of making the flags into jackets, which was a stroke of genius. It was probably highly illegal, to deface the flag, but look what it did. Before that, you never saw a Union Jack anywhere, except up a bloody flagpole. After we did that with it, Union Jacks were on everything. People forget that. It was The Who that started that. We didn't get the idea from a carrier bag. The carrier bag came from The Who.

Nancy Lewis (journalist, *Fabulous*): They sent me an advance copy of the single. It had this exploding cover and they said it was gonna be a great hit. Hype, hype on the phone. And the first time I didn't like it at all 'cause it was very unusual for its time. I mean there was like explosive noises and feedback and things on it which were totally foreign elements then.

Kim Kerrigan: That was when Keith introduced me to the pills. I was ready for it. I loved it.

Chris Stamp: They were like these two children together, these two incredible beauties. They were besotted. They couldn't keep their hands off each other.

22. Astoria Ballroom, Rawtenstall.

24. The Who record a version of "Anyway, Anyhow, Anywhere" for BBC radio at the Aeolian Hall, Studio 2, London. Later they play at the Majestic, Reading.

25. Marquee, Soho, London.

27. "Anyway, Anyhow, Anywhere" enters the UK singles chart, where it will peak at No. 10. The Who play at the Assembly Hall, Worthing.

Chris Stamp: Our first record had been a hit and this second one was virtually a flop, comparatively speaking . . . but whereas the first one was just a single, "Anyway" really showed the fans and the business where The Who were actually going.

28. Ricky Tick Club, Windsor.

29. The Who feature, playing a pre-recorded live session, on BBC radio show "Saturday Club". Later in the day they record TV show "Thank Your Lucky Stars" at Alpha Television Studios, Birmingham, then finish the day off with a show at the Pavilion Ballroom, Buxton.

30. Mojo Club, Sheffield.

31. When The Who arrive at TWW Studios, Bristol, to mime an appearance on "Discs A Go Go", they are refused permission to appear because there is a piano on the record, but they have no pianist.

Chris Mercer (producer, "Discs A Go Go"): I regarded the piano as very important and wanted it represented visually.

Mid-1965

Pete Townshend is seen wearing a jacket made from a Union Jack flag.

Roger Daltrey: Kit came up with the idea for that jacket. He should be posthumously knighted for it. Prior to that the Union Jack had only ever been flown on buildings as the national flag. When we walked into a Savile Row tailor and said, "Will you make a jacket out of this?" they said, "No." They thought we'd go to jail.

June 1965

1. The Who play their first European date at the Olympia, Paris, France.

2. Club Au Golf Drouot, Paris, France.

4. Trentham Gardens, Stoke-on-Trent.

5. "Anyway, Anyhow, Anywhere" is released in the US. On the same day, The Who play at Loyola Hall, Stamford Hill, North London.

6. St. Joseph Hall, Upper Holloway, North London.

7. Marquee, Soho, London.

8. Public Hall, Wallington.

9. Il Rondo, Leicester.

11. Co-op Ballroom, Nuneaton.
12. Town Hall, Dudley.
13. Manor Lounge, Stockport.
14. Recording live session for BBC radio show "Top Gear" at Maida Vale Studios, London.
15. Town Hall, High Wycombe.
16. Town Hall, Stourbridge.
17. Recording UK TV show "Top Of The Pops" at BBC Television Studios, Manchester, followed by a gig at Bowes Lyon House, Stevenage.
18. Floral Hall, Morecambe.
19. The Who, Spencer Davis Group, Marianne Faithfull, John Mayall and Long John Baldry are among the artists performing at the Uxbridge Blues and Folk Festival. Later in the day, The Who fit in another gig at The Cavern in Central London.
20. Blue Moon, Hayes.
24. Town Hall, Greenwich.
25. Ricky Tick, Windsor.
26. The Who play at the Town Hall, High Wycombe, then an all-nighter at Club Noriek, London, where they are recorded live for broadcast the following night on Radio Luxembourg's show "Ready Steady Radio!".
27. Starlite Ballroom, Greenford, West London.
28. Manor House Ballroom, Ipswich.
29. Burton's Ballroom, Uxbridge.
30. Town Hall, Farnborough.

July 1965

1. Marquee, Soho, London.
2. UK TV show "Ready Steady Go!" features The Who, Manfred Mann, Nina Simone, The Ad Libs, The Majority and comedy duo Peter Cook and Dudley Moore.
3. "Anyway, Anyhow, Anywhere" reaches its UK peak of No. 10.
5. Assembly Rooms, Tunbridge Wells.
7. The Who play at the gala opening of The Manor House, London.

Chris Welch: The gig was in a tiny little upstairs room, packed with mods and very hot. I was reviewing it for *Melody Maker*, and I managed to get right down the front so I could see exactly what was going on.

It was a great gig, but Moon played with such manic energy that he collapsed at the end of the set and slumped forward over his drum kit. A couple of roadies rushed on, looking very worried, and dragged him out feet first, down the stairs and out into the open air, where he recovered quite quickly. Pete and Roger disappeared soon after, leaving Keith and John stranded, so I had the pleasure of driving them in my car to the Scotch of St James nightclub afterwards.

Keith Moon: When The Who started, I began playing a constant drum solo throughout the act and Chris Welch saw us and probably thought, "I've noticed the drummer for the first time." In that era, nobody ever took any notice of the drummer. It was all guitars and singers. When I started twirling the sticks and standing up and those kind of things, nobody else did that kind of thing in rock. I'm a total extrovert, I love to be involved. I don't like this great big kit in front of me and the audience. I envy the guitarist who can go over and get that much closer to the audience. I can't do that, I have to sit at the back, so I acted in a different way and started to draw attention to the drums in a different way by acrobatics and all the tricks.

So, a lot of people used to say, "God, look at the drummer!" So I suppose there was a certain amount of revolutionizing the drummer's role. Actually bringing the drummer out as an integral part of the group. The group wasn't just made up of a singer and a lead guitarist. You used to watch pop shows on TV and they'd just show the singer, the rest of the band being just a backup group and nothing else.

9. Locarno Ballroom, Basildon.

10. Winter Gardens, Ventnor.

11. Savoy Ballroom, Southsea, Portsmouth.

12. The Moody Blues throw a party at their house in Roehampton. Guests include The Beatles' Paul McCartney, his girlfriend Jane Asher, George Harrison and Patti Boyd,The Who, Rod Stewart, Marianne Faithfull, Sandie Shaw, Doris Troy, Long John Baldry, Viv Prince (The Pretty Things), Hilton Valentine (The Animals), Twinkle and Goldie & The Gingerbreads.

13. Marquee, Soho, London.

14. Locarno, Stevenage.

15. Ritz, Llanelli.

16. Town Hall, Cheltenham.

17. Town Hall, Torquay.
28. The Pontiac, Putney.
30. The Fender, Kenton.
31. The Wilton, Bletchley.

August 1965

1. Britannia Pier Theatre, Great Yarmouth.
4. The Witch Doctor, St Leonard's-on-Sea.
6. After recording another appearance on "Ready Steady Go!" at Wembley Studios, London, The Who go on to appear at the 5th National Jazz and Blues Festival, Richmond, where Moon's performance is fuelled by taking 20 amphetamine pills beforehand.

Chris Welch (*Melody Maker*):

Keith Moon's drum solo was an explosive firing on all tom-toms. Keith looked like a white tornado, dressed in slacks and T-shirt soaked in sweat.

7. Loyola Hall, Tottenham, London.
8. Britannia Pier Theatre, Great Yarmouth, with Donovan.
13. Central Pier, Morecambe.
15. Britannia Pier Theatre, Great Yarmouth, with Donovan.
20. Pavilion, Bournemouth.
21. Palais, Peterborough.
22. Britannia Pier Theatre, Great Yarmouth, with Donovan.
23. Corn Exchange, Colchester.
24. Town Hall, High Wycombe.
26. City Hall, Salisbury.
27. Town Hall, Torquay.
28. Matrix Club, Coventry.
29. Mojo Club, Sheffield.
30. Sophia Gardens, Cardiff, Wales.

September 1965

3. Recording another appearance on "Ready Steady Go!" at ATV's Wembley Studios, London.
4. The Who's stage gear is stolen from their van, which is parked outside Battersea Dogs' Home in London, but that night they play a show at the Spa

Royal Hotel, Bridlington.

John Entwistle: The police found it the next day, but not before we got another consignment from Vox. They all blew up in the end. We took them back to the Vox factory and piled them up outside in the rain. They never charged us for them.

6. Town Hall, Farnborough.

11. Imperial Ballroom, Nelson.

20. Recording a Dutch TV show at Studio Bellevue, Hilversum, Netherlands.

21. De Marathon, The Hague, Netherlands.

25. Folkets Hus, Helsingor and K.B. Hallen, Aarhus, both in Denmark.

26. In Aarhus Hallen, Aarhus, Denmark, Roger Daltrey punches out Keith Moon and is almost thrown out of the band. Later that night, they play a second gig in Fredrikstorv, Aalborg.

Roger Daltrey: There was a tour of Europe where they were doing speed more and more and more – I couldn't do speed, because it'll dry your throat up – but we did this tour and we were all so out of it and the music was going down the tubes, it was fucking dire.

Pete Townshend: In Denmark, they were really wild. In Aarhus, they got completely out of hand. That's a farming area and the hall was packed with four to five thousand young farmers, a rather rough audience . . .

Svante Borjesson (audience): Violence lay in the air of Aarhus Hallen even long before The Who were to perform. They had to do their set rather early in the schedule, to be in time to do a show in Aalborg as well. The thousand-strong audience were tearing their chairs apart, and throwing pieces, along with bottles and trash, at the supporting groups.

By the time The Who got on stage, the audience had turned into a riot mob. Again, kids tried to get up on stage. George Mitchew once more tried to push them back. Instead, he was pulled down into the audience where he was beaten and kicked. The Who only played half of one song before the situation got completely out of hand. The kids stormed the stage, took the instruments that were still there and began smashing them. The Who and their management had already escaped through the back exit, once they realized what was happening.

Keith Moon: I was taking a lot of speed. Roger wasn't because it used to fuck his voice up. Roger was drinking and we were all speeding . . . Roger blew up, "You're all fucking junkies! The group's finished as far as I'm concerned." And he took a swing at me.

Roger Daltrey: I was so fed up with it, I went in the dressing room and there was Moon's big bag of pills and I just threw them down the toilet. Moon went absolutely apeshit and came at me with a tambourine . . . I was heartbroken. I didn't want to fall out with him.

Chris Stamp: Roger was not liked by Keith at all. They were bitter enemies. Roger got the close-ups on TV, Roger got the girls, Roger was the singer. He was in front of Keith most of the time.

John Entwistle: We were sorting out the pecking order. Everyone wanted to be the most important member of the band. I decided to be the best musician in the band. Pete Townshend went his own way, wanted to do most of the writing. Roger and Keith were the ones the little girls screamed for, and they were fighting for that.

Pete Townshend: We were in the dressing room, yelling and hitting each other when a photographer called Bent Reg appeared and started taking pictures and writing things down. We all stood to attention and saluted, but he went back to England and told everyone what had happened.

Roger Daltrey: I was slung out of the band there and then. I calmed down and was apologizing for what I'd done. I had a terrible temper. I'm embarrassed to think about it now. I was horrible.

Svante Borjesson: The concert in Aalborg was something of an anti-climax. Still, The Who played a good concert to almost ecstatic kids.

27. The Who consider the implications of Daltrey being thrown out of the band.

Pete Townshend: Kit was into forming a double group. Keith on drums, John on bass, me on guitar together with the band Paddy, Klaus and Gibson. That was Kit and I just groping for something that might keep the band together.

Roger Daltrey: Fortunately, management stood by me, and I promised never to fight again.

October 1965

2. The Who make their US debut playing "I Can't Explain" on "Shindig".

John "Binky" Philips (fan, viewer): I had never seen amplifiers before and Townshend had his big super Beatle with a Union Jack draped over it. I dug the Stones a lot and Daltrey didn't really hit me because I was into Jagger so much, but Townshend's face, especially his nose, and Keith Moon really blew my head. I had only seen a drummer like Charlie Watts and here was this guy just making faces, closing his eyes, blowing his cheeks up and swinging his arms like a maniac. I really dug them.

6. With Daltrey back in the band, The Who play at the Kinema Ballroom, Dunfermline, Scotland.

Pete Townshend: Kit Lambert intervened and said, "Give him another chance," and said to Roger, "In the future, if you want to make a point, it's got to be discussed sensibly, no more getting things done by violence." Roger said, "From now on, I'll be Peaceful Perce . . ."

Roger Daltrey: I said, look, I promise not to fight any more. At that time, I didn't know any other way to articulate my feelings. I was brought up a lot rougher than them. Pete was middle class and so was John. I was this little guy, and the only way I could solve anything was to have it out there and then. I decided to learn to bite my lip. Moon, of course, had a field day. He made me this figure of fun and there was nothing I could do about it.

John Entwistle: There was a certain amount of pride swallowed on each side. Roger promised not to hit us and we promised to behave.

8. City Hall, Perth, Scotland.

9. Market Hall, Carlisle.

10. Two shows in Sweden – a matinee at Johanneshovs Isstadion in Stockholm (supported by The Overlanders and The Lee Kings) and an evening show, the Pop Gala, at Cirkus Lorensbergs in Gothenburg.

Lasse Sandegren (drummer, Lee Kings): There was no time for The Who to bring anything but their guitars to the late show. They had to borrow our amps and drums. Keith obviously liked my Ludwig kit a lot, because this evening in Gothenburg he wanted to borrow my drums again even though he had his own. I remember he broke a drum head, but I got one of his spares.

Monica Tromm (Swedish music critic): The Pop Gala was very boring, all instruments were intact. Roger walked around dragging a microphone stand, but that was also the most exciting . . .

11. Parr Hall, Warrington.

12. Recording "A Legal Matter" and "The Ox", at IBC Studios, Portland Place, London.

Roger Daltrey: For the *My Generation* album, there was nothing to be nervous about in them days. We used to take every day as it came. Every day was just a gig and I think we did the recording between gigs, literally. We did the whole album in two afternoons and by the end of the week we were playing the stuff onstage. That's how wonderful it was in those days.

13. Recording "My Generation" and "The Kids Are Alright" at IBC Studios, Portland Place, London.

Pete Townshend: I wrote the lines of "My Generation" without thinking, hurrying them – scribbling on a piece of paper in the back of a car. For years I've had to live by them, waiting for the day when someone says, "I thought you said you hoped you'd die when you got old. Well, now you are old. What now?" Of course, most people are too polite to say that sort of thing to a dying pop star. I say it often to myself.

I wrote it just after I did "I Can't Explain". We had loads of rows about doing it. Chris Stamp was all for it, but the others kept wanting to put their own bits in. The ending is a natural progression of what's come before. It's the way it happens on stage . . . It was meant to get back more to the general theme at the end, but it doesn't.

Roger Daltrey: The demo of "My Generation" was very Bo Diddley, jink-ajink-ajink – ajink-jink, and it was only when we got into the studio that Moon got to grips with it. Moon hated playing that stuff. It was all too much for him. He loved to bash on the on-beat, on the one, so he soon changed the original rhythm.

Then, as I was singing the words, the idea for the character to stutter came from Kit Lambert.

Keith Moon: Pete had written out the words and given them to Roger in the studio. He'd never seen them before, so when he read them the first time, he stuttered . . . Kit said, "Leave in the stuttering." When we realized what had happened, it knocked us all sideways. And it happened simply because Roger couldn't read the words.

Shel Talmy (producer): I think the stuttering bit was a gag that came about screwing around during rehearsal, and then when it came to the "f%$£ off" it seemed even funnier and something we could get away with, and I guess we did. Of course, the BBC banned the record, because it was detrimental to the stutterers of the world, which helped immensely.

John Entwistle: A lot of the solos I played were much faster and more interesting than the ones that finally went on the record. I'd play a really fast solo, and they'd say it hadn't recorded properly, so I'd play something simpler. I was using a Danelectro bass with very thin strings, which were inclined to break, but you couldn't buy replacement Danelectro strings in Britain then, so I'd have to buy a new guitar. I went through three guitars at £60 a time during the recording of "My Generation". In the end, they decided to record it one more time, and I bust a string again and there literally weren't any more Danelectros in the country. I went out and bought a Fender Jazz bass and put the trebliest strings I could find on to it – tape-wound La Bella strings – and played the solo on that.

Pete Townshend: Perhaps if I had died before I got old, I might have been forgotten. You tend to hope you'll become James Dean or Jimi Hendrix, but a lot of dead people aren't remembered at all . . . But I've tried to compensate by actually making myself happy.

14. Skating Rink, Camborne.

15. Hillside Ballroom, Hereford.

16. Baths Ballroom, Scunthorpe.

20. Top Rank, Southampton.

22. Social Centre, Milford Haven, Wales.

23. Rhodes Centre, Bishop's Stortford.

24. Carlton Ballroom, Slough.

25. Trade Union Hall, Watford.

28. The Who release "My Generation" in the UK and play at The Locarno, Swindon.

Pete Townshend: By the time we'd made our third record, I was realizing that what was going on was that I was writing the material, we were going in and [Shel Talmy] was just sitting there, and this man called Glyn Johns, the engineer, was doing all the work.

John Entwistle: All Talmy seemed to do was replace us with other people to make his job easier. He was there to rush us along, basically. Glyn Johns was the one that got the sounds. So eventually we went to Glyn as a producer.

29. Starlite Ballroom, Greenford, West London.

30. Manchester University.

Colin Jones (photographer): They used to do two shows a night. I can remember we went to a new club in the break and they got through all these bottles of Mateus Rose . . . When you were with them you tended to go towards Townshend rather than the others. Keith Moon didn't say very much at all, he just wanted to get pissed. Roger Daltrey was like a boxer who'd just won a big fight. He wasn't in the same league as Townshend. None of them were, except Keith Moon, musically, as a drummer.

31. The Who play their only date ever at The Cavern, Liverpool.

November 1965

1. St Matthew's Hall, Ipswich.

2. Marquee, Soho, London.

3. Locarno, Stevenage.

Colin Jones: Entwistle would stand like a lamp-post for the whole gig, maybe tapping his foot, and Roger Daltrey would be sticking his crotch out at the audience. He was always the sex symbol, the Adonis of the group. He had that conceit. There was an I-love-myself sort of thing when he performed.

4. "My Generation" by The Who enters the UK singles charts, and The Who cancel a gig at Queen's Hall, Barnstaple, because Roger has a throat infection.

Pete Townshend: If there was ever a period when The Who might have split, it would have been in the days of "My Generation". We had an image of no time for anybody and mod arrogance, in a period when we were actually a very ordinary group. We hadn't really done anything good, but we knew we were capable so we managed, over a period, to get it together.

5. Recording UK TV show appearance on "Ready Steady Go!" at Wembley Studios, London.

6. Pete Townshend explains "My Generation" in *Record Mirror.* In the evening, the band plays at St George's Ballroom, Hinckley.

Pete Townshend: The guy who's singing "My Generation" is supposed to be blocked. It's reminiscent in a way because mods don't get blocked any more. They get drunk or other things. Pills was a phase . . . No, he's not blocked, he just can't form his words.

7. Mojo Club, Sheffield.

11. Gig in Paris, France.

12. Gig in Paris, France.

13. La Locomotive, Paris, France.

15. Pavilion, Bath.

16. Recording "The Kids Are Alright" at IBC Studios, London, followed by a gig at the Winter Gardens, Malvern.

Colin Jones: Roger used to have trouble remembering the words. The way they worked then, it was all done very fast, so they'd be in a studio making a record and then it would be on the street the next day. Roger would have to sit playing his Dansette, writing down the lyrics.

19. After recording a "Ready Steady Go!" appearance at Wembley Studios in the early evening, The Who go on to play at the Glad Rags Ball in London, where Daltrey storms off stage fuelling rumours that the band is about to split.

Roger Daltrey: We dashed there straight from "Ready Steady Go!" I tested the mikes before things started. They were no good. We couldn't get the sound we wanted. I wanted to use our amps – with their gear behind them. But they said, "No, use ours and like it!" It was only because we didn't want to disappoint the kids that we went on at all. We thought of jacking it in altogether.

Pete Townshend: We were more or less about to break up. Nobody really cared about the group. It was just a political thing.

John Entwistle: Keith and I were going to leave and form our own group.

Pete Townshend: The first two years of The Who were absolutely horrible. The music is light-hearted and funny but, underneath, it was agonizingly sad. No real friendships, honesty or trust. We weren't very nice people. I wouldn't go through that again for anything.

20. The single "My Generation" is released in the US. On the same day, *Melody Maker* publishes a front-page story claiming that Boz Borrel of The Boz People might soon replace Roger Daltrey in The Who. That night, the band plays at the Florida Rooms, Brighton.

Pete Townshend: Kit used to brief us before we went into interviews about what to say. Sometimes to be as objectionable, arrogant and nasty as possible. And oh, those outrageous lies we told. I remember telling Jonathan Aitken "I have four cars – a Lincoln Continental, a Jag XK150, a Cortina GT and a London taxi," – and all I had was an old banger. Then I said to somebody else that I was spending between £40 and £50 a week on clothes, and had to borrow money to go to Carnaby Street and buy a jacket in order to pose for a picture.

22. The Who record live versions of "My Generation", "The Good's Gone", "La-La-La-La-Lies", at Aeolian Hall, Studio 1, London for the BBC Radio show "Saturday Club".

Roger Daltrey: We didn't care, really. We did "My Generation" and went through the whole rigmarole of smashing up the gear – on the radio. And we used to do this in front of an audience. The audience reaction was completely, um, BBC disgusted.

24. Town Hall, Stourbridge.

25. Dorothy Ballroom, Cambridge.

26. The Palais, Wimbledon.

27. "My Generation" by The Who reaches No. 2 in the UK singles chart. The Who play at the London School Of Economics.

28. Oasis, Manchester.

29. St Matthew's Hall, Norwich.

30. Town Hall, High Wycombe.

December 1965

1. Wolsey Hall, Cheshunt.

3. The Who appear on "Ready Steady Go!" at Wembley Studios, London, performing "My Generation". They also release their debut album, *My Generation.* In the evening they play at the Goldhawk Social Club, Shepherd's Bush, London.

"Irish" Jack Lyons (audience): The air hummed with excitement as everyone waited for The Who to appear on stage. They hadn't played the Goldhawk for six months but they'd decided to do a thank-you gig for all their mod followers at the Shepherd's Bush club where they used to play regularly, Friday nights. There was a distinct atmosphere of "the heroes return" about the occasion. For the first time in the history of the Goldhawk a huge queue lined the street outside. I'd gone in with their co-manager Kit Lambert, which gave me a buzz because it looked like I was his assistant or one of the band's brothers. The last time The Who played the Goldhawk they were paid £50, this time they were on £300.

I stood on the steps of the stairs that led to the bar. With me were some Goldhawk regulars – Martin Gaish and his brother Lee, Peter Campbell, Tommy Shelley, Joey Bitton, Jez Clifford, his mate Chris, and Alan Bull. We stood tier-like on the stairs, from where we had a clear view of both The Who on stage and the audience jammed together like sardines on the floor below.

They were reaching the end of a pulsating set and the adrenaline reached fever pitch as we anticipated a murderous final assault. They thanked all the

Goldhawk mods for their loyal support which was greeted by hearty cheering and much stamping of feet. Before the cheering died away they launched into a thunderous version of "The Ox", which was to be the last song The Who ever played at the Goldhawk.

4. Two editions of US TV rock show "Shindig" are taped at Richmond, UK, featuring The Who, The Animals, Georgie Fame, and The Yardbirds. In the evening The Who play at the Corn Exchange, Chelmsford.

5. White Lion, Edgware, London.

6. At Eltham Baths, Eltham Hill, South London, The Who play a gig with Viv Prince of The Pretty Things standing in for Keith Moon, who has fallen ill with whooping cough. Keith will not return to the band until the 17th.

Phil May (vocalist, Pretty Things): I always remember Keith coming and standing in front of our set, watching the gig, right in front of the drums. 'Cause Viv was amazing. He'd hit anything – mike stands, fire bucket, just anything he'd play. Drummed on the floor, on the guitars themselves. Keith, later, would also say he idolized Viv. Before that, playing drums was quite sedentary. Boring. And, through Viv, you'd suddenly realize you could be a drummer but also an extrovert.

You could be a star and play your drums too. I think Keith realized he could be Keith, and didn't have to switch instruments. He could still play the drums and let out all his lunacy through the drum kit.

8. Corn Exchange, Bristol.

9. The Who play at the Guild Hall, Portsmouth, and are seen on the first part of US TV show "Shindig's" special edition "Shindig Goes To London", performing "Anyway, Anyhow, Anywhere".

Binky Philips: They did "Generation" and, during the break, Daltrey took his mike stand and started bashing the drum set. Moon was going berserk! His hair was plastered to his head because it was so wet. Townshend looked furious. He'd play a few chords and every few seconds walk up to his amp and turn it up. He was playing a Rickenbacker and suddenly he takes it off, holds it over his head, and rams it into the speakers. I fell off my bed.

I wasn't supposed to watch TV during the weekdays, so I had the volume real low. I was flipping, so I turned it up and couldn't give a shit any more. He was getting weird noises now by wrenching it around in the speaker and when he pulled it out the neck from the third fret up was gone.

He looked at it and got furious so he threw it over the amps into the curtain. He stalked off stage like a robot with an incredible scowl on his face. You could see people stand next to the amps with their mouths open. Townshend stalked the stage with another Rickenbacker and finished the song. I wouldn't shut up about it the next day at school.

11. Southampton University.

12. New Barn Club, Brighton.

13. Federation Club, Norwich.

15. Students' Union, University College of Swansea, Swansea, Wales.

16. Town Hall, Kidderminster.

17. The Who tape an appearance on UK TV show "Ready Steady Go!" at Wembley Studios, London, then play a gig at the Ricky Tick, Windsor where the newly returned Keith Moon collapses on stage. Viv Prince stands in again.

18. The Birdcage, Portsmouth.

19. Plaza Ballroom, Guildford, Surrey.

21. Marquee, Soho, London.

23. Pavilion, Worthing.

24. An all-star edition of "Ready Steady Go!" is aired featuring The Kinks, The Hollies, The Animals, Herman's Hermits and The Who. In a *Cinderella* parody, Keith Moon plays Buttons and Townshend is the Wicked Stepmother. Later in the day The Who play at the Pier Ballroom, Hastings.

Keith Altham (journalist, *NME*): It was to be a pop panto, with the stars miming to appropriate pop records. Cilla Black was the storyteller. The presenter, Cathy McGowan, was Cinderella. Ray Davies of The Kinks and Hilton Valentine of The Animals were the Ugly Sisters, Herman was the Prince, and two of the Hollies, Graham Nash and Bobby Elliott, were the pantomime horse. It was Pete Townshend, though, who brought the house down as the Wicked Stepmother, mugging hysterically to Peter Cook and Dudley Moore's "Goodbyee".

Peter Noone (Herman, of Herman's Hermits): Keith Moon was supposed to walk on from stage left but instead he decided to barge straight through the scenery. He just ripped right through this fake door. It was chaos.

Keith Altham: While all this was going on The Who's John Entwistle was in one corner of the studio, playing the William Tell Overture on his French horn, which was not at all appreciated by the studio manager.

Pete Quaife (bassist, Kinks): My only memory of that day is that I had

cystitis. I really had to pee very badly all the way through the show.
25. The Who's debut album, *My Generation*, is released and enters the UK album charts, where it will peak at No. 5.
30. The Who are seen on "Shindig Goes To London", performing "Daddy Rolling Stone".
31. Recording a special late-night edition of "Ready Steady Go! – The New Year Starts Here", with The Rolling Stones and The Kinks.

1966

January 1966

1. Trade Union Hall, Watford.
5. A new BBC TV show begins in the UK – "A Whole Scene Going". The first edition includes The Who, whose Pete Townshend admits to using drugs. Other artists featured are Lulu and comedian Spike Milligan.
7. Mister McCoys, Middlesbrough.
8. The final edition of US TV show "Shindig" is aired, starring The Who and The Kinks. The Who play at the Jigsaw Club, Manchester.
9. Cosmopolitan Club, Carlisle.
13. The Who play at the Embassy Ballroom, Swansea, Wales, and later at the Ritz Ballroom, Skewen, Wales.
14. Municipal Hall, Pontypridd, Wales.
15. The Who play at the Two Puddings Club, Stratford, East London, followed by an all-nighter at the In Crowd Club, Hackney. On the same day, UK pop paper Disc runs the headline "Who's Keith Moon: Home Boy At Heart", detailing Keith's happy life at home with his parents; pregnant girlfriend Kim Kerrigan is moving in with them at Wembley.

Kim Kerrigan: It was lovely being part of that family. They were wonderful, absolutely incredible.
16. Agincourt Ballroom, Camberley, Surrey.
21. Glenlyn Ballroom, Forest Hill, London.
22. The Who play at the Adelphi, West Bromwich, followed by an all-nighter at The Baths, Smethwick.
23. The Co-op, Warrington.
26. Locarno Ballroom, Stevenage.
28. The Who play "Circles" for "Ready Steady Go!" at Rediffusion Studios,

Wembley, then drive to Edgbaston for that night's gig at Birmingham University.
29. Imperial Ballroom, Nelson.
30. Beachcomber Club, Leigh.
31. Youth Centre, Newport.

February 1966

1. Britannia Rowing Club, Nottingham.
4. The Who begin a mini-tour headlining over The Merseybeats, The Fortunes, The Graham Bond Organization and Screaming Lord Sutch, at the Astoria, Finsbury Park, London.

Nick Jones (reviewer, *Melody Maker*):

> The scene was set for The Who to take Finsbury Park by storm but, as often happens, the big occasion was too much. Daltrey's mike seemed to be off all night, and Keith Moon's drums were inaudible, the acoustics only permitting an occasional cymbal crash to get through. Despite these difficulties, The Who played immaculately . . .

5. The Who's mini-tour proceeds to the Odeon Theatre, Southend-on-Sea.
6. The Who's mini-tour ends at the Empire Theatre, Liverpool.
8. Town Hall, Farnborough.
11. Palais, Wimbledon.
12. Dreamland Ballroom, Margate.
13. Community Centre, Southall, West London.
14. Panto Ball, Liverpool University.
15. Squire Club, Sheffield.

Roger Daltrey: Moon always thought the drums should be at the front of the stage. I was the poor sod that had to stand in front of him. That was a headache in itself. He'd always be doing things behind my back and I never knew what was going on. I was blissfully ignorant of the fact that he was taking the piss out of me every night. We were over-testosteroned young men barely out of our teens. Of course it created friction.

17. Club A Go Go, Newcastle.
18. Drill Hall, Dumfries, Scotland.
19. Memorial Hall, Norwich.
20. Oasis, Manchester.
21. Beachcomber, Preston.

Keith Moon: We've got forty-eight 12-inch speakers, which is about 600 watts worth of power and, with my drums, it makes £3,000 worth of equipment on stage every night. That's why we have three road managers to get the stuff erected. In some clubs, we have to turn the speakers sideways to get them all on the stage.

23. A second version of "Anyway, Anyhow, Anywhere" is recorded at Olympic Studios, Barnes, London.

24. Victoria Ballroom, Chesterfield.

25. Wellington Ballroom, Wellington.

26. Starlight Ballroom, Boston.

28. Eltham Baths, Eltham Hill, London.

March 1966

2. Wolsey Hall, Cheshunt.

4. The Who release a new single, "Substitute", on the Reaction label (a Polydor subsidiary) in the UK, and play at the Social Club, Pontypool, Wales.

Pete Townshend: On the demo, I sang with an affected Jagger-like accent which Kit obviously liked, as he suggested the song as a follow-up to "My Generation". The lyric has come to be the most quoted Who lyric ever. It somehow goes to show that the "art, not the artist" tag that people put on Dylan's silence about his work could be a good idea. "Substitute" makes me recall writing a song to fit a clever and rhythmic-sounding title. A play on words.

John Entwistle: I changed basses every day, looking for the perfect instrument. Basically, I wanted to play with my fingers but ended up playing with a plectrum because it was easier to record the top-end part of my sound that way. Probably the first record where you can hear me playing with a pick was "Substitute".

Pete Townshend: The stock, downbeat riff used in the verses I pinched from a record played to me in Blind Date, a feature in *Melody Maker*. It was by a group who later wrote to thank me for saying nice things about their record in the feature. The article is set up so that pop stars hear other people's records without knowing who they are by. They say terrible things about their best mates' latest and it only makes the pop scene snottier and more competitive. The record I said nice things about wasn't a hit, despite an electrifying riff. I pinched it, we did it and you bought it.

John Entwistle: Pete was always being influenced by other artists. "Substitute" was an attempt to play the introduction from "I Can't Help Myself" by The Four Tops. He played me the demo of it and I thought it sounded great. We didn't want it to sound too Motown so I played a Gibson SG medium scale bass with wire-wound strings. When it got to the solo, because we were recording and mixing it virtually live, I thought, yeah, this should be a bass solo, so I turned my volume up and they couldn't mix me out, so it ended up as a bass solo.

Pete Townshend: "Substitute" was a bloody amazing session. Keith can't even remember it. That was the first Who-produced session. Kit didn't slide naturally into the seat of producing The Who – he kind of arrived at the position of producing The Who because we needed a producer. It was obviously logical that I should produce The Who, even then.

So it was logical that when it came to "Substitute", and we got out of Shel Talmy's clutches, we should enjoy ourselves. We went in and played through the thing . . . Keith doesn't remember the session. Roger was gonna leave the group.

John Entwistle: After we'd done "Substitute", Keith phoned me up in a raging temper and shouted "How dare you record without me!" He was convinced he hadn't been at the session. Actually, he was drunk at the session, out of his head, and just couldn't remember it. I told him to listen to it, because he would always scream during difficult drum breaks, and you could hear him on "Substitute". So when he heard that he realized how far gone he was.

He really thought we were trying to throw him out the band. He was on some weird downer pills. Somebody had told him they were uppers but they made him paranoid. He'd run into some ego problems where he was trying to become friendly with The Beatles . . .

5. Drummer John Steel plays his last gig with The Animals, at Birmingham University. Shortly after, at Le Kilt club in London, Keith Moon asks if he can join The Animals.

Dave Rowberry (keyboards, Animals): He spurted it out – he wanted to join The Animals. I don't think he was very happy where he was. I think he saw us as more of a happy band, because we did get on well together. And The Who didn't.

9. An injunction is taken out by producer Shel Talmy, preventing further sales of the Reaction/Polydor version of "Substitute", because he had produced the B-side, "Circles", for Brunswick.

Shel Talmy: When The Who was firmly established in the minds of pop fans around the world, I received a letter in the post saying something to the effect that my services were no longer required, we consider the contract terminated.

Pete Townshend: We did two versions of "Circles", which were both identical because they were both copies of my demo. Shel put in a High Court injunction, saying there was copyright in recording. In other words, if you're a record producer and you produce a song with a group, and you make a creative contribution, then you own that sound.

He took it to the High Court judge and he said things like, "And then on bar 36 I suggested to the lead guitarist that he play a diminuendo, forget the adagio, and play 36 bars modulating to the key of E flat." Which was all total bullshit – he used to fall asleep at the desk. Glyn Johns [engineer] did everything.

John Entwistle: Because we were trying to get out of our contract with Shel Talmy, "Substitute" came out on two different labels, Reaction and Brunswick, with four different B-sides. The B-side was originally called "Instant Party", and we'd recorded it with Talmy. We tried renaming it "Circles" but that didn't work, so then we wrote a song called "Circles". Finally there was "Waltz For A Pig" by The Who Orchestra which was really The Graham Bond Organization with Jack Bruce.

Shel Talmy: Lambert, who was a lot older than all of us, became jealous of my alleged influence with "his boys" and, along with Polydor abetting him, breached my contract. Note that Polydor came on the scene to ferment discontent only after The Who were already a huge band. So where were they when I was looking for a deal?

10. On the same day that "Substitute" enters the UK singles chart, The Who play at The Ram Jam Club, Brixton, London.

11. Attempting to upstage the Reaction/Polydor release of "Substitute", Brunswick Records release "A Legal Matter" by The Who. On the same day the band plays at the Market Hall, St Albans.

12. The Birdcage, Portsmouth.

13. Starlite Ballroom, Greenford, West London.

15. In an attempt to circumvent the Shel Talmy lawsuit, Reaction/Polydor release a new version of "Substitute", backed with the instrumental "Waltz For A Pig". The Who record live versions of "Substitute", "Dancing In The Street" and "Man With Money" at Aeolian Hall, London for BBC radio's "Saturday Club".

John Entwistle: "Man With Money" was a stage song we used to do. The Everly Brothers had an album called *Blues* and there wasn't any blues on it. There was that one song on it. We copped a lot of Everly Brothers.

17. Keith Moon marries Kim Kerrigan, at the registry office in Brent, Middlesex.

Keith Moon: It was my managers' idea to keep the marriage a secret . . . at the time, I didn't care, I just wanted to marry Kim, but my managers and publicist did care about what I did.

Kim Kerrigan: It wasn't the way I planned it, but I really, really loved him. I wouldn't have done it otherwise.

I was very young, and things were changing. There were different facets to Keith, and other facets were coming out. He wanted to marry me, he wanted to possess me, he loved the idea of us having his baby, but on the other hand, there was all this other . . . This was a very small part of his life. There was everything else opening up. The Who were big. So he was very confused, obviously. I said I didn't want to get married, he was sure he did, but at the same time he had all this confusion. It would manifest itself in the aggression, he would get very frustrated. And also the pills . . .

18. The Who appear on "Ready Steady Go!", then play a gig at the Locarno Ballroom, Basildon. On the same day, Shel Talmy's injunction against Polydor is lifted, and the group signs to Robert Stigwood's newly formed Reaction label.

19. King's Hall, Stoke-on-Trent.

23. Tower Ballroom, Great Yarmouth.

24. On the same day that "A Legal Matter" enters the UK singles chart, where it will peak at No. 32, The Who play at the Starlight Ballroom, Crawley.

25. Corn Exchange, Hertford.

26. St George's Ballroom, Hinckley.

27. Central Pier, Morecambe.

28. The Who record an appearance on "Top Of The Pops", to be transmitted on the 31st.

29. The Who fly to Paris to appear on the TV show "Music Hall De France".

30. The Who appear on "Music Hall De France".

April 1966

1. A special edition of "Ready Steady Go!", suitably renamed "Ready Steady Allez!", is broadcast from La Locomotive Club, Paris, starring The Who and The Yardbirds.

2. The Who remain in Paris and play two shows at La Locomotive Club. Meanwhile, in the US, the second version of "Substitute" (with "Waltz For A Pig" as the B-side) is released.
3. The Who fly back to London.
4. At the High Court in London, an injunction is granted to Shel Talmy, temporarily preventing The Who from recording. The Who play at the Town Hall, Chatham, Kent.
8. Queen's Hall, Leeds.
9. Pavilion Ballroom, Buxton.
11. Floral Hall, Southport.
14. Package tour featuring The Who, The Spencer Davis Group, The Merseys and The Jimmy Cliff Sound begins at the Gaumont Cinema, Southampton.

Phil Wainman (drummer, Jimmy Cliff Sound): He [Keith Moon] was ever such a regular bloke. He couldn't believe his luck. It was like, "Bloody hell, look what I've done." He never came across as "I'm better than you," or "Aren't I great?" He was like a puppy, always his tail wagging . . .

15. Package tour featuring The Who and The Spencer Davis Group plays at the Fairfield Halls, Croydon.
16. "Substitute" by The Who peaks at No. 5 in the UK singles chart. Package tour featuring The Who and The Spencer Davis Group plays at the Odeon Cinema, Watford.

Nick Jones (reviewer, *Melody Maker*):

They didn't let up, and haven't played as well – or as hard – for some time . . . a fast-moving, powerful, show.

17. Package tour featuring The Who and The Spencer Davis Group plays at the Regal Cinema, Edmonton.

Roger Simpson (reviewer, *Tottenham & Edmonton Weekly Herald*):

Keith (the loon) Moon, wearing a white T-shirt with a printed medal on it, went crazy on the drums, throwing his drumsticks high into the air and crashing them down on to the skins. Their version of The Beach Boys' recent hit "Barbara Ann" was a disappointment, but their present Top Ten number, "Substitute", was well done. They ended the act with "My Generation", lead guitarist Pete Townshend bringing out every conceivable weird sound from his guitar.

19. In a break from their package tour, The Who play at the Town Hall, Walsall.
21. Locarno Ballroom, Stevenage.

22. Package tour featuring The Who and The Spencer Davis Group resumes at the Odeon Cinema, Derby.
23. Package tour featuring The Who and The Spencer Davis Group plays at the Odeon Cinema, Rochester.
24. Package tour featuring The Who and The Spencer Davis Group plays at The Hippodrome, Brighton.
25. Package tour featuring The Who and The Spencer Davis Group ends at the Pavilion, Bath.
26. Lynx Club, Borehamwood, London.
28. The Witch Doctor, Savoy Rooms, Catford, London.
29. Tiles Club, London.
30. Corn Exchange, Chelmsford.

May 1966

1. When The Beatles play their last ever UK live gig, the NME Pollwinners Concert at the Empire Pool, Wembley, The Who are also on the bill.

Chris Stamp: The Who by this time were very into their Union Jack period and looking incredible . . . Pete did his feedback thing and we had smoke bombs going off. And we did this destructive ending with Pete's guitar. And Keith, who had knocked over a few drums here and there, really went for it.

Kit Lambert: He [Keith] more or less stole the show by building up into a drum climax, which finally resulted in the whole drum kit disintegrating and falling into the audience, which left Keith drumming on a single drum.

Chris Stamp: I think they even fell off the stage, he made a huge mess. He did it to be with Pete, to top Pete, and to also make The Who's presence felt, make sure the Stones and The Beatles had to follow this.

2. Pavilion, Bath.
3. Winter Gardens, Malvern.
4. Town Hall, Stourbridge.
5. Town Hall, Kidderminster.
6. Top Hat Ballroom, Lisburn.
7. National Boxing Stadium, Dublin.
8. Arcadia Ballroom, Cork.
11. Corn Exchange, Bristol.
12. Pavilion, Worthing.

13. Palais, Wimbledon.
14. Palais, Bury.
16. Keith Moon secretly participates in a recording session with Jeff Beck and Jimmy Page, John Paul Jones and Nicky Hopkins, for the track "Beck's Bolero".

Jeff Beck: That was a momentous recording session. We had a half-baked song, Jimmy and I. We didn't have to play it more than twice before the others were on to it. There was not an ounce of work in it. We didn't deliberate, we just played it through. Everyone in the control room was aghast: "These guys don't even need to rehearse." We did four or five cuts and it just sounded and felt like we shouldn't go anywhere else. We should just get rehearsing and carry this band.

At the same moment that he [Moon] screams, he knocks the microphone off the stand. The cymbal fill is so wild that he actually smashes the mike, deliberately. Boff! Kicks the mike off with a stick, and then you don't hear the drums again. And that's the tape we used.

What he was doing was giving a two-fingered gesture to The Who. Once he found security in the knowledge that he could do this, he probably went back and said, "Right, I know I'm safe with these guys if all else fails," but it didn't.

Chris Stamp: Keith was always looking round for other options. He always thought he was going to be The Beach Boys' drummer, The Beatles' drummer, the Stones' drummer . . .

Roger Daltrey: We only ever wanted to be The Beatles. At the height of The Who's fame, Keith would have dropped our band just like that to join The Beatles.

20. With Beach Boy Bruce Johnston in the audience, Pete Townshend clobbers Keith Moon with a guitar, for turning up late to a show at the Ricky Tick, Newbury. Moon quits the band for a week.

Bruce Johnston: I don't know what sparked it off. I just remember watching from the side of the stage and, all of a sudden, they got in the biggest fight I've ever seen. Guitars are swinging, everybody's just in a frenzy.

Pete Townshend: Keith had a row with me. I got angry and threw a guitar at him and he threw a drum at me. He hurt himself, lacerated his leg. At the time, he was intending to join Jeff [Beck]'s group.

John Entwistle: We went to find our manager and told him we were splitting and were going to form our own band. We sat in different nightclubs and planned our new career. I thought of the name Led Zeppelin and Keith came up with the cover of the Hindenberg going down in flames. The Who thing had become too much for us, and we were heading into the sunset. But we ended up being apologized to and going back to The Who. I often muse on what would have happened if we'd gone away and formed Led Zeppelin.

Keith Moon: It was incredibly violent for a time. It was common knowledge in England because there were a lot of people coming to see our shows and we came on with sticking plasters, bleeding. There were even fistfights on stage. Every five minutes somebody was quitting the group.

23. Locarno, Blackburn.

26. Locarno, Ashton-Under-Lyme.

27. The Who's manager Robert Stigwood announces that Keith Moon has returned to the group. He has been missing for a week after the Newbury Ricky Tick club show during which Pete Townshend hit him with a guitar.

28. South Pier, Blackpool.

29. Winter Gardens, Morecambe.

30. Sincil Bank Football Ground, Lincoln.

June 1966

1. The Who touch down at Arlanda airport, Sweden, to begin a tour.

Hempo Hilden (drummer in Swedish band, Why): The promoter for the Swedish tour was a girl from [Hilden's home town] Soderhamn, named Carola Lundstrom. Her company's name was Music City, and she also did tours with Spencer Davis, Manfred Mann, The Kinks and so on. She knew us from her school days in our town, but she was now a big-shot manager, so we had these long-distance phone calls, all the way from Stockholm from her.

Being fourteen years old, you can imagine the stunning surprise in our band when we were asked if we would like to be the support act for The Who, because The Who were to hit our little town one special Saturday in June.

2.Gröna Lund, Stockholm.

3. Liljekonvaljeholmen, Uppsala.

Magnus Sjostedt (journalist/radio presenter): The four of us arrived a little late, about 7.30 p.m. They [The Who] arrived at the same time. They drove through the gates in a modest standard limousine followed by a van, which I believe carried their equipment. To this day, I cannot quite understand how they managed to set up amps, speakers, PA, mikes, drums, in such a short time. A soundcheck was out of the question.

The Who were to follow a rather obscure local group called Whobos. I have completely forgotten what the Whobos looked or sounded like. But I remember that afterwards, a screen was pulled across the stage for a few minutes. Then it was fronted by an also-forgotten compere, introducing The Who as "The guys that do whatever they fancy with their instruments". The screen was pulled back. There they were, on the stage, The Who.

Much to my surprise, they looked exactly like they had done on record sleeves and TV promotions. I do not remember their clothes in detail, but Keith Moon wore a T-shirt, while Roger and Entwistle looked more Carnabetian in colour, and Townshend more strict. He also had his Rickenbacker, and Moon his double drum kit.

They burst into "Heatwave", an unexpected opening. In one hour, in that small faraway place, in front of a small Swedish audience they went for it. Pete blew the fuses, furiously stabbing the loudspeakers. Keith really kicked hell out of his drums in "The Ox", until they appeared to explode. Roger tossed the mike into space and screamed his lungs out, and John acted cool and blew the English horn.

Then they were off. They left me breathless. The bright sunny evening turned into a starry summer's night. The four of us went to see the two remaining Swedish acts, while The Who were on their way to their next Swedish amusement park.

3. Kungsparken, Kungsör.

Rolf Inghamn (promoter): Folkparks are a very Swedish phenomenon. Kungsparken was a typical folkpark. The parks were always a fenced green area, often with both an outdoor stage and an indoor dance-salon. You could buy hot dogs, coffee, sweets and pop – never alcohol in those days.

Folkparks had their glory days in the mid-fifties (245 parks in 1958), but go back to 1891, when the first park was built. They were built as a meeting place for the labour movement, but also for recreation and pleasure. From the beginning, local talents and travelling artists performed in the parks. During the jazz era, American stars toured the parks. When the British pop invasion struck Sweden in the early sixties, the parks became the natural place to host these English guests in many Swedish small towns.

Ulf Eneroth (audience): Five Swedish crowns for the bus, 10 crowns entrance.

Kungsparken was the Eldorado for rock'n'roll lovers in 1966. Today, Kungsparken is just a hill covered with grass and bushes. John's enormous bass play, Roger singing "Barbara Ann", and Townshend's treatment of the guitar – however it survived the show. But drummer Keith Moon showed his taste for wildness when he ended the show by kicking the drums off stage.

There I was in the audience, 13 years old, shouting and enjoying myself. Not even the pounding in my ears could take away the experience. The night bus arrived home at three o'clock in the morning, and a very worried and very angry father was there to meet me. But a very happy young man fell asleep that night.

4. Two gigs, first at Berget, Soderhamn, supported by The Panthers and Why, then at Högbo Bruk, Sandviken.

Hempo Hilden: It was a warm, sunny day in June and all the support bands arrived very early at the venue, discussing who would play first, second and so on.

During these discussions, a dark blue Ford Transit appeared at the venue and two skinny guys jumped out and started to unload a lot of Marshall cabinets and amps, plus an enormous amount of red sparkle Premier drums. That was the first time I ever saw a Marshall amp.

It took the two roadies about eight minutes to get the stage set for The Who. The term "soundcheck" did not exist at that time. Everything was ready and set when a white Opel Admiral cruised into the venue, driven by Carola Lundstrom, who was transporting the guys in the band.

There was no security whatsoever, except for one police officer who was off duty because he was working at the venue as stage manager. At that time, his job was to switch the power off if he thought that the band was too loud.

He had never seen so much amplification on that stage before, so in his mind, the band was too loud even before they hit a single note. So there were two operations done very quickly by Carola Lundstrom. One was to tell a lie to this police officer that there was a traffic jam and trouble with a crowd outside the venue. Number two was to replace the main fuses in the electric system with three-inch needles, and bypass the main switch before the police officer got back.

The band came on stage and started the intro of "Substitute" and were halfway through the song when the police officer got back on the scene. We still don't know if he tried to switch the power off or not, but The Who played their show without interference.

The Who gave an impressive performance and we were amazed how the small Selmer amplifier could produce Roger Daltrey's vocals over the massive wall of sound coming from the Marshall stacks. We had read about The Who's violent stage act, but they did not destroy any instruments at this show, because they had another show later the same day.

5. The Who appear on Swedish TV show "Popside" and play two shows, one at Träffen, Nyköping, and one at Idrottshuset, Örebro.

Gunnel Larsson: I was working at the Shell petrol station in Vrena when this group of young Englishmen came in. They introduced themselves as The Who and explained that they were going to appear on television in just 10 minutes. They asked where they could find a TV set.

Since there weren't any at the station, I invited them back to our house. They rushed in, wild and exhilarated, and jumped on the sofa, put their feet on my table. They liked the programme and thanked me by giving their autographs to my nine-year-old daughter, Ann-Christine.

Rolf Gildenlov (promoter): The Who's roadies carried instruments and amplification in record time, including the PA system, on stage. In less than 20 minutes everything was settled, soundchecked and ready.

Then all hell broke loose. No one had expected the assault from the audience, that started with the first chord. Lots of youths were squeezed towards the stage and for some moments the situation became life-threatening. Several girls fainted, not through exultation but through lack of oxygen. Of course, some tried to invade the stage in order to get closer to their idols, but were roughly pushed back by the police and the guards. The police didn't have much experience in such situations in those days. When the panic started, the police tried to press the crowd backwards while pressure gained from behind as everyone tried to get closer to the stage.

After only a few songs, the police lost control of the situation, and the officer in charge ordered me to cut the power to the stage immediately, to prevent what could have turned into a catastrophe. I tried to protest but the policemen more or less pushed me through the corridor towards the power switch, and together we unscrewed fuse after fuse until it finally became quiet. The stage lighting cut off. But the situation didn't improve. After a brief period of silence, surprised by the sudden darkness, a roar rose from the crowd.

In a matter of seconds, I was eye to eye with a furious Mr Townshend, who questioned our capability concerning the power supply. He thought the lack of electricity was due to technical problems and got even more furious, if possible, when he realized it had been ordered by the police. The next moment we screwed on all the fuses again. Sound and lighting came back and Pete rushed up on stage to continue where he had left off. The police started another attack against the power plant but The Who's staff did their best to defend it. But after a couple of minutes, it was all dark again, only Keith continued drumming as if nothing had happened, and the audience enjoyed an improvised drum solo.

Meanwhile, Pete and his men swore at the Swedish police force now guarding the power plant. I was in the middle of it all trying to prevent a fist fight. A policeman tried to stop Keith Moon but Keith, who usually beats up his drums, had now gotten a glint in his eye indicating his desire to beat up the policeman. But when the policeman got too close he gave in, pushed out his set of drums and left the stage. A sad ending . . .

7. The Scandinavian tour ends with two dates, one at the Tivoli, Copenhagen, and another at Fyens Forum, Odense.

8. The Who fly back to the UK.

11. European radio stations mistakenly announce the death of Roger Daltrey of The Who.

14. The Who record "Disguises" at Pye or IBC Studios, London.

15. The Who record "Disguises" for the BBC TV show "A Whole Scene Going", in London.

16. UK dates resume with a gig at Hull University.

17. City Hall, Perth.

18. Market Hall, Carlisle.

19. Britannia Pier, Great Yarmouth, supported by The Merseys and Max Wall.

Malcolm Cook (stage manager): Robert Stigwood had organized a series of nine concerts in Great Yarmouth to be headlined by The Who. The great music hall entertainer Max Wall was down on his uppers, and Stigwood decided to revive his career by putting him on this bill with The Who. As it happened, The Who all stood at the side of the stage in hysterics at Max Wall, but the teenage audience didn't care for him at all.

Next up was an act called Oscar, later very successful as Paul Nicholas. I noticed that he kept wincing and grimacing. Then he pointed down at the orchestra pit, and there's Daltrey and Moon of The Who flicking bottle tops at him while he's performing. I had to go down and drag them out by the scruff of their necks.

When it came time for The Who to get on stage, Townshend was nowhere to be seen. I had the other three all ready to go on without him when he turned up at the last second, in a foul temper about something. So they went on, did one number, and then the stage was plunged into darkness by their roadie.

I'm peering into the dark and I suddenly realize they're not on the stage any more. They'd nipped off and out of the theatre. Next thing I know, I'm called to the front of the house where there's a man being stretchered away into an ambulance with a huge mark on his forehead. Moonie had thrown a drumstick at him from the stage. The audience was furious, and the manager, Mr Powell, had half his clothes torn off. The Who were banned, and didn't do any more of those shows.

20. Gaytower Ballroom, Birmingham.
21. Winter Gardens, Malvern.
23. Leeds University.
25. College Of Further Education, Chichester.
26. Britannia Pier, Great Yarmouth.

July 1966

The Merseys release a cover version of the Townshend song "So Sad About Us".

Roger Daltrey: It's a great song. It's very melodic but there's an angst behind it. I can't really remember whether Pete wrote it as a single for The Merseybeats . . .

Pete Townshend: . . . in the living room of the home of my friend Speedy Keene's parents in Hanwell, West London . . .

Roger Daltrey: . . . and they did it first or whether we did it first and they covered it. I know they covered it and had a hit single from it. I think that's one of the few hit singles Pete's had with any other artists.

1. Winter Gardens, Eastbourne.
7. Locarno, Streatham.
8. Top Rank, Cardiff.
9. Westminster Technical College, London.
10. Keith and Kim Moon go bowling at Heathrow, London.

12. A baby girl, Amanda, is born to Kim and Keith Moon at Central Middlesex Hospital, London.

Kim Moon: If we went out together after I had Mandy, if someone talked to me, he'd lose it. We'd go home and he'd start a fight with me. Sometimes, I wouldn't go home with him. I'd get home and he'd be throwing things out of the window, smashing things up.

15. Tiles Club, London.

16. Civic Hall, Barnsley.

22. Central Pier, Morecambe.

23. Spa Royal Hall, Bridlington.

24. Britannia Pier, Great Yarmouth.

27. Flamingo Club, Redruth.

28. Town Hall, Barnstaple.

30. 6th National Jazz and Blues Festival, Windsor Racecourse Balloon Meadow.

August 1966

1. The Who begin work on their next single, "I'm A Boy", at IBC Studios, London.

12. Brunswick Records release a new single, "The Kids Are Alright", in the UK.

18. Palace Ballroom, Douglas, Isle Of Man.

24. Orchid Ballroom, Purley.

25. Dreamland Ballroom, Margate.

26. The Who release a new single, "I'm A Boy", on Reaction/Polydor.

Pete Townshend: The chord structure in "I'm A Boy" and the opening chords in "Pinball Wizard" were directly influenced by that piece of music by Purcell, which I'm sure a lot of our fans will flinch at.

John Entwistle: That was done in two versions. There was a much longer version which was supposed to go on the album. It had horn parts. It was kind of a forerunner of *Tommy*. I remember the bass was just straight pumping on a note and I changed it to the operatic-sounding part. I wrote that.

29. Ultra Club, Downs Hotel, Hassocks, Sussex.

September 1966

1. "I'm A Boy" enters the UK singles chart. Simultaneously, "The Kids Are Alright" enters the chart. The same night, The Who play at the Locarno,

Coventry.
2. Locarno, Basildon.
4. Belle Vue, Manchester.
6. Palais, Ilford.
8. Locarno, Stevenage.
9. Pier Pavilion, Felixstowe.
10. "The Kids Are Alright" peaks at No. 41 in the UK singles chart.
11. Ultra Club, Downs Hotel, Hassocks, Sussex.
13. The Who record live versions of "I'm A Boy" and "Disguises" at The Playhouse, London, for the BBC radio show "Saturday Club".
15. Gaumont Theatre, Hanley.
16. Odeon, Derby.
18. De Montfort Hall, Leicester. The remaining 11 concerts of the tour are cancelled to let The Who finish their album.
21. Pete Townshend is fined £25 for dangerous driving.
23. Keith Moon and John Entwistle go to see The Rolling Stones open a UK tour at the Royal Albert Hall, London.
24. On his first day in the UK, Jimi Hendrix is taken to meet Pete Townshend.

Pete Townshend: I was very unimpressed with Jimi that day. He was wearing a beat-up US Marines jacket, and he looked scruffy, jet-lagged, and pock-marked. I thought "Ugh!" Two days later, I saw him play at Blaises and it was devastating.

October 1966

2. "I'm A Boy" peaks at No. 2 in the UK.
8. Palais, Peterborough.
9. Winter Gardens, Bournemouth.
10. Pavilion, Bath.
14. Queen's Hall, Leeds.
15. Corn Exchange, Chelmsford.
16. Starlite Ballroom, Greenford.
18. Recording tracks for "Ready Steady Go!" at Wembley Studios, North-west London.
19. Appearance on Dutch TV show "Rooster", and gig at Club 192, Casino Oberbayern, Scheveningen, The Hague, Netherlands.

20. Recording Danish TV show "Klar i Studiet" (Ready in the Studio), a local version of "Ready Steady Go!", followed by two gigs, one at K.B. Hallen, and another at Herlev Hallen, Copenhagen.

Chris Hutchins (*NME*): Over 2,000 Danish fans screamed and yelled as they went through numbers like "Heatwave", "Barbara Ann" and "Substitute". Pete spotted a few empty chairs in the centre of the auditorium and suggested people from the back came forward to fill them. Chaos followed as more than a thousand fought for those few seats.

Order was never restored and no one sat down again. It was like The Beatles all over again as the stage filled with burly protectors ejecting fans left, right and centre. The four took no notice and stormed through "Legal Matter" and "I'm A Boy". Finally, they reached "My Generation", and Townshend tried hard to smash his new guitar through an amplifier. Hysteria prevailed even after they had returned to the dressing room.

21. While The Who are in Gothenburg, Sweden, performing at Liseberg Konserthallen, they are seen performing tracks from their new EP *Ready Steady Who!* on UK TV pop show "Ready Steady Go!".

Gosta Hansson (Swedish reviewer):

> The Who sold out two shows at the Konserthallen. There were no interruptions. Neither did the members fight between each other, nor smash any instruments. Pete Townshend made several attempts to attack the speaker, but that was about all that happened.

Pam Nettleship (viewer): The Who's "Ready Steady Go!" appearance was more of a disaster than a happening. Even smashing up the equipment was done with little conviction. As a Who fan, I was choked and if I didn't know better I would wonder why kids rave about them.

John Entwistle: The reason we had "Batman" on the *Ready Steady Who!* EP was that Keith and I used to sit and listen to Beach Boys records and Jan and Dean and The Rip Chords, and we both went out and bought this rare *Jan And Dean Sing Batman* album, because Batman was the big thing on TV then. We figured it would be fun to burst through a big paper Who sign at the start of the "Ready Steady Who!" TV show, so we recorded Batman really as an intro for that.

"Bucket-T", "In The City" and "Barbara Ann" also came out of Keith's interest in The Beach Boys.

22. Gislovs Stjarna, Simrishamn and Jägersbo-Höör, Höör.

Mats Malmsstrom (audience): With plenty of time to spare before the show at Jägersbo, me and my friend grabbed two places in front at the outdoor stage. Just before The Who were about to come on stage, two guards came up to us. They wanted me to move away from the stage, as there was a risk of getting squeezed if the audience started to press forward. My friend, who was two years older than me, told the guards he would look after me, and they seemed satisfied with that answer.

The show started. It was a fantastic feeling and my first pop concert ever. Keith broke several drumsticks and threw them into the audience. I stood right below Pete, when something suddenly came rolling along the scene. I grabbed it immediately and put it in my pocket. After a short while I picked it up and looked at it. It looked like some kind of control. I looked around and noticed there was a knob missing on Pete's guitar. And I still have it in my possession.

When Roger told the audience that it was time for the last song, Pete picked up another guitar. A green rather shabby one. The last song was "My Generation". During the song Pete tore one string after another. When the last string broke he took the guitar off and banged it to the floor several times. Then Keith laid back, aimed and kicked his drums to the audience.

23. MFF Stadion, Malmö, Sweden and Fyers Forum, Odense, Denmark.

24. Folkparken, Halmstad, Sweden.

25. Nalen, Stockholm, Sweden.

Lars Dahlberg (audience): On stage there were lots of Marshall amps and speakers looking as destroyed as I'd seen on photos. We forced our way towards the stage (not very easy). People were arriving in a steady stream. Then the music started. What a sound. And what volume. What a feeling.

The crowd waved back and forth, one second three metres from the stage, the next right in front of it, where I noticed John's nails didn't look very clean. I guess there was some kind of panic, you couldn't do anything but follow the waves. I got a terrible feeling someone had fallen down on the floor we jumped around on, and there wasn't anything I could do about it.

Then Pete started to smash his guitar and his speakers, and I started shivering. Somebody let off a smoke bomb. It was total chaos. Pete ended the berserk by pushing his whole Marshall stack into the audience. This was of course the heaviest live concert I had ever experienced in my life. After the smoke vanished, a guy jumps up on stage trying to steal a piece of speaker cloth from a Marshall, but he got caught by the guards and violently taken behind stage.

27. "Reach Out I'll Be There" by The Four Tops is the new UK No. 1 single.

Pete Townshend: I was going up to Stanmore to visit my girlfriend Karen, whom I was utterly crazy about, and I wasn't sure where the relationship was gonna go. While I was at her house, one of her younger brothers had had some trouble with maths, and I met his schoolteacher who had been a real brute: I remember him beating me with a ruler in the corridor at school. I walked in and he was there. He looked at me, then he looked at Karen, who was really quite beautiful, and it was my little moment of triumph. I left, got into my Lincoln Continental, switched on the radio – one of those big bassy American car radios – and "Reach Out I'll Be There" by The Four Tops came on. It sounded like fucking classical music, like Wagner. I pulled over, and I thought, "I live in this world, and I've got this music that I fucking found, and that's my girlfriend." I felt fucking omnipotent, and whenever I hear it I get this rush. It's not healthy, but . . .

28. It is announced that The Who have finally settled their differences with Shel Talmy out of court.

30. After a gig at the Sportpalast, Berlin, Germany, co-manager Chris Stamp is injured in a street fight.

Neville Chester (road manager): The promoter asks us to come out to a club. At the first one, Keith's messing about with other people's women, then we go to another and we're followed by some guys. The next I know we're out on the street and there's a fight and Keith walks away: "Chris, you talk to them." And Chris Stamp and myself are in the thick of it. Chris got quite badly kicked around, and he's not a small guy. And it was totally Keith's fault. I can still see him now, he just wouldn't shut up.

November 1966

1. Recording TV show "Beat Beat Beat" in Frankfurt TV Studios, Frankfurt, Germany.

2. Live performance for Radio Bremen, in Bremen, Germany.

4. Kassel, Germany.

5. Messehalle 10, Saarbrucken, Germany.

6. Kongresshalle, Cologne, Germany.

7. Düsseldorf, Germany.
10. The Who begin work on "Happy Jack" at CBS Studios, London.
11. The EP *Ready, Steady, Who!* is released in the UK by Reaction/Polydor. On the same day, Brunswick Records release "La-La-La-Lies".
12. Filming for US TV show "Today", at Duke Of York's Barracks, King's Road, Chelsea.
17. Locarno, Glasgow, Scotland.
18. City Hall, Perth, Scotland.
22. Pete Townshend appears on US TV show "Where The Action Is".
24. Pavilion, Worthing.
25. Pete Townshend attends a press reception for Jimi Hendrix at the Bag O' Nails, London.
26. Recording at IBC, where they are visited by Jimi Hendrix, then gig at the Spa Royal Hall, Bridlington.

Roger Daltrey: Kit Lambert brought him in, having just signed him . . . Jimi had all this wild hair and we were like, "Fuckin' 'ell, who's he?" He was such a gentleman and a quiet bloke, but he looked like a raving madman. Kit said, "He's a guitarist we've just signed."

Pete Townshend: Jimi sort of wandered in looking peculiar, just really peculiar, and Keith Moon was in a nasty mood and said "Who let that savage in here?" I mean, he really did look pretty wild and very scruffy.

Chas Chandler asked me what kind of amplifiers Jimi should buy. And I said, "Well, I like HiWatts – or Sound City, as they were then called – but he might prefer Marshall." And Jimi said, "I'll have one of each."

Anyway, he walked around for a bit, gave me a lukewarm handshake and then I never saw him again for a while.

29. Winter Gardens, Malvern.

December 1966

1. Town Hall, Maidstone.
2. "Happy Jack" is released in the UK.

Pete Townshend: My father used to play saxophone in a band for the season on the Isle of Man when I was a kid. There was no character called Happy Jack, but I played on the beach a lot and it's just my memories of some of the weirdos who lived on the sand.

John Entwistle: "Happy Jack" was the best my bass ever sounded on a single. Keith always tried to creep in and do the high parts in our backing vocals, but he sang out of tune, so we'd try to keep him out. When we'd finished "Happy Jack", Keith kept hanging about, and we told him to go home but he wouldn't. He was hiding in the studio while we did the backing vocals, "laugh laugh laugh" and "lap lap lap", and he was singing behind us. And Pete turned round at the end and said, "I saw you!"

I had to develop a very melodic style because there's only two guitars in the group, and there had to be something going on over the power chords. I think Pete finally realized that I'm not a bass player. I'm a bass guitarist. I play the guitar but lower.

3. The Who release their second album, *A Quick One*, in the UK.

Pete Townshend: On our second LP we really discovered The Who's music for the first time, that you could be funny on a record.

John Entwistle: We had 12 minutes of time left to make up on the album. Kit Lambert had the idea. He said to Pete, "Why don't you write a mini-opera and squeeze a bunch of songs into it?" And that's basically what happened. He wrote a lot of short songs and it became the mini-opera but it didn't take us aback because we were expecting it.

Pete Townshend: Entwistle wrote for the first time. He wrote "Whiskey Man" and "Boris The Spider". My reign, set aside as an individual from the group, was over and the group was becoming a group. It was only then we started to work musically together.

John Entwistle: Around that time we were very short of money. We couldn't earn it on concerts because we were smashing up so much equipment and buying clothes, so the costs were ridiculous. So the idea came up that if we each wrote two songs for the *Quick One* album, it would put some money in our pockets because we'd get publishing advances of £500. Now that was more than we'd seen in the whole year. We were on £20 a week, which just about paid for the booze.

John Entwistle: Kit had us marching in band formation around the studio (for "Cobwebs And Strange"). Pete was playing recorder, I followed up with my tuba, taking great care to avoid Roger's trombone slide. After Roger came Keith Moon with a pair of big cymbals . . . It worked OK until we came to double-track. We started marching up and down again but once we passed by the monitor speaker we couldn't hear it. By the time we came back we were hopelessly out.

Actually the first song I wrote was "Whiskey Man". Then "Boris", which was the fastest song I've ever written. One night I'd been sitting with Bill and Charlie of the Stones getting drunk at the Scotch Of St James, and we started talking about names for animals, Barry The Badger and so on. I came up with Boris The Spider, after Boris Karloff, and it made us all laugh.

So a couple of days later, after we'd rehearsed "Whiskey Man" in the White Hart Hotel, at the end of Laxton Road where I lived, Pete asked to hear my second song. I didn't want to seem lazy, not having written one. So I said it was about a spider called Boris. Of course then Pete asks me to play it, so I just made it up as I went along.

Then I rushed down the street and demoed it on my old tape machine to make sure I didn't forget it. It's become like my trade mark. I still get people throwing rubber spiders at me at gigs. I've quite a collection of them in my barn.

Keith saw a guy in a club wearing a necklace of a big silver spider so he bought it off him and gave it to me. It had the body of a stag beetle but the legs and the head were a spider. It eventually fell apart, but I'd had so many comments about it and so many women came and chatted me up about it, I decided to have a black one made. Now I've got about six of them. I like to have it with me. I have actually gone to gigs and been unable to go on without the spider. I send people back to get it.

A lot of Lambert's input was with Pete before the song was actually presented to us. Especially in the mini-opera. We had between nine and 12 minutes left to complete the album. It meant writing three more songs, so Kit suggested writing lots of little songs to make a nine-minute miniature opera. Really it was just to fill up a gap.

Roger Daltrey: Kit's idea was to do something more than a three-minute song (for *A Quick One While He's Away*) and he encouraged Pete to come up with a total concept.

John Entwistle: We wanted to put cellos on the track, but Kit said we couldn't afford it. That's why we sang "cello cello cello" where we thought they should be.

John Entwistle: Moon didn't come through with two [songs for the album], actually. "Cobwebs And Strange" was me. Basically, I made the brass part up and it just went on from there.

Keith Moon: I wanted to write something with an Indian flavour. The end product is an Eastern tune with a brass band treatment.

John Entwistle: ["I Need You"] was a song about The Beatles. Keith had gone through an experience with The Beatles where they were talking their own language. He had gone through all this paranoia thinking that The Who could speak the language as well. Everything you said, "What does that mean, what does that mean?" He was on these little yellow pills at the time. Yellow paranoia pills.

Keith Moon: It's solely a musical illustration of a transport cafe. The melody is typical of the sort of record that would be on the juke box. If you listen to the whole thing, you'll hear our transport cafe sound effects. We rustled bags of crisps, clinked tea cups and we even got our Liverpudlian road manager to say a couple of things into the mike to get the effect of people passing the juke box. It was not a Lennon impression, as some people seem to think.

4. Midnight Sun, Birmingham.

5. Locarno, Streatham, South London.

9. Drill Hall, Dumfries, Scotland.

10. "I'm A Boy" is released as a single in the US. The band plays at the Empire, Sunderland.

15. On the same day that "Happy Jack" enters the UK singles chart, a new roadie, Bob Pridden, joins the crew for a gig at the Locarno, Streatham.

Bob Pridden: We rehearsed for the afternoon, and that night they went on stage and I couldn't believe it. I'd never seen anything like it in my life. Pete came on stage looking very hip, John was dressed well too but didn't move all evening. Roger twirled mikes around and Keith's sticks were going everywhere. At the end, they just smashed everything to pieces. I thought, "Oh, my God!" I was in a state of shock. They walked off stage and Roger turned to me and said, "Bobby, get it all fixed for tomorrow."

15. Official opening date of The Speakeasy club in London.

Barry Gibb (Bee Gees): The most vivid scene, for me, was this underground club called The Speakeasy. The only people who knew of or got into it were the top end of British pop – The Beatles, the Stones, The Who. It was set like a 1920s funeral parlour. You entered through a coffin door that swung open, and suddenly there were the Stones and Beatles sitting round.

I met Pete Townshend there, and he introduced me to John Lennon, who was actually wearing the Sgt Pepper clothes. I don't think John knew who he was being introduced to. He was talking to somebody else and he went like that and shook my hand, and went "How ya doing?" and carried on talking.

I don't think he was being rude, just preoccupied. Pete certainly didn't behave as if John was likely to be rude. He kept saying, "John . . . John . . . John, I want you to meet this kid," but it didn't really go any further.

16. At Ryemuse Studios, London, a backing track is recorded for use on the following week's "Ready Steady Go!"

17. The Who's second album, *A Quick One*, enters the UK album charts, where it will peak at No. 4.

21. Upper Cut, London. Townshend also finds time to check out Jimi Hendrix at Blaises Club.

Chris Welch (reviewer, *Melody Maker*): That was quite an eventful night for me, with The Who first and Hendrix afterwards. The club had been quite recently opened, and it was owned by Billy Walker, the British champion boxer. The Who played a good set, and I remember that they did "My Generation" extremely fast which seemed odd at the time but, in retrospect, I imagine they were keen to get the show over with so they could go and see Jimi, who was then fast becoming the hot new guitar-slinger around London.

Pete Townshend: Eric Clapton called me and suggested that we check him out. It was kind of keeping an eye on the competition. We arrived at the show a little late as I was stuck in the studio and, just as we arrived, Jeff Beck was walking out. I asked Jeff, "What's the matter, mate? Is he that bad?" Beck could only roll his eyes upward and say "No, Pete, he's that good!" When Eric and I saw his show, we knew what Jeff meant. He was doing everything – the blues, rock, and things I still can't name. He was playing the guitar with his teeth, behind his back, on the floor. It was unbelievable.

It was tough for me and Eric because we'd appropriated this black American blues and imported it for the 14 to 20 year olds in London. Now here's Hendrix saying, "I'm taking it back. You've finished with it. I'll show you where it goes next."

23. The Who appear on the very last edition of "Ready Steady Go!"

30. London's psychedelic venue The Night Tripper changes its name to UFO, and quickly becomes the in place for rock artists like Pete Townshend..

Pete Townshend: I used to frequent the UFO club, which is where I met Mike McInnerney and [future wife] Karen and all that lot, everybody. We used to get that Swiss stuff [LSD], which was real Sandoz stuff, which is really incredibly pure.

Craig Sams (macrobiotic restaurateur): UFO was every other weekend, so on a lot of the alternate weekends [painter] Michael [English], his girlfriend Angela, and Pete Townshend and Karen, his girlfriend, and me would get together at Karen's place in Eccleston Square and trip the night away. We had our own little UFO. That gave us something to do on the alternate Fridays. Once we were all walking down the street just past the Victoria Coach Station, it was really freezing cold but Townshend had stripped down to his shirt – "Cold is just a state of mind, man" – and we were all barrelling along, just full of our own incredible strength, and some car pulls up. The classic scene: a head comes out and somebody says, "Hi, Pete Townshend. I think your last album was fucking great!" and then the guy drunkenly heaves all down the side of the car. Suddenly you realized the huge distance between where we were going, into spiritual realms, and 15 pints of lager, which was where a lot of the mods had gone. But we'd all come from the same roots – soul, dancing and mild pharmaceuticals.

31. The all-night Psychedelicamania happening takes place at The Roundhouse, London, featuring The Who, The Move and Pink Floyd.

Nick Jones (reviewer, *Melody Maker*):

> The Who almost succeeded in winning over the show with an immediate flurry of smoke bombs and sound-barrier smashing . . . After playing most of their new album tracks rather half-heartedly, Pete Townshend wheeled upon a fine pair of speakers and ground them with his shattered guitar into the stage. It was fair comment. The group had thrice been switched off as well as constantly being plunged into darkness by a team of lighting men – none of whom seemed to know where, in fact the stage, or the Who, were positioned.

1967

January 1967

Although it never sees the light of day, Townshend is reported to be working on a full-scale pop opera in his Wardour Street studio.

Pete Townshend: I'm now anxious to start moving musically. This opera is an exercise I want to see if I can write. It takes place in the year 1999, when China is breaking out and is about to take over the world. The hero loses his wife and decides to go and live in this tiny country, which is about to be overrun by the Chinese. The hero goes through hundreds of situations, and there is music for each.

He goes out in a boat and gets shipwrecked, he has a bad nightmare, and so on.

6. Marine Ballroom, Central Pier, Morecambe. Pete Townshend, having been involved in a car crash on the M6, is replaced on this gig by Mike Dickinson of support band The Doodlebugs.

Mike Dickinson: Before we went on we had a 10-minute conference backstage and decided to do stuff like "Dancin' In The Street" and "In The Midnight Hour" and a few Who hits, which I busked through, trying to keep up with John and Keith. I played a full set with The Who that night. Except for the last number, "Boris The Spider", when Roger asked me to leave the stage as they were going to smash a few things up.

12. "Top Of The Pops", playing "Happy Jack".

Pete Townshend: When we had a hit with "Happy Jack", which was a very different sound for us, it became obvious that the musical direction of the group was going to change. I'd gone back to being influenced by the Stones again.

13. Festival Hall, Kirkby-in-Ashfield.

15. Recording for German pop show "Beat Club", at Radio Bremen, Hamburg.

17. The Who record live versions of "Happy Jack", "See My Way", "Run Run Run" and "Boris The Spider" at The Playhouse, London, for the BBC radio show "Saturday Club".

John Entwistle: On the studio version of "See My Way", Roger wanted the drums to sound like cardboard boxes, but Keith's drums always sounded like biscuit tins being hit. We couldn't make them sound like cardboard boxes. So Keith went out the back of the studio for a while, and when he came back, he started playing and Roger said, "That sounds perfect! How are you doing that?" It was two cardboard boxes Keith had found outside.

18. Orchid Ballroom, Purley.

21. "Happy Jack" peaks at No. 3 in the UK. A 9.30 show at Leeds University is cancelled when Townshend arrives late.

Godfrey Claff (Entertainments Secretary, Leeds University): They decided at 10.20 that they would have to cancel their performance. Pete Townshend appeared soon afterwards and still expected to play.

Jerry Howarth (student): He was very concerned about it all. His car ran out of petrol on the A1 and he even offered his guitar as surety as he had no money to pay. He went to a police station and managed to raise money by ringing up home, but it was too late by the time he got here. He offered to appear again when the Union wanted and he said he would pay the group's expenses.

25. Kingsway Theatre, Hadleigh, Essex.

26. Locarno, Bristol.

28. Tofts Club, Folkestone.

29. The Who, supported by The Jimi Hendrix Experience, play a tribute concert for Brian Epstein, at The Saville Theatre, London.

Pete Townshend: Kit Lambert, our manager, had just signed Jimi up to our label [Track] and put him on backing us up. I couldn't really believe it, you know? I thought, Jesus Christ, what's going to happen? So he went on and he did his thing. He knocked the amplifiers over, he practically smashed it up . . . and I went on afterwards and I just stood and strummed.

Glen Coulson (fan): Townshend came out on the stage and said, "Well, we're not gonna top that. You lot might as well all go home now."

Pete Townshend: I'm not ashamed to say he blew us away.

31. Palais de Danse, Ilford.

February 1967

2. Locarno, Coventry.

4. Birdcage, Portsmouth.

5. The *News Of The World* runs the headline "Pop Stars And Drugs – Facts That Will Shock You". It reveals that The Moody Blues have hosted parties at which Pete Townshend of The Who and Ginger Baker of Cream took LSD. It also claims that Mick Jagger had participated when the Stone involved was actually Brian Jones. In the evening, The Who play at the Waterfront, Southampton.

10. Gaiety Ballroom, Grimsby.

11. Royal Links Pavilion, Cromer.

12. Starlite Ballroom, Greenford, West London.

21. Town Hall, High Wycombe.

23. The Who set off on a brief four-day Italian tour, starting at Palazzetto dello Sport, Turin.

24. Palazzetto dello Sport, Bologna, Italy.

25. Palalido, Milan, Italy.

26. Palazzetto dello Sport, Rome, Italy.

March 1967

1. The Who record "Pictures Of Lily" in Pye Studio No. 2, London.

Roger Daltrey: I think "Pictures Of Lily" is a great song. It's another rip-off from The Kinks . . . Think about Ray Davies singing that, and it would be more of a Kinks song than it ever really was a Who song.

Pete Townshend: It's all about a boy who can't sleep at night so his dad gives him some dirty pictures to look at. Then he falls in love with the girl in the pictures, which is too bad . . . because she's dead.

John Entwistle: It's all about wanking . . . Townshend going through his sexual traumas, something that he did quite often. I sometimes think you could say that record represents our smutty period or, to be more refined, our Blue period.

I pretty much completely rewrote the bass line. I joined the whole thing together, made it more complicated. The thing I hate about "Pictures Of Lily" is that bloody elephant call on the French horn.

I also hated the backing vocals, the mermaid voices, where we'd sing all the "oooohs". I hated "oooohs". I'd much rather sing "aaaaah". But it was always "oooooh". Maybe because we were The 'Oo. I could never sing "oooohs" in tune. Singing backing vocals with The Who, especially once we had louder gear on stage, was like singing with headphones on. You can't hear your voice. It's like when you see people on planes listening to the in-flight headsets and singing along out of tune. You can't tell if you're in tune.

2. Marquee, Soho, London, recording live tracks for Radio Bremen's "Goes To London" show.

Randy Bachman (Canadian band, The Guess Who): We came face to face with our dream when our single "His Girl" charted in England and we had the opportunity to go there to tour.

We weren't able to get around to see a lot of bands because we didn't have the money but we did manage to meet The Who at the Marquee Club in Soho one afternoon. They were recording a live set for one of the British pop television shows. We were strolling by, heard the noise, and just walked in and sat at a table to watch.

"Who are you? What are you doing here?" asked one of their crew.

"We're The Guess Who from Canada."

"Oh."

The Who in the garden of Keith Moon's home, Tara.
Kim Moon: **"We led separate lives under the same roof. He'd get up in the morning and decide to be Hitler for a day."**

Pete Townshend in his home demo studio.
Glyn Johns (producer): **"The demos Townshend makes are invariably better than the records that are released."**

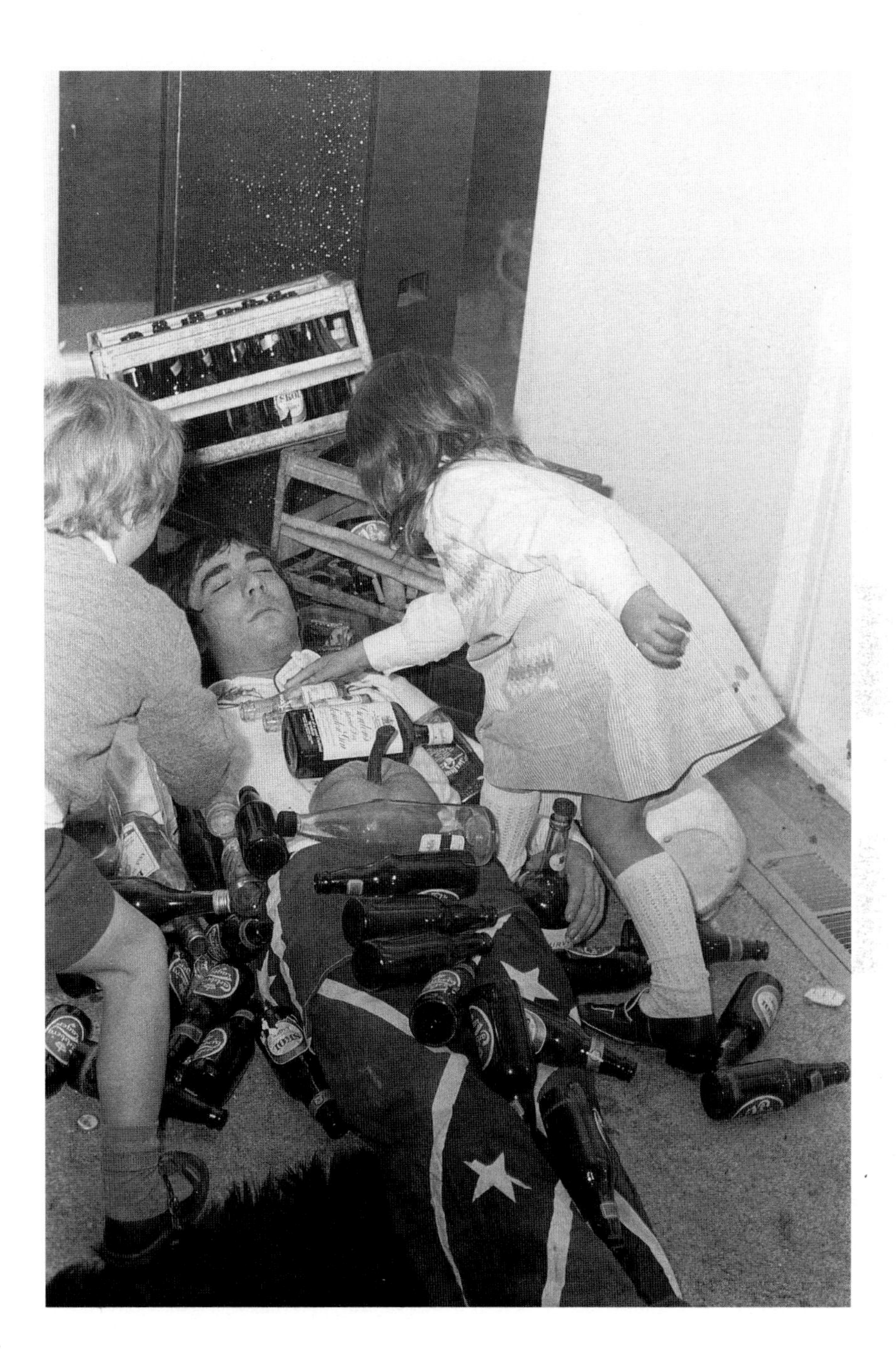

Keith Moon relaxing at home.
John Entwistle: **"Moon would pass out before a gig, sober up just before we went on, play like a maniac, and go back on the bottle as soon as we finished."**

The Who on TV in the mid-60s.
Cathy McGowan (presenter, *Ready Steady Go!*): **"I said to Keith Moon, 'Don't talk to me like that. Nobody's interested in what you're doing anyway, quite honestly.'"**

The Who promote Magic Bus via a bus ride around London.
John Entwistle: **"On stage, Magic Bus was always a complete bore for me. I'd be playing the same note, A, for six minutes. It wasn't so bad when we recorded it because that was only three minutes."**

Daltrey makes the most of his legendary fringed jacket.
Chris McCourt (photographer): "**Daltrey was interesting to photograph, actually, because of his American Indian suede fringe jacket thing with the tassles, plenty of movement.**"

Poster for an early single by Pete Townshend's father, Cliff.
PeteTownshend: "**My father had a dance band called the Squadronaires. I travelled with them until I was about seven, so I got an early taste of the road.**"

Keith Moon (centre) in The Beachcombers.
Norman Mitchener (guitarist, Beachcombers): **"He was good, he was loud. He had something in his playing. His snare work was heavy and it was drivey".**

"We need to talk to you."

"Well, just sit there."

The Marquee is like someone's basement, it's so small. The Who had stacks of Marshall amplifiers and were playing so loud our ears were ringing like someone had fired a gun beside our heads. We didn't want to look rude or uncool by plugging our ears but it was painful. They were smashing their gear and smoke bombs were going off. The director kept stopping them.

"Turn it down!"

"Okay."

Then they would just crank it up again blasting away. John Entwistle was playing his bass guitar with a metal pick cut from the aluminium trim around an Arborite countertop or table, whacking the strings like a hammer.

Finally they finished, the director had enough footage, and they laid down their instruments and came over to talk with us.

"We need to straighten out the name. We're The Guess Who and we're getting confused with you guys."

John Entwistle looked us up and down and simply mumbled, "Oh, bugger off. There's the Byrds and Yardbirds so there can be a Who and Guess Who, so bugger off."

4. California Ballroom, Dunstable.

10. Top Rank, Swansea, Wales.

11. King's Hall, Stoke-on-Trent.

13. Granby Halls, Leicester.

17. Exeter University.

18. Devonport Forum, Plymouth.

20. Pavilion, Bath.

22. The Who fly to New York.

Pete Townshend: We stayed at the Drake Hotel. We spent $5,000 in four days at the hotel alone. We had to tip the man at the door $250 before they would let us have our baggage. That was the kind of world we were suddenly thrown into, and we couldn't figure the whole thing out.

Nancy Lewis (journalist): I'll never forget the rehearsal The Who did the first time they went to the RKO 58th Street Theater. It was the first time they had been seen in America and Frank Barsalona [a US bookings agent] and all those people were there. The Who came on and they looked incredible that day –

Townshend had on his white pants and Union Jack coat, they looked sensational and they went out for their dress rehearsal and they just did a 20-minute set and at the end destroyed all their instruments, blew up smoke bombs, and all the people in the audience at rehearsal just couldn't believe it. It absolutely freaked everyone out.

25. The Who and Cream play their US concert debut, as part of DJ Murray The K's nine-day season of concerts under the heading Music In The Fifth Dimension, at the RKO 58th Street Theater, New York.

Roger Daltrey: Paul Simon was the first guy to bring us here. He made Murray The K aware of us and he [Murray] brought us over here for the Easter show.

Pete Townshend: The first time we came to America we played along with Cream, supporting Mitch Ryder & The Detroit Wheels and Wilson Pickett at Murray The K's show at the Academy of Music in New York.

Ben Palmer (road manager, Cream): It was a big bill, a lot of acts, and it was supposed to be five shows a day. I think the first curtain was at ten in the morning – the kids were on holiday – and the last show would go on not far short of midnight, and that was for the supper crowd coming out of the theatres.

Eric Clapton (Cream): The audience were mostly 13 to 14 year old teenyboppers. Everybody went down well and, as we only had one or two numbers each, everybody pulled the stops out. The Who stole the show. They only had to smash everything up and everybody was on their feet.

Pete Townshend: As an institution, that sort of show was falling to pieces. It wasn't filling up. The kids weren't coming. Smokey Robinson was billed to appear with Wilson Pickett. Diana Ross was a guest at one point. In the end, it turned out to be an opportunity for Murray himself to come out in his new bimbo's wigs. I mean the guy was a tremendous indictment of the American music industry. He had wonderful stories to tell. But they were all of pathos as far as we could see.

Keith Moon: One and a half minutes of "My Generation", one and a half of "Substitute", then smash your fuckin' instruments and rush off.

Pete Townshend: I spent more time as a carpenter, glueing guitars together than as a musician.

Binky Philips (critic, *Record World*): I've never seen anything so loud and brutal [as The Who]. They were the absolute epitome of flash. Townshend dressed in white, with pants up to his chest, Daltrey's hair was all puffed up – they were gorgeous. Townshend would throw his Stratocaster 20 feet up into the air and catch it. When he was tired, he would let it slam on the floor. Such a gas.

Roger Daltrey: We did everything to Murray The K. I broke every microphone on the show and the last one left was his own personal gold-plated microphone. We would do four or five shows a day. But they were two songs [each show]. We used to do something like "Substitute". We always used to do "Generation". We'd do one song and then smash all the gear up. And we had Bobby Pridden backstage permanently gluing guitars back together.

Pete Townshend: Simon & Garfunkel had come to that Murray The K show. I think Neil Diamond might have done a guest thing. There were some big names for the time, American names. But Bill was just cutting through all that stuff and giving people time to play and perform and the audience time to sit down and relax.

What was happening at the Murray The K show, which should have been a lesson for the promoters to realize, was that the kids were coming in and they were staying all day. They were staying all day because they liked the music. They weren't staying all day because they wanted to get away from school. If that had been the case, they would have gotten bored. They stayed because they liked the music they were hearing and they wanted to hear it again and again and again.

26-31. Six further nights at the RKO 58th Street Theater, New York.

April 1967

1. Eighth night at the RKO 58th Street Theater, New York.

2. Ninth and last night at the RKO 58th Street Theater, New York.

Eric Clapton: We had all these 14lb bags of flour and some eggs we were going to use on stage on the last night, but Murray got to hear about it and said we wouldn't get paid if we did. So we spread them all around the dressing rooms instead. The whole cast joined in and Pete Townshend ended up swimming around in his dressing room, fully clothed, when his shower overflowed. It was rumoured that Murray spent $30,000 on the show and lost $27,000. He was very distraught, wandering about, throwing his hands in the air.

Pete Townshend: During the psychedelic era we [Townshend and Clapton] started to see quite a lot of each other because of the atmosphere that prevailed in London. We were mixing with a lot of the same people. We socialized a fair bit and went to see Pink Floyd a couple of times together because we both had a passion for Syd Barrett. Then we got a bit closer during the Murray The K shows in New York, when The Who and the Cream were together on the bill. But, in 1969, after the Cream finished, he disappeared completely from my life.

3. The Who fly back to London.

6. Recording session in London for next album.

7. Spot Studios, London, recording "Doctor Doctor" for next album.

John Hudson (staff member, Spot Studios): It was just around the corner from Robert Stigwood's management office in Brook Street, so most of his artists recorded there. It was one of the first small, friendly studios.

The company name was Ryemuse Ltd, from a Mr Rye who owned it, and the studio's name changed from Spot to Mayfair around 1973. Spot was above a chemist's shop and there was no lift, with the studio and control room on the second floor, so all the equipment had to go up two flights of stairs. There was no window between the studio and the control room, because there was a corridor between, so there was no visual communication between the two. That room sounded fantastic, though I think it was a fluke.

8. Twelve-day German tour, supported by John's Children, starts at Meistersingerhalle, Nürnberg.

Simon Napier-Bell (manager, John's Children): John's Children weren't much of a musical group, so the only point in being on stage was to make a great show and upstage The Who. They hadn't had hit records, so they wouldn't get any attention by playing their music. And of course, we knew The Who had a pretty amazing act, so we had to do something even more amazing.

So that first night, I got the band to destroy a chair on stage, knowing that the audience would respond by doing the same thing. I think there were ten thousand broken chairs in the hall by the end of John's Children's set.

10. Jaguar Club, Herford, Germany.

Simon Napier-Bell: I think it was the next night that we bought a couple of kilos of duck feathers, and the band scattered them liberally around the hall like a snowstorm that went on and on.

Of course, when The Who came on, the feathers were still floating around and got into Roger's throat, making it very difficult for him to sing. Kit was my best friend but he'd agreed to have my band on the tour, and they had to get some benefit from it. He really quite admired what we did, because it was exactly in the tradition of what he would have done. But he couldn't allow it, because we were upstaging his band. The Who were very good to our faces, but they were giving Kit a terrible time every day saying we had to be thrown off the tour.

11. Rheinhalle, Düsseldorf, Germany.

Richard Green (publicist, Track Records): They had a tour manager, but for some unknown reason, I had to collect the money. If you know anything about Kit Lambert and Chris Stamp, that wouldn't surprise you. Kit told me, "You look after them but, whatever you do, dear boy, don't let anyone have any money."

So Moon said, one night in Düsseldorf, "Beast [nickname for Green], I want £200." I said, "Keith, Kit said you can't have any." So he said, "Right, I'm not going on." And he disappeared. I asked one of the roadies where he'd gone and he said, "He's just caught a cab." So I had to get a cab and say, "Follow that cab!" Mooney had gone to some bloody club at the other side of town that he must have known about, and when I got there, he'd gone back to the concert hall. When I got back, having paid this taxi driver however much, Keith turns to me and says, "Now can I have the money?"

12. Friedrich-Ebert Halle, Ludwigshaven-am-Rheine, Germany.

Simon Napier-Bell: The place was totally wrecked. We were making it very difficult for The Who, because the audience, having just seen John's Children, really expected something incredible from the headline act. That put a lot of pressure on them. I'm not sure The Who even played that night.

13. When The Who play at Circus Krone-Bau, Munich, Germany, Marc Bolan of support group John's Children writes a letter to his girlfriend.

Marc Bolan:

The tour's going OK. The Who are a drag, but we're going down quite good . . . we were out-playing The Who in most shows.

14. Halle Munsterland, Munster, Germany.

Simon Napier-Bell: By now, Kit had had enough headaches from John's Children and he told me that if we did anything more to overshadow the Who, we'd be off the tour. So, of course, we did it again the next night.

15. Siegerlandhalle, Siegen and Rhein-Maine Halle, Wiesbaden, Germany.

16. Oberschwabenhalle, Ravensburg and Donauhalle, Ulm, Germany.

19. Live recording for TV show "Beat Club", in Fernsehstudio, Osterholz, Germany. DM6,000 of The Who's money is stolen from a dressing room.

21. Arts Festival, the Dome, Brighton.

Ian Grant (audience): The night I saw my first gig. Wasn't too impressed with the opening acts [Crispian St Peters and The Merseybeats] but when Cream hit the stage I was transfixed. When The Who performed their set I was totally blown away. I felt I had to be involved in some way. This was the night it all started. I would have never dreamt the 30-year journey I have been on since. [Grant later became a top rock manager.]

22. The Who release their new single, "Pictures Of Lily", in the UK. It is the first release on the new label, Track Records, set up by managers Kit Lambert and Chris Stamp. "Pictures Of Lily" will peak at No. 4.

24. Pavilion, Bath.

25. Town Hall, High Wycombe.

26. Recording for next album at De Lane Lea Studios, London.

27. The Who appear on "Top Of The Pops", performing "Pictures Of Lily", which also enters the UK singles chart on this day.

28. Recording session in London for next album.

29. Ten thousand hippies turn up to see Pink Floyd, The Crazy World Of Arthur Brown and other bands at the 14 Hour Technicolour Dream at London's Alexandra Palace. Although The Who do not perform, Pete Townshend is in the audience.

Drachen Theaker (drummer, Crazy World Of Arthur Brown): It was a wild act, but it wasn't that wild musically. We were just an R&B group underneath. It wasn't like the Pink Floyd, because we took our cue from the whole US mid-sixties soul music invasion. What made it psychedelic was Arthur's acting ability and the fact that Vince and I just overplayed to death at gigs. We made a hell of a noise for two people.

Vincent Crane (keyboards, Crazy World Of Arthur Brown): Arthur was a soul singer then. We did psychedelic soul music and that's why you've got things like "Money" on the album. A lot of people used to think he was coloured.

Pete said he wanted to produce us when we met him at the Technicolour Dream gig. So we went to his home studio and cut some tracks, which he eventually placed in *The Committee* film.

Arthur Brown: Townshend had been interested in signing The Bonzo Dog Doo Dah Band, but Track Records missed them, as they had just been signed by another label. So Townshend told Track that if they didn't hurry up and sign our band, then we would get picked up too. At the time, we were being wined and dined by every record company in England. We never had so much free food in our lives. The record companies could tell . . . Something was going to happen with this band. So Track Records signed us up.

30. Scandinavian tour begins in the Ice Hall, Helsinki, Finland.

May 1967

2. Njardhallen, Oslo, Norway.

3. Lorensbergs Cirkus, Gothenburg, Sweden.

Gosta Hansson (Swedish reviewer): It seems that many in the audience came just to see The Who destroy their equipment. They were surely satisfied. But the fans that came for the band's musical qualities were not disappointed either. The group had developed tremendously since their last visit.

4. Masshall, Norrköping, Sweden, supported by The Jokers, followed by Rogoletto, Jönköping, Sweden.

Ove Nilsson (guitarist, The Jokers): The instruments arrived only one hour before the show. The unpacking didn't take more time in those days. The Who did the soundcheck on stage before their act. They checked the guitar sound and the microphones and kicked off.

Unfortunately the guitars were too dominant in those days. That goes for most of the bands in the sixties. The PA system was seldom more than 50 watts.

Jan Elgstrom (audience): What we remember most of all – like yesterday – was Keith's treatment of his drumsticks. On one side of his drum kit he had lots of drumsticks, and when he broke one, he just took another. On one occasion, he threw his drumstick high up in the air, took another stick, kept the beat going, threw it away and caught the first one on its way down. Fabulous.

Lotta (reviewer, Norrköpings Tidningar):

> Having played "Substitute", "Run, Run, Run" and "Boris The Spider" without any response from the audience, they continued almost desperately with "Happy Jack" and "I'm A Boy", but nothing happened. When they finally closed with "My Generation", they simply let an amplifier explode in anger and disappointment.

Jan Elgstrom: Pete made a lot of noise by holding his guitar in front of his amps and speakers. At the end of the show, Keith stood up and spread his drums on the floor. No one had ever seen anything like it before. We thought it was a good concert and felt very satisfied. But most importantly, we had seen them live – that was the big thing.

Lotta:

The sweaty drummer threw his drums all over the stage. When the havoc was complete, the four Englishmen left both a delighted and confused audience behind. The Who will probably never forget the "ice-cold" audience in Norrköping.

Ove Nilsson: The Who ended their act by smashing the guitar on the floor, and kicking the drums off the stage. Our drummer got Keith's T-shirt afterwards.

5. Sporthallen, Eskilstuna, Sweden.

Christer Thunell (audience): I went to Eskilstuna with one thing in mind, now there's going to be pop-circus on stage with broken amplifiers, smoke bombs and a lot of wattage. But all The Who managed to create was the latter, plus a couple of songs delivered in an extremely bad mood.

The evening started when Pete Townshend came in. He looked at the stage, tested it, got in a car and left. He came back after a while and explained he would not play on a stage that was too small and situated metres above the heads of the audience. And that was that.

The security guards expected riots, and were getting more and more nervous. But, after threats of withdrawn money, The Who did five songs without any joy at all. Pete Townshend, who usually carries around three guitars, brought only one as he stood waiting to enter the stage. After a couple of songs, drummer Keith Moon had wasted dozens of drumsticks which fell to the audience, who did their best to grab a piece of the broken tool. These were the only incidents.

Finally, the first chords of "My Generation" came from the speakers, and Pete started to play his guitar with a microphone stand accompanied by the cheering crowd. He turned over a couple of speaker cabinets and a smoke bomb exploded. That was all we got for our money.

6. Kungliga Tennishallen, Stockholm, Sweden, supported by The Maniacs and Pete Proud.

Peter Stolt (vocalist, Pete Proud): We spent all afternoon getting the sound right. Right before we were going on stage, The Maniacs came in and asked if they could go first because they had another gig later. They used our equipment, played, and took off. Everything went wrong when we came on stage. I was supposed to sing the lead but got the wrong microphone. The guitar was drowned in drums and rumbling bass. We heard that something was wrong but we were totally stressed and didn't have any experience. We went through the set but our mood plummeted. It was a total disaster. We left everything on stage and ran off with tears in our eyes.

Ludwig Rasmussen (concert reviewer):

> The Who started out with their speakers on full power trying their best to surprise the audience, which was successful at first. But after a while, the concert turned lame . . .

Peter Stolt: Townshend started swinging his guitar around and broke some of our equipment.

Ludwig Rasmussen:

> The indispensable final number, "My Generation", became the most destructive The Who had presented in Stockholm. Roger swung his microphone into the drums. Pete hit his guitar into another microphone so it broke. Keith pushed out his entire set of drums. Speakers and amps fell, Townshend's guitar was smashed to pieces. Luckily, the finale was chaotic, otherwise the audience probably would have been disappointed.

Peter Stolt: We went into their dressing room later to explain what had happened. A manager signed a cheque and tossed it over his shoulder. We were crushed. I headed to Club Liverpool, a club on a boat on Soder Malarstrand, and drifted around, hidden behind dark sunglasses. I ended up spending the night sleeping in the band's touring van.

7. Following an afternoon show at Sommarlust, Kristianstad, a full-scale riot erupts on the last Scandinavian tour date, at MFF-Stadion, Malmö, Sweden.

Ingmar Fallhammar (sound engineer): It was with mixed feelings that I accepted the task of taking care of the sound when The Who visited Malmö for a concert at MFF-Stadion. According to reviews, they demolished instruments worth SEK30,000. Their pay was, if I'm not mistaken, SEK3,500, which meant that they would have to do very short tours or their debts would grow out of control. I did some calculating and the real figure came closer to SEK28.50.

The guitar he smashed was a stand-in for the one he actually used. The stand-in had a simple arrangement on the backside of its neck. Just before the smash he pulled a little switch – the guitar folded over his knee – accompanied by the cheering audience. Later when the audience had left, the guitar could easily be restored to its former state. Cost: SEK0.

"The wild guitarist hit his guitar through a speaker. When he pulled it out grey-coloured paper fell out." But the speaker wasn't connected, and the paper, which was to be assumed coming from the speakers, was the same kind kids use in school. Costs per concert: SEK6.

"The drummer ended a solo by jumping on a cymbal so it was bent out of shape like an umbrella in stormy weather." After the concert he bent it back to normal over his knee. Cost: SEK0. These expenses, along with strings, were approx. SEK28.50. Unfortunately this destructive spirit spread to two generations of musicians.

8. The Who fly back to the UK.

10. Top Rank, Swansea, Wales.

13. Shoreline Hotel, Bognor Regis.

15. Keith Moon hangs out at The Speakeasy with Paul McCartney.

Paul McCartney: The first time I ever heard "A Whiter Shade Of Pale" was the night I met Linda. We met at the Bag O' Nails, and we went on to The Speakeasy, and they played the record of it there. We were with Keith Moon of The Who and Eric Burdon of The Animals, and we were all trying to figure out who it was. We all thought it must be Stevie Winwood, but it turned out to be Procol Harum. We just said, "This is the best song ever, man." And it became mine and Linda's song, so that's why I have a special affection for it.

17. John Entwistle breaks a finger when he punches a picture of "a well-known pop star" backstage at the Locarno, Stevenage. Further recording for *The Who Sell Out* is thus delayed.

20. A momentous day for The Who as "Happy Jack" enters the US singles chart. Simultaneously, "Pictures Of Lily" reaches No. 4 in the UK. The same day, The Who also play at the Wolu Festival, Brussels, Belgium.

Simon Napier-Bell: Kit was getting in a bad way with drugs by then. He'd sit in the office with ten drugs laid out on his desk and whoever phoned up, he'd take the right drug to enable him to deal with them. For one person, he'd need uppers, and then for the next one, he couldn't speak to them until he'd gulped down a handful of downers. But at least heroin wasn't in the mix then.

Kit never had money. Even when he was a millionaire, he always had money problems. It was as if he loved being broke. I remember he pawned the cufflinks his father had given him to pay to get Roger's teeth fixed, and he pawned his record player to pay their wages one week.

23. Recording for *The Who Sell Out* in London.

Pete Townshend: I can remember pacing around his [Chris Stamp's] office, wildly brainstorming. Chris had a bemused expression on his face, waiting for me to come up with something. I needed an idea that would transform what I regarded as a weak collection of occasionally cheesy songs into something with teeth. Suddenly I hit on it – we would turn the entire album into a pirate radio segment and actually sell advertising space to manufacturers and fashion houses.

Roger Daltrey: I love *Sell Out*, I think it's great. I love the jingles.

John Entwistle: We did most of the commercials in one day. Me and Keith went out to a pub and we got a few commercials thought up like "Rotosound Strings" and "Premier Drums".

Roger Daltrey: It was Chris Stamp's idea [to include radio jingles], because at that time we relied heavily on the pirate radio stations. You have to understand that at that time in England the BBC Broadcasting Service, they played probably two rock'n'roll records a day! That was it. So all these kind of renegade people set up in ships off the shore and beamed in rock'n'roll. And it was incredible because for the first time ever we had DJs who were just so happy to be playing the music they loved.

It was so different from today, where you get DJs who are told what to play because of the marketing and all this shit. There's a few left who play what they love. But in those days it was really special. That album was recorded when the government had brought in legislation to sink them. They said, "You can't broadcast." They did some international thing where they had to go so far off shore that it became almost impossible for them to survive. *Sell Out* came out literally within the first week of them being turned off. To placate us the government gave the BBC their own pop station and it was awful.

John Entwistle: The jingles were added later. I had an idea for a couple of tribute jingles to the pirate stations that had just been deposed. We owed a lot to the pirate stations because the BBC wasn't very good to us at all.

Roger Daltrey: The whole thing as an album is a wonderful piece of work.

Roger Law (sleeve designer): I had worked at the *Observer* with Peter Cook, so I was something of a satirist. They picked up on that attitude.

John Entwistle: Actually, for that cover I was supposed to be in the beans and I rang up and said I was going to be a bit late and they said, "You're going to have to hurry up because the baked beans are drying up." And I said, "What baked beans?" And they said, "The baked beans you're going to be sitting in." So I figured if I left a little bit longer someone else would arrive and have to sit in the beans. So I got there real late and I got the girl and Roger got the beans.

Roger Law: We couldn't get any beans that hadn't been in a cold store. We poured them all into a bath. And then we had poor old Roger Daltrey in there. He didn't complain. They were all very good actually.

Pete Townshend: There was some kind of lottery as to who would do the baked beans. Roger didn't exactly volunteer, but he was very sporting about it and jumped in. He actually got cramp very quickly.

Roger Daltrey: I was the last one to be done. They all grabbed the easy ones and I was basically last and they thought, "Oh, we'll let Daltrey get in the tub of baked beans." It was awful. I got very sick because they had just got the bloody things out of the freezer. So they were freezing cold. Then I think it was Moon who had the bright idea about putting an electric fire around the back of the tub. I was cooking, one half of me was cooking. My feet were freezing and it made me very ill.

Pete Townshend: I was a little worried about wearing no shirt, in order to apply giant Odorono. But looking at the sleeve again today, I find myself wishing I still had a body as elegant and Byronically aristocratic.

24. "Pictures Of Lily" is released in the US.

25. The Who appear on "Top Of The Pops" performing "Pictures Of Lily".

27. Townshend's guitar is stolen after a gig at the May Ball in the Grand Marquee, Pembroke College, Oxford.

28. While recording the song "Melancholia" at Advision, London, Keith Moon strains stomach muscles while throwing his drums around. He is rushed to St George's Hospital and is unable to play for two weeks.

Sam Hutt (doctor): Keith Moon came into St George's and I was then working for two surgeons and he came in to have his hernia repaired. He bashed the drums so hard that he'd given himself a hernia. I assisted at his hernia repair. Got very pally with him. A lovely bloke – a lunatic and a bit dangerous and all that, but a lovely bloke at heart. And I'd go down The Speakeasy from time to time and visit with Keith and watch him spill champagne everywhere and get arseholed. I wasn't a great Speakeasy goer. I tended to go with Moony and the typical thing was [imitates Moon's Cockney accent]: "A bottle of champagne!" and it comes along and, "Fuck me, I've fucking knocked it over! Let's have

another bottle, all right, hey! Fucking champagne, eh. Fucking cunt! All right!" High-class drunken lunatic.
29. Julian Covey of The Machine stands in for Keith at the Locarno, Glasgow, Scotland.

June 1967

3. Julian Covey of The Machine stands in for Keith at the Floral Hall, Southport, as "Happy Jack" gives The Who their first US Top 30 entry, at No. 24.
4. Chris Townson of John's Children stands in for Keith at the Guildhall, Southampton. Later, Pete attends a farewell party for US singer Mitch Ryder in London, along with Jeff Beck and John's Children.
5. Chris Townson of John's Children stands in for Keith at the Top Rank, Swansea, Wales.
7. Recording "Early Morning Cold Taxi" at CBS Studios, London.
9. Keith Moon returns to the drum stool for a gig at the Magilligan Golden Slipper Ballroom, Derry, Northern Ireland.
12. College Ball, Christ Church, Cambridge, with The Moody Blues and Georgie Fame.
13. Flight to America.
14. US tour begins at The Fifth Dimension, Ann Arbor, Michigan.
15. The Cellar, Arlington Heights, Illinois.
16. Fillmore Auditorium, San Francisco, run by legendary promoter Bill Graham.

Kit Lambert: you should have seen their faces when they were told just how long they were expected to play . . .

Pete Townshend: We played two 45-minute spots each night. It was a gas. It was like going back to the Marquee Club. We were immediately thrown into panic by not having enough numbers, but we got by. Ended up rehearsing in our hotel. And the amplification at the Fillmore is too much. The bloke who runs the Fillmore really worried about what we thought of his place and whether the amps were OK.

Chris Stamp: This was really vital to us. The publicity preceded us to Monterey, and from that moment on, we knew that we had arrived in the States. It also was vital because at the Fillmore they had the best of equipment, certainly the best light-show scene going at the time, and they were on show to thousands of people in the very best of surroundings. It helped them enormously to be able to play well – their confidence was enormous too.

17. Fillmore Auditorium, San Francisco, supported by Santana.

Pete Townshend: Some of it was a bit sad in a way. It was sad to go see the Haight-Ashbury, which was already very, very commercial.

Bill [Graham] was extraordinary because he was like a rock in the middle of this. For us, coming from the outside, he was very important. Because you sort of felt that without him, all these airheads would fall to bits. He wasn't doing acid. He wasn't drinking. He didn't seem to be the kind of guy who would be interested in anything except keeping that ballroom going.

There was a feeling that he was a serious promoter and that he was making money. And that was important. Obviously, not lots of money. Because he was the only promoter known in the history of the music business to spend any money on a PA system. And he was obviously taking the ticket money that he earned from top bands like The Who and passing it on to people who weren't selling tickets at that time like Cannonball Adderley, with whom we played the Fillmore the next time through. Cannonball still had his brother Nat with him then and these guys were just great heroes to me. They both really liked The Who and it was interesting to feel that what we were doing was acceptable to people like that.

I remember feeling very secure when we worked for Bill. I didn't feel secure at Monterey.

18. Final day of the Monterey Pop Festival, California, featuring The Jimi Hendrix Experience, The Who, Blues Project, Dionne Warwick, The Impressions, Johnny Rivers, The Mamas & The Papas.

Chris Stamp: The Who had barely broken into the American market, so I felt the Monterey exposure would be great. Everyone was blissed out – even the local cops had flowers in their hair. We truly felt we were at the beginning of a great movement towards change. It certainly changed my life, and The Who's.

Pete Townshend: Over in England, the LSD revolution was much more politicized at the time than it was in San Francisco. It was smaller and very cliquey. We were very surprised when we went to Monterey at how wet everybody appeared to be. Kind of emotionally wet. They were using those borrowed, secondhand catchphrases. You know, "Peace and love." People were spray-canning it on the walls. But they were still beating the shit out of one another.

Over in England, there were people like Tariq Ali and Richard Neville of the *Oz* magazine and the *International Times*. So it was much harder. Monterey did change the way we thought because we didn't like the atmosphere there. All the same, my wife and I, who was then my girlfriend, we did meet a lot of people at Monterey who are still our friends today.

I took Karen with me – we weren't married then, and the famous Owsley showed up. He's The Grateful Dead's sort of road manager and drug producer. He was on the research team that invented LSD and knew how to make it and used to make his own brand called STP which was much more powerful . . . and it was bloody terrible. I mean, you wouldn't believe it. I mean I had to . . . You know when they say under Japanese torture occasionally sometimes if it's horrific enough the person actually gets the feeling that they're leaving their body. In this case I had to do just that, abandon my body, there's no doubt about it, that's exactly what happened. I said, "Fuck this, I can't stand any more." And I was free of the trip. This is really the truth, right. And I was just floating in mid-air looking at myself in a chair, for about an hour and a half. And then I would rest and I would go back in again and it would be the same. And I was just like zap, completely unconscious as far as the outside world was concerned, but I was very much alive, in that, you know, like alive, crawling alive. Anyway, the thing about STP as distinct from LSD is the hump, the nasty bit. It goes on for about 16 hours rather than 10. And just to walk or just to do anything fundamentally organic is very, very tricky. But eventually it tailed off and then you get like, instead of a night's lovely planning it, nice colourful images, you get about a week of it, and you get a week of trying to repiece your ego, remember who you were and what you are and stuff like that. So that made me stop taking psychedelics.

Roger Daltrey: The dressing rooms at Monterey were under the stage and one memory that will live with me forever is of sitting under there with Jimi during the changeover between two acts. Jimi was playing "Sgt Pepper" on his guitar but, and this was the amazing thing, he was playing all the parts. He would go from a bit of orchestration, to a vocal part, to a solo – the whole thing on one guitar, and he was accompanied by me, Mama Cass, Brian Jones, Janis Joplin and a bunch of other rockers, all of us banging on anything that came to hand. I'll never forget that.

John Entwistle: The guy that was doing road management for Hendrix used to be our road manager and he told us about the plot where Hendrix was going to go on first and steal our act. We were pretty pissed off about that. I know Keith was and Pete was. I mean, Pete will now look back . . . he looks back favourably on Hendrix . . . but at the time Hendrix was being an asshole and so was his manager, Chas Chandler.

Henry Diltz: Backstage, Townshend and Hendrix had been going back and forth about who should follow whom. John Phillips finally resolved the issue by flipping a coin. The Who lost, which is why they came out and played with such a vengeance.

Pete Townshend: They wanted to know what was gonna come first, and we couldn't really decide. I said to Jimi, "Fuck it, man, we're not going to follow you on." He said, "Well, I'm not going to follow you on." I said, "We are not going to follow you on and that is it."

Brian Jones was standing with me, and Jimi started to play. He stood on a chair in front of me and he started to play this incredible guitar, like "Don't fuck with me, you little shit"' And then he snapped out of it and he put the guitar down and said, "OK, let's toss a coin." So we tossed a coin and we got to go on first. He went on immediately after us. Jimi said, "If I'm gonna follow you, I'm gonna pull out all the stops."

John Phillips (The Mamas & The Papas): The Who knew how good Jimi was and wouldn't be outdone, so they blew the entire stage up with bombs and fireballs and things.

John Entwistle: Monterey was kind of a non-event for me. I hated every minute of it once we were on stage.

Country Joe McDonald: Watching a rock band, you didn't expect that to happen. [Keith Moon's] drumsticks flying in the air, arms flying all over the place, microphone stands and equipment being thrown down. It was kind of a combination of wrestling and music.

Eric Burdon (The Animals): When The Who began smashing up the stage, which in America I suppose was a taste of brutal theatrics, Bill [Graham] was right in the middle of the mêlée thinking it was a terrorist attack of some sort. I was standing right there and I could see the look of horror on everybody's faces. I think maybe that particular incident made Bill wake up and realize what he already knew. A little peace and brown rice may be all right, but there was still a monster running amok, and it was still alive and kicking. That fascism was still bubbling under.

What brought it all together for me was the following act [Jimi Hendrix]. You had two expressions of violent action on that stage at Monterey. Although the actions were the same, they amounted to totally different statements. One was brutality, rape, and one was erotic. I saw Jimi Hendrix take the stage flashing to the max and almost transgress from male to female while the music still remained male.

Pete Townshend: I went out to sit with Mama Cass and watch Jimi, and as he started doing this stuff with his guitar, she turned around to me, she said to me, "He's stealing your act." And I said, "No, he's not stealing my act, he's doing my act." And I think that was the thing. For me it was an act, and for him it was something else. It was an extension of what he was doing.

23. John Entwistle marries Alison Wise at Acton Congregational Church.

John Entwistle: Keith tried to stop me getting married. He was always finding beautiful women, saying, "Look, you won't be able to have this when you're married" . . . As far as he was concerned, the wife and kid, they stay at home, but he knew that if I got married, I would be a homebody and not be able to hang out any more.

24. "Pictures Of Lily" is released as a single in the US.

25. Keith Moon attends The Beatles' live recording of "All You Need Is Love" on the satellite-broadcast TV special, "Our World", at EMI Studios, Abbey Road, London.

Tony Bramwell (Beatles aide): I went off the evening before to find guests for the broadcast. You could find nearly everyone down The Speakeasy, The Cromwellian, the Bag O' Nails and The Scotch Of St James. So we got Eric [Clapton] and his girlfriend, then Mick [Jagger] and Marianne [Faithfull]. I found Moony [Keith Moon] in The Speakeasy, absolutely enjoying himself, throwing peanuts everywhere. It was just, "Here you, party tomorrow, two o'clock, EMI," and he said, "Right, I'd better go home then," and his chauffeur took him home.

Despite his reputation as a wild man, Moonie was as good as gold.

29. The Who record two Rolling Stones songs, "Under My Thumb" and "The Last Time", at De Lane Lea Studio, London, as a protest against the Stones having been arrested on drugs charges.

Roger Daltrey: Keith and Mick had been jailed for smoking grass, or had been caught with cannabis anyway, and we did it as a gesture. All the proceeds were gonna go to legal things to mount a campaign to get them out. We thought it was a disgraceful sentence.

It was fun to sing somebody else's song. And they got jailed in the afternoon the previous day and we went in the studio at eight o'clock the next morning to record that. John was on vacation so Pete played the bass.

30. "The Last Time"/"Under My Thumb" is released as a single in the UK.

July 1967

1. "Pictures of Lily" enters the US singles chart.

2. Townshend goes to see Cream play at the Saville Theatre, London. Later Townshend and Moon go on to The Speakeasy to see The Toys perform. Also in the throng are Beatles guitarist George Harrison, Jeff Beck, Monkees Mike Nesmith and Mickey Dolenz, Lulu and Spencer Davis.

5. Recording "I Can't Reach You" and "Glittering Girl" at De Lane Lea, London.

7. Malibu Beach and Shore Club, Lido Beach, New York.

8. Village Theater, New York, supported by Blues Project and Richie Havens.

13. Calgary Stampede Corral, Calgary, Alberta, Canada.

14. As support act to Herman's Hermits, The Who start their first full-length US tour at Memorial Coliseum, Portland, Oregon.

Keith Moon: For me it was a tour of discovery. It was three months with 'Erman's 'Ermits. Backing up the 'Ermits was ideal. It was a position that suited us. We weren't on the line. If the place sold only a portion of what it could 'ave sold, the disaster was never blamed on us, it was blamed on 'Erman's 'Ermits. We didn't have the responsibility. We had time to discover. We found the good towns.

Pete Townshend: On the Herman's Hermits tour the fucking plane crashed, and nobody whimpered, nobody said a word. Nobody. Nobody CARED. Crash landed . . . that was in the days of the Herman's Hermits tour but it's still insanity.

15. Center Coliseum, Seattle, Washington.

16. Memorial Auditorium, Sacramento, California.

17. The Agrodome, Vancouver, British Columbia, Canada.

19. Lagoon Terrace Ballroom, Salt Lake City, Utah.

21. State Fair Arena, Oklahoma City, Oklahoma.
22. Sam Houston Coliseum, Houston, Texas.
23. Memorial Auditorium, Dallas, Texas.
24-25. Recording material in Nashville, for *The Who Sell Out*.

Keith Moon: We played in 55 different towns and averaged about 2,000 miles a day . . . We're still doing a lot of recording but the Nashville session was easily the most interesting. There was this guy, something to do with Decca Records, who had his own private studio. Outside was a huge lake, around which lived people like the Everlys and Roy Orbison. It was beautiful.

26. Redemptionist High School Football Stadium, Baton Rouge, Louisiana. At home in the UK, The Who's double A-sided cover version of two Rolling Stones tracks, "The Last Time"/"Under My Thumb", enters the singles chart, where it will peak at No. 44.
28. Garrett Coliseum, Montgomery, Alabama.
29. After the show at the Auditorium, Birmingham, Alabama, Keith Moon is attacked by five men outside his hotel.

Keith Moon: It was like a scene from those Al Capone films. These guys had two cars waiting for them with the motors running. And as soon as I walked out, they grabbed me and pushed me right through the plate glass door. But by the time I got up, they were gone.

30. Convention Hall, Miami Beach, Florida.
31. Bayfront Center, St Petersburg, Florida.

August 1967

1. Mississippi State Coliseum, Jackson, Mississippi.
3. Dane County Coliseum, Madison, Wisconsin.
4. Rosenblatt Stadium, Omaha, Nebraska.
5. International Amphitheatre, Chicago, Illinois.
6-7. Recording "Relax" plus an early version of "Mary Anne With The Shaky Hand" for *The Who Sell Out* at Mirasound Studio, New York.

Keith Moon: When we had to fly to Toronto from New York, somehow or other I managed to leave my passport in a laundry basket at the hotel, and almost got left behind. But someone pulled strings. I got on to the plane. My passport was sent on another plane.

9. Maple Leaf Gardens, Toronto, Ontario, Canada.

10. Townshend goes to see Jimi Hendrix at the Ambassador Theatre in Washington.

Pete Townshend: I hadn't touched psychedelic drugs for a year when I saw him at some concert in Washington or somewhere in the States, and he was pulling those old psychedelic stunts again. And you have to see him to know what I'm talking about. He did things which were magical. I don't think he knew he was doing them or that he could do them, but he'd do things with his body that were very, very beautiful to look at, yet accompanied by these incredibly wild noises. It was some kind of strange alchemy. He took the drug culture and made it into something by demonstrating that there was actually such a thing as physical poetry in rock, something that was very close to ballet. I'm not saying he danced 'cause he didn't, but he was very beautiful to look at, and you felt pain in his presence and in the presence of that music. You felt small and you realized how far you had to go. What was also painful was to meet him afterwards and realize he didn't know what he was doing. He had no idea of his greatness. There was also a feeling that he was going to burn out very, very quickly. He was so insecure and shy. Sweet guy. Really nice guy.

11. Civic Center, Baltimore, Maryland.

12. Convention Hall, Asbury Park, New Jersey.

13. Constitution Hall, Washington, DC.

Nils Lofgren: There was a huge show with The Blues Magoos, Herman's Hermits and The Who. This was the original Who with Keith Moon, and they were just spectacular.

14. Rhode Island Auditorium, Providence, Rhode Island.

15. The Marine Offences Act plugs the legal loophole which had allowed pirate radio to flourish in British offshore waters.

John Entwistle: Once they stopped the pirate radio stations, you had no choice but to play for the BBC. It was kind of the one little bit of England that seemed very communist.

15-16. Another attempt at recording "Mary Anne With The Shaky Hand" for *The Who Sell Out* at Bradley's Barn, Nashville, Tennessee. "Someone's Coming" is also recorded, and work is done on "Rael".

Pete Townshend: The idea that I worked on before *Tommy* was called "Rael", and that was condensed into a four-minute single. It turned out to be a track on *The Who Sell Out* album and immediately after that, I started to think I should really get to grips – it was a personal thing I think. I was thinking that it might even be done outside The Who. In other words, I'd write a few singles and things to keep the band happy but, in the meantime, I'd be working on this rather grand thing on the side.

17. Memorial Auditorium, Chattanooga, Tennessee.

18. "We Love You", the new single by The Rolling Stones, is released in the UK and US simultaneously.

Pete Townshend: I suppose what I wanted was to rescue the pop song which seemed to me to be in serious trouble in the late sixties, partly because of the kind of post-psychedelic wetness that seemed to be everywhere. You could write a song that went "Weee love you, weeee love you." And it would get to No. 4 in the charts. I was outraged and desolate because I knew I was too much of a cynic to ever be able to do that. I was a believer in what a certain group of writers like Ray Davies, Bob Dylan, and certain moments in Lennon and McCartney, were occasionally uncovering.

20. Civic Auditorium, Fargo, North Dakota and Minneapolis Auditorium, Minneapolis, Minnesota.

21. New Edmonton Gardens, Edmonton, Alberta, Canada.

22. Winnipeg Arena, Winnipeg, Manitoba, Canada.

John Einarson (audience): It was an oddball billing, to be sure. While most of the 9,000 squealing teenyboppers were there to sing along to "Henry The Eighth" and "Mrs Brown You've Got A Lovely Daughter", amid the sea of pedal-pushers the few bona fide rockers were anxiously awaiting The Who's assault.

Though barely known beyond their recent pop hit "Happy Jack", those of us who followed British music knew full well the musical mayhem a Who performance entailed. The Blues Magoos came out first and proved to be the one-hit wonders they would ultimately become, in spite of their much-vaunted electric suits (merely dayglo under blacklights), but they received a heartier ovation than The Who due to their recent hit "We Ain't Got Nothin' Yet".

The Who's appearance next didn't generate much of a rush from the crowd but nonetheless the quartet gave a brief, spirited set, Townshend's windmill thrashing and Moon's manic drumming earning cheers from the crowd. Winnipeg had never seen anything like it (though our own Guess Who, recently back from Britain having witnessed a Who show at the Marquee, had adopted their trademark equipment-smashing finale and performed it to startled

Winnipeggers months earlier). Despite the group's best efforts it wasn't a stellar performance as the group seemed to be going through the motions, knowing full well that the audience was more in Herman's corner than theirs.

Ending with "My Generation", as if on cue Townshend thrust his Rickenbacker through a Vox Super Beatle, Moon kicked over his drums in a hail of smoke bombs, and they were gone. Polite applause from most, howls for more from my buddies and I to no avail; as the smoke cleared, a grinning Peter Noone took the stage to rapturous screams. It must have been frustrating for The Who to endure this night after night.

23. Atwood High School Stadium, Flint, Michigan. Later, The Who celebrate Keith's 20th birthday party in the local Holiday Inn. Legend has it that Moon drove a Lincoln Continental into the swimming pool, but . . .

John Entwistle: He never drove a car into the swimming pool. He couldn't even drive.

Nancy Lewis (journalist): The first thing he did was pick up the cake, and hurl it against the wall and then a whole mêlée started to break loose. Herman was involved too. They had a big cake fight right there. It was total chaos.

Keith Altham (journalist): What happened was that there was a pretty wild party going on, and the hotel manager came up to complain.

Tom Wright (roadie): I told him we'd wind it down and so on, and he left. At one minute after twelve he comes running back and says, "God damn it, this sounds more like a revolution than a birthday party. We're having complaints and you can't do this and you can't do that."

He was just about to go into a big deal when Keith picked up what was left of the five-tiered cake and just shoved it into this guy's face. Everybody in the room went silent, including this guy. All this stuff, like, just drips. And you can't even laugh because it's so shocking.

Keith Altham: When the cops finally arrived, they found Keith in the nude, covered in birthday cake. Keith decided it was all really a movie, and made a break for it, slipping on a piece of cake and breaking his two front teeth.

Nancy Lewis: It ended up with Keith walking around without any trousers on and we were trying to escort him back to his room so he could cover up. As he was going out the door he fell over flat on his face and knocked out his two front teeth. He was so out of it he wasn't even aware what happened so he had to be rushed to the dentist.

John Entwistle: He hit the sheriff with the cake, because the person he threw it at ducked, and he started running, except he was so pissed he tripped and fell over and smashed his teeth. So the sheriff drove him to the dentist's and we all waited while they operated on him without any anaesthetics . . . 'cause he was drunk. He was whimpering for about two days. He didn't even see a swimming pool that night.

Keith Altham: Waking up in jail the following day, he found to his dismay that the rest of The Who had flown on without him and he was to make his own way to Philadelphia. This he did, by the simple expedient of hiring a Lear Jet. Suffice it to say that the bill for the party reached five figures and The Who sportingly chipped in their share.

Pete Townshend: It's important to say that when we say we often "hated" hotels, because they were a cold component in our lonely lives, we also appreciated their comfort, the clean sheets, the maids who cleaned, the people who brought food to our rooms, who prepared it, the people who made sure we had rooms in the first place. We're not stupid or ignorant. We were too young and spoiled to know any better at the time, so sometimes we made trouble. It was the people I've just mentioned who suffered. I'd like to apologize to them now [February 2000], and tell them that whenever I see a Holiday Inn sign I feel WARM . . . there must be a solid piece of American travelling salesman in me. I suppose that's what we were, travelling salesmen.

24. Civic Center Convention Hall, Philadelphia, Pennsylvania.

25. Keil Opera House, St Louis, Missouri.

26. Fort William Gardens, Fort William, Ontario, Canada and Duluth Arena, Duluth, Minnesota.

27. Music Hall, Cincinnati, Ohio.

28. Sioux Falls Arena, Sioux Falls, South Dakota.

29. Municipal Auditorium, Atlanta, Georgia.

30. War Memorial Auditorium, Rochester, New York.

31. Public Meeting Hall, Cleveland, Ohio.

September 1967

1. Indiana Fairgrounds Coliseum, Indianapolis, Indiana.

2. Ohio State Fairgrounds, Columbus, Ohio.

3. Ohio State Fairgrounds, Columbus, Ohio, and Civic Arena, Pittsburgh, Pennsylvania.

4. Ohio State Fairgrounds, Columbus, Ohio.
5-7. Recording in Los Angeles for *The Who Sell Out.*
8. Convention Center, Anaheim, California.
9. Final date of US tour, International Center Arena, Honolulu, Hawaii.

Keith Moon: We were in Hawaii and I said I must surf. Jesus, I've been buying surfing records for years, you know. I've got to try it. So I rented a board and paddled out with all these other guys. The wahines were on the beach. Woodies. Surfers' paradise, right? I look off in the distance and there's a huge wave coming. I said to one of the guys, "What do I do?"

And he said, "Well, okay, buddy, all you got to do when you see that wave there comin', she hits boy, she hits and you want to be travelling at relatively the same speed, so you paddle." Perfectly logical. I said, "Great." And then this solid wall of water came. All of a sudden, this bloody thing hit me up the arse and I move from like doing two miles an hour to two hundred! I'm hanging on to the sides of the bloody board, y'see, and I hear: "Stand up, man!" Stand up? So I stand up and I look up and there's water all around me, I'm in a great funnel, a great big sort of tube of water.

And then I see the coral reef coming up. I'd only been on me feet for about two seconds, but it seemed like a fucking lifetime. Sod it! Sod it! I fell off, the wave crashed down on the reef, the board went backwards and then was thrown up in the air by the water. I surfaced, shook me 'ead and relaxed. Then I looked up and saw this bloody board coming from about 60 feet in the air straight at me 'ead. I went underwater and it went ssshhhhwwwooomm!

I've got a bald patch ever since where it scraped me skull.

John Entwistle: We played 30 concerts and earned $40,000 – and I still had to borrow $100 to get home. It was heartbreaking.

15. CBS TV studios, Los Angeles. When The Who record an appearance on US TV's "Smothers Brothers Comedy Hour", transmitted two days later, the gunpowder charges under Keith Moon's drum kit ignite rather more explosively than intended.

Roger Daltrey: He [Keith Moon] just got the pyrotechnic guy drunk and paid him a few hundred dollars, and the guy put on four or five times the amount of charge that should have been there. It went off like a grenade. It was a huge explosion. Huge!

Pete Townshend: The drum exploded so fiercely my hair was singed, and

Keith crawled from the wreckage covered with blood. Bette Davis and Mickey Rooney, who were also on the show, were having heart attacks. They had to be stopped from rushing on to help us.

Roger Daltrey: The Smothers Brothers nearly got sacked for that. They got into a lot of trouble for that. We did "I Can See For Miles" and "My Generation" and that was live vocals too. That's a live vocal to a track on both those songs.

16. Recording "I Can See For Miles" at Goldstar Studios, Los Angeles.

Pete Townshend: Quite a fiery Wagnerian piece. I spent a lot of time working on the vocal harmonies and structuring it.

It was written about jealousy but actually turned out to be about the immense power of aspiration. You often see what it is you want to reach, and know you can't get at it and say, "I'm gonna try." Those words start to move you in a direction, as long as you say, "I can see what I want, but there's no way I can get it."

John Entwistle: That was the first time we'd used a four-track tape recorder. Up until then it was all mono. We still kept the bass and drums on one track in mono, and everything else is stereo. It was the best recorded sound we'd got to date. When I remixed that for *The Kids Are Alright* movie we had a pile of tapes in the studio that was 12 feet wide and nine feet high. Mono. Optical mono. Four track. Eight track. Sixteen. Twenty-four. All different formats.

Roger Daltrey: The first slow track we did was "I Can See For Miles". I mean, slow! It took a whole day, and most of that day was taken up on doing the harmonies. I mean, the actual track and the lead vocal was done literally in a couple of hours and then we spent eight hours overlaying harmony after harmony after harmony. It was the ace future single that didn't do that well.

It was a big single in America but in the rest of the world they didn't seem to take to it at all. I still think it's probably our best single. I really love it. The energy of that record is incredible.

Mid-September 1967

The Who fly back to London.

Chris Rowley (journalist, I*nternational Times*): This rich Californian, who had a credit card and rich parents, had this apartment on Shaftesbury Avenue above the Shaftesbury Theatre. When he left the McInnerneys moved in and they lived there for a little while . . . I was at this apartment when Pete Townshend, a friend of McInnerney's, had just come back from LA. He, Daltrey and Moon, but I think not Entwistle, had just done LSD or STP, they didn't know what, on the plane! The dims! Thirteen hours you're in the plane. Even if you're the Who and you're rich and people treat you well, 13 hours in a plane on acid! Later on McInnerney did the cover of *Tommy*.

October 1967

2. "Early Morning, Cold Taxi" is recorded at CBS Studios, London.
4. Another version of "Mary Anne With The Shaky Hand" is recorded at De Lane Lea Studios, London.
10. The Who record versions of "I Can See For Miles", "Pictures Of Lily", "A Quick One While He's Away", "Boris The Spider", and "My Generation" for the BBC radio show "Top Gear", at De Lane Lea Studios, London.
11. Recording "Heinz Baked Beans" and "Odorono" for *The Who Sell Out*, at IBC Studios, London.

John Entwistle: Most of the commercials that we recorded ourselves were done at Kingsway Studios. Me and Keith thought them up in the pub next door.
12. Recording "Tattoo" for *The Who Sell Out* at IBC Studios, London.

Pete Townshend: "Tattoo" was written as an album track. I wrote it when we were on the road with Herman's Hermits in 1967. Jimi Hendrix was already in our lives . . . I was feeling very eclipsed by him as a guitar player . . . so I decided to write a different kind of song, which is why I started to write story-songs, cameos, essays of human experience, and "Tattoo" was one of those songs, concerning not only what it's like to be young, but trying to look at the generation divide and what made men men.

When I was 11 or 12, street guys always had a mass of tattoos down one arm. You really felt, "Jesus, that's gonna happen to me sometime." It was such a relief when I finally got to be 16 or 17, and you didn't have to do that any more. There were marches for Ban the Bomb and against nuclear war that was impending. Bigger issues than going down to the funfair and standin' there with your arm covered with tattoos listening to Elvis Presley records. My characters are all slightly manufactured, you can't constantly go on writing about your experiences and your own feeling. You can write from them, and sometimes you have to disguise it, I suppose.

And "Tattoo" again is me examining what divided me and Roger, and his idea of what made a man a man and my idea. I thought it was going to be one of those songs where Roger would turn round and say to me, "No, you sing this. I don't need to question whether I'm a man or not." But he did sing it, and he sang it really well. And I realized then, "Hey, he doesn't know. He doesn't know if he's a man or not. He's got the same insecurities I have."

13. Keith Moon appears as a guest on a new UK TV show, "New Releases".

14. The Who's new single, "I Can See For Miles", is released simultaneously in the UK and the US.

18. "I Can See For Miles" enters the UK singles chart.

20. Recording "Armenia City In the Sky", for *The Who Sell Out*, at IBC Studios, London.

John Entwistle: Everyone always thought it was "I'm An Ear Sitting In The Sky". That's Speedy Keene. He was a friend of Pete's and he had written the song and we liked it so we did it.

Pete Townshend: Basically [Speedy Keane] was just a friend. We'd both been formed by a lot of the same experiences, we'd had the same flashes and we progressed from there. He had incredible potential. I knew that straight away, but it was all unrealized and disorganized.

He was amazingly insecure. He wouldn't expose himself in any way. Every time he made a move towards expressing something real, he'd suddenly draw back, and he'd cut off dead. He was suspicious of everyone and everything, which you could understand, and that made him paralyzed.

John Entwistle: *Sell Out* had a lot more melody in the album. We had to think about melody a lot more. I did "Silas Stingy" for the album. When we started recording it Pete thought it was all in a minor key. And I was saying it was all major and he was playing minor chords and it sounded really peculiar.

21. Appearance on new UK TV show "Twice A Fortnight".

22. Saville Theatre, London, supported by Vanilla Fudge.

Chris Welch (reviewer, *Melody Maker*):

Pete played double-necked guitar, Keith galvanized his nine-drum kit, Roger and John sang and played with drive and enthusiasm. It was a welcome return to Britain for The Who . . .

Derek Boltwood (reviewer, *Record Mirror*):

They ran through most of their hits with the audience going absolutely wild.

24. Final recording of "Mary Anne With The Shaky Hand" at De Lane Lea, London.
28. Start of UK tour at City Hall, Sheffield with Traffic, The Herd, The Tremeloes and Marmalade. Meanwhile, in the US, "I Can See For Miles" enters the Top 40 chart.
29. Townshend's guitar is smashed when the curtain is mistakenly lowered during The Who's set at Coventry Theatre, Coventry.

Ken Hillman (reviewer, *Coventry Evening Telegraph*):

Townshend shouted for the curtain to be raised, threw his guitar on the stage and kicked angrily at the footlights. Then he picked up a footlight and used it to hammer the floats. Finally, he swung at the lights with a microphone stand . . .

Pete Townshend: I used to break a guitar every performance – if not two sometimes – and they would always cost around $150. They would always cost me an incredible amount of money to find – they'd cost, like, road manager's time and my time to look through pawn shops, local music stores and things like that.
30. City Hall, Newcastle.

November 1967

1. Empire Theatre, Liverpool.
2. Recording "Sunrise" at IBC Studios, London.
3. Granada Cinema, Kingston upon Thames.
4. Granada Cinema, Walthamstow.
5. Theatre Royal, Nottingham.
6. Town Hall, Birmingham.
7. Recording an appearance on the 200th edition of "Top Of The Pops" at BBC Television Centre, London.
8. Granada Cinema, Kettering.
9. Granada Cinema, Maidstone.
10. Adelphi Cinema, Slough.
11. Final date of UK tour at the Imperial Ballroom, Nelson.
17. First date of second US tour, as support to The Buckinghams, at Sahwnee Mission South High School Gymnasium, Overland Park, Kansas.

John Entwistle: On our second US tour, we worked from coast to coast, revisiting all the places we had done well at before. But the money just went. We even had $5,000 stolen from a bedroom.

18. Festival of Music, Cow Palace, San Francisco, headlined by The Association and The Animals, and also featuring the Everly Brothers and Sopwith Camel. Back in the UK, "I Can See For Miles" peaks at No. 10.

Pete Townshend: To me it was the ultimate Who record, yet it didn't sell. I spat on the British record buyer.

19. Hollywood Bowl, Los Angeles.

21. When washrooms are damaged by fans at the Civic Auditorium, Fargo, North Dakota, The Who are banned from ever appearing there again.

22. Southfield High School Gymnasium, Southfield, Michigan.

23. New Barn, Lions Delaware County Fairgrounds, Muncie, Indiana.

24. Swinging Gate, Fort Wayne, Indiana.

25. Village Theatre, New York. The Who have their first US Top 10 entry when "I Can See For Miles" peaks at No. 9.

26. Village Theatre, New York.

29. Union Catholic High School Gymnasium, Scotch Plains, New Jersey.

December 1967

1. US tour ends at Long Island Arena, Commack, New York, supported by Vanilla Fudge.

5. Keith Moon attends the opening of The Beatles' new Apple Boutique, Baker Street, London.

6. Sky Line Ballroom, Hull.

16. The Who release their concept album *The Who Sell Out* in the UK.

Roger Daltrey: I think *The Who Sell Out* came out in the same month that the last pirate ship went off the air. So that was a protest record, saying, "Well, fuck you. You might have sunk them, but we'll just release records that sound like them." We had nothing else. I mean, we had the BBC playing these dreadful middle-of-the-road bits of music, usually by their own orchestras. We didn't even get great Frank Sinatra songs – we got the BBC version of it. It was pure pap.

20. In the Isle Of Man, Pete Townshend breaks a finger, obliging The Who to pull out of Christmas On Earth Revisited – a major psychedelic happening featuring Jimi Hendrix, Pink Floyd, The Move and Soft Machine, held at Olympia in London two days later.

30. Pier Pavilion, Hastings.

1968

Pete Townshend: I'd been in the pop business two years, and I was rich and famous. But I had got there through frustration. I felt as if a bomb had gone off in my head and there was a demolition site inside. I had to find something to fill the empty space.

Roger Daltrey: Around 1968 there was a clique of groupies that were the best ever. They were really great in bed – incredible, fantastic fucks. They were proud of being groupies – totally servile – groupies have to be servile. Groups on the road are absolute pigs; they have to be in order to survive because it's such an unnatural life – town-to-town-room-to-room. You get very little time on the road to romance anybody, so groupies make life easier. There is no way you can say, "I'd like to get to know you." It's just, "Stay here and fuck – or else fuck off."

Groupies don't actually suggest going to bed with you. You just say, "Get your clothes off," and they get their clothes off. Or else you get into bed – there's three women there and it just happens. They just want to fuck you to score you up. Groupies don't have special techniques in bed – they are just very easy to get there. But a few of them do know some tricks; baby oil and a cold wash cloth – they rub the baby oil all over your prick – put a cold wash cloth on your balls – and then give you head. Very nice. Or whipped cream over the whole body – then fucking. It's really great. Only trouble is, it dries up and goes a bit sticky, but when you first do it, it's really fantastic.

January 1968

1. Baltaberin Club, Bromley.

4. At Goldstar Studios, Los Angeles, The Who record Entwistle's song "Dr Jekyll And Mr Hyde".

John Entwistle: I wanted my songs to be like no one else was writing. And no one was writing that sort of black kind of stuff. And also, the idea for me to write "Silas Stingy" and "Dr Jekyll And Mr Hyde", they were all meant to go on a kids' rock album. Young kids love "Boris The Spider" and a lot of the other songs I'd written. So we were gonna release a children's album with all these snakes and spiders and creepy things. So they all ended up being used for B-sides on albums that came afterwards. And I just got this black image but the song was written for a children's album, a project that Kit Lambert thought of.

6. *The Who Sell Out* is released in the US.

12. The Royal, Tottenham, North London.

Roger Simpson (reviewer, *Tottenham & Edmonton Weekly Herald*):
On one number Keith Moon, having mercilessly battered his nine-piece drum kit, took a hammer and crashed it down on a cymbal . . . Daltrey repeatedly threw his microphone at Moon's drums, while Moon kicked part of his drum kit off the stage. Townshend pushed the amplifiers to the ground and bounced his guitar on the fallen equipment.

13. Third album *The Who Sell Out* enters the UK chart, where it will peak at No. 13. Later that night, they play at the Dreamland Ballroom, Margate.

18. Flight from Heathrow to Australia to begin a tour with The Small Faces and Paul Jones.

John "Wiggy" Wolf (production manager): My first memory of the Australia tour was that it was difficult to get them on the plane, because Pete thought he ought to go first class, so he really put me through it. In fact, they weren't going to go. Pete didn't want to go from the beginning. It was a bit of a job. Kit and Chris, they bottled out and left me the job. To me, it was a great adventure, but Pete, I don't know, maybe he got out of the wrong side, after a late night. It was all "I want to go first class", so I got him a first class upgrade.

Pete went up to first class for a while, but he didn't like it, so he came back and joined the rest of us, and after all that, I couldn't get a rebate!

He'd gone up, and got all these freebies, enough to get Keith and me completely pissed. Moonie and I got stuck into the free drinks very early . . . plus we had our little substances so we were up and we were the only two on the plane who were up and still raving! We were conned rather nicely by the stewardess who we thought we'd befriended and we'd fallen in love with, you know how it is on a plane! Anyway, she took us back up to the galley, because obviously we were keeping everybody awake with our ravings. We went back up to the galley, looking for "more" . . . She came out with some pills and she said, "You look as though you're high," because we were on speed and she gave us these things and we thought, "Yeah, this is happening, she's given us some more leapers!" But they were Mickey Finns, designed to knock you out! So she gave them to us, we took them and I just about made it back to my seat. Moonie collapsed, he couldn't quite make his seat, so he collapsed on the floor taking up the space of the three seats and that's where he stayed till Cairo!

When we got to Cairo, Keith and I wanted to get out into the Casbah and all the nonsense. We were meant to be in transit, but we just sort of wandered out. We got our passports and we wandered out into Egypt, looking around, thinking this is great. We bumped into this voluptuous belly dancer called Samika when we were just outside and I think she was going to lure us off like these two nice young English boys. She signed our passports "Samika" and her phone number, for when we came back through. Luckily, I suppose in a way, we got apprehended by one of the officials – police or some other official there – and they were talking like Tutankhamen, which we didn't understand, and they led us back to the airport like naughty schoolboys!

Keith, John, and I bought some ivory elephants in Karachi. We were just like the classic tourists because everything seemed to be ridiculously cheap. Even with what little money we had, we were able to buy half the continent of India with our meagre handouts.

19. The Who arrive at Mascot Airport, Sydney, Australia.

John "Wiggy" Wolf: It was quite horrific really. Not for me, but for them, because everybody was just knackered. You're supposed to get off looking like a pop star and we were all looking like tramps. I think there was a little bit of resentment right from the beginning somehow. Pete was always quite acerbic. I think he spoke his mind and they didn't like that particularly. Pete got off on the wrong footing, right from the start.

20. After a gig at the Festival Hall, Brisbane, Keith Moon drives off in a rental car . . .

Ron Blackmore (tour manager): He'd been on at me all day to get him a rental car. I said to Wiggy, "Should I give him a car, or shouldn't I?" He said, "Yeah, give him a car, he'll be all right. It'll be worse if you don't!" I said, "Well, what happens if he doesn't come back?" And Wiggy said, "No, no, he'll be all right, give him a car."

So we got Keith a rental car and he took off. When he came back, he got home about 2.30 in the morning and he'd driven the car in through the doors of the Park Royal Motel. The electric doors have opened and the car has come in, and he's now parked in front of the reception desk. The car's facing towards the elevators, with the headlights on and the door open, and I've got a phone call from some poor night porter in reception. He's rung up and said, "Mr Blackmore, can you come down straight away?" And I've gone, "What's the problem?" And he said, "It's Mr Moon!" I thought, "Shit!"

I've dropped the phone, got my pants on, and shot down there. As I've come out of the elevator, I'm looking at a car. I sized up the situation, looked at this guy and said, "Well?!" And he's stammering, "W-well, Mr Moon, he's driven in, pulled up there, got out of the car, thrown me the keys, and told me to park it! What do you think I should do?" "Park it!" I said, got back in the lift and went back to bed!

21. The Who return to Sydney and check in at the Sheraton.

Steve Marriott (Small Faces): The Australian trip was a total disaster. It was fun – midgets on manoeuvres. It was fun and we had a lot of laughs on it, but we came away owing money, smashing up rooms and stuff like that.

Roger Daltrey: It was crazy, because Australia was really a backward country then. We couldn't afford to take our own equipment so we had to hire what was there. We used these systems from, like, World War II. It was the PA. It was unbelievable. And the Aussies at that time had no sense of humour and they threw us out after three weeks. They didn't like us at all. The Small Faces were fun to be with. We did that whole tour with them.

22. At Sydney Stadium, Sydney, Australia, the rotating stage comes to a sudden halt during the show.

Ron Blackmore: The sound system was exactly the same one used for wrestling and boxing matches. They had three great metal horns, issued during World War II, which was what they had to sing through, and these were aimed at the four seating sections. The microphone cables came up through the centre of the stage, so the stage could only turn so many times in one direction. Then you had to throw a switch to get it to turn the opposite way because, as it turned, it was twisting up all the microphone cables. In total there were eight amplifiers, 16 cabinet speakers, two drum kits, one Hammond C3 organ with two Leslie cabinets, a great big row of these double-stack Marshall amps, the drums and a piano. We had all this on the revolving stage in the middle of the stadium, and there was so much weight that it wouldn't turn. There were red-coated bouncers everywhere trying to make it turn round.

Geoff Quayle (reviewer, *Sydney Morning Herald*):

> Among the wild screaming one could just detect the driving sounds of "Substitute", the record which got the group moving in the Australian charts.Townshend cavorted around the stage, which obstinately refused to revolve as he hoped, and plunged his group and the audience into a

startling rendition of a pop opera which Townshend wrote.

23. During the second night at Sydney Stadium, The Who borrow some gear from The Small Faces.

Ron Blackmore: Something went wrong on stage, so Pete plugged in to one of the Faces' Marshalls. At the end of the show, he speared one of the cabinets with his guitar. There was a bit of a scene but, luckily, we were able to get a speaker for that cabinet and repair the damage.

Paul Jones: I liked all of them. I respected Townshend, who I thought was the most thoughtful and intelligent. John was very quiet and kept himself somewhat to himself. I was wary of Keith and Steve Marriott who were manic and hell-for-leather. That wasn't my way at all. The person that I seemed to get on most well with was Roger, who had a more down-to-earth side to him.

Ron Blackmore: I used to have to go up and divert the attention of the hall people away, while Bob [Pridden] got down and drove all these bloody nails in to hold down Keith Moon's drum kit. We'd distract everybody, and then we'd set up the smoke bombs and we used to hide them beside and around the amplifiers, so that nobody would know what we were gonna do because, if they did, they would definitely have stopped us.

24. The touring party flies from Sydney to Essendon Airport, Melbourne, where Townshend hits a reporter during a press conference.

Kenney Jones (drummer, Small Faces): They kept asking Townshend and all of us what drugs we were on. So I said, "I don't take drugs." But they were like, "You do take drugs, and you're bringing them over here." I told this reporter where to go, and then he looked at Townshend and said, "So what kind of drugs are you on, then?" Townshend just decked him – knocked him straight out.

25. By the time of the first gig at Festival Hall, Melbourne, Pete Townshend and Ronnie Lane of The Small Faces have become almost constant companions.

Ronnie Lane: I was reading a couple of Sufi books, and he was reading this book about a guy called Meher Baba, that had this thing called "Sufism Reoriented". So I started to learn about Baba, and he seemed like an all right guy, and Pete and I had fun.

Pete Townshend: Every time I came up with a worldwide theory that had taken me years to get clear, [a friend of mine] would say, "That's such a coincidence, man, this guy Meher Baba said something similar in this book *The God Man.*" I just had to look at this book. What I saw, apart from a photo on the front cover of a strange and elderly man, was shattering.

Sure enough, each theory I expounded, many to do with reincarnation and its inevitability when considered in the light of the law of averages, were summed up in one sentence . . .

What was so sneaky about the whole affair was the way Baba crept into my life. At first his words were encouraging, his state of consciousness and his claims to be the Christ exciting and daring; later they became scary. I began to read of his astoundingly simple relationship with his disciples and of his silence for 40 years. It became clear that the party was over. If I read any more lines like, "What I want from my lovers is real unadulterated love, and from my genuine workers I expect real work done," I would have to decide once and for all whether the whole thing was really for me or not.

26. Festival Hall, Melbourne.

Ron Blackmore: I was out there trying to find guitars every day from guitar shops. I'd loosen the neck and try to get it ready, and hope that Pete could just drop it, so that it fell in half, and didn't smash it completely, because we couldn't replace the bits.

Ian Clothier (audience): Townshend smashed up a Strat, and hurled what was left of it into about the fourth row. I can still see my mate, Les Wellstead, emerging from the pack with the neck of the ill-fated guitar in his possession, being chased by souvenir hunters. However, the security waited until we were filing out and, in that post-concert dreamy state, we were extricated from the crowd and the souvenir inexplicably confiscated.

27. Being entertained by a groupie, Pete Townshend misses the flight to Adelaide for this night's gig at Centennial Hall, which is delayed by more than an hour.

Ron Blackmore: We may have started off with eight to ten cabinets, each containing two 15-inch speakers, but by about the fifth show, probably only about 50 per cent of them were working. There were no speakers that we could replace, and the Who weren't aware of that. They didn't know the damn things were stopping. I remember, at the end of the tour . . . the Marshalls were fine but, for the Sunns, we needed a dozen 15-inch JBL speakers from the Sunn factory in Oregon, to recone them.

28. While flying from Adelaide to Sydney, The Who, Small Faces and Paul Jones are asked to disembark at Melbourne for bad behaviour and "making a hostess cry".

Doug Parkinson (touring crew): I remember on the bus from the hotel in Adelaide, Stevie Marriott showing me this big bag of dope. It was the first time I'd ever seen grass, which was really scarce in Australia at the time. He was sitting in the back, busy rolling joints before we got to the airport.

Ronnie Lane (Small Faces): We got on the airplane early one morning. We'd been up raving the night before and I fell asleep on the plane. But an Australian support band was also on the plane, and they'd brought aboard a couple of cans of beer . . . They started drinking them and, in those days, it was illegal to drink on planes. So a couple of stewardesses took a very dim view of this . . . and refused to serve us any coffee. I woke up with Paul Jones very loudly demanding his coffee. The stewardess burst into tears and went up to the pilot and reported this whole incident.

Ron Blackmore: Next thing I know, I'm sitting in my seat, looking up the aisle, and I could see this guy (the captain) in a uniform and hat on. He's walking down the aisle, and he's looking at all the seat numbers as he's coming down. I remember thinking out loud, "This guy's looking for me!" I would have been the only name he would have had, because all the tickets were bought in the name of Aztec Services.

He stopped right at my seat and he said, "Are you the leader of this mob?" And I said, "I'm the tour manager, if you're referring to the group of people that are on your flight." He said, "Well, as far as I'm concerned, they're a mob, and I'm here to tell you that they'll all be arrested on arrival at Melbourne airport."

John "Wiggy" Wolf: We all just guffawed with laughter.

Steve Marriott: We were deported. The police saw us out of their country.

29. Jacqueline Daltrey, wife of The Who's singer Roger, sues for divorce in London. On the other side of the world, The Who play at the Town Hall, Auckland, New Zealand.

Steve Marriott: New Zealand was enjoyable. We got to the airport and Pete Townshend immediately smashed one press guy's camera – throws it. Oh, here we go again! But they kind of understood, because I don't think they're too keen on Australians either.

John "Wiggy" Wolf: Marriott, myself and Moonie caught the clap down there. It was from Australia, but I think it was in New Zealand that it showed up. We were all comparing how bad we were. We all shared a taxi to go along to this clap doctor, paying out a few quid for the shots. I think it was because I was the most obvious, but all the others had been with the one I'd been with, so they had to get a whole load. Our whole life on that tour was dedicated to women, drinking and partying.

31. Town Hall, Wellington, New Zealand.

Paul Rodgers (reviewer, *New Zealand Truth*):

They took nearly 8,000 teenagers for $2.60 to $3.60 each. All the kids got for their money was an ear-splitting cacophony of electronic sounds that was neither musical nor funny . . . the two Wellington performances turned out to be the most hopeless flops ever staged there. Without the aid of recording technicians, this bunch of long-haired boors were worthless.

Steve Marriott: In Wellington it was my 21st birthday, and they gave me the only suite in the hotel, which was really nice of them. Me and Keith Moon and Wiggy (The Who's road manager, John Wolf) destroyed the place. I'll tell you how it started. EMI had given me a little portable record player as a birthday present, so I'd gone and bought a bunch of great records that you can get over there, because they're so far behind you could still get stuff you couldn't get in England. I started playing it and it fed back into itself and made a terrible humming sound that you couldn't get rid of, so I threw it over the balcony.

And Wiggy went down and got it and I threw it over again, and before you knew it, there were chairs, TVs, settees, everything was over the balcony and through the windows – mirrors, everything, the whole fucking deal. There was quite an audience watching it all come down. It was ridiculous, I was hurting with laughter, it was so funny at the time – pissed as newts. We'd be lying on the floor gasping for breath, and someone would see something that wasn't broken, and then break it and sling it over the balcony and it would start again.

Anyway, we were sort of lying there wondering what to do. When we came to, we could see what we had done – all the French doors were gone, every window, there's nothing in the room 'cause it's all on the pavement. I think Ronnie and Pete were there to begin with, and Pete said to Ronnie, "This ends in the nick," and they split and left the three of us to do it – me, Moony and Wiggy.

We were the culprits, I'm afraid. So I had a great idea – "Let's say someone's broken into our room and complain about it." So that's what we did, and the police were there interviewing us and all that. So Keith Moon rings up the reception and says, "Look, what kind of security do you have? Our room's been broken into and vandalized, and we paid good money for these . . ." The police came and like, Wiggy was seen carrying an armchair and throwing it over. He's got a bald head, and there's this wig hanging by the bed, and they're talking to him, "Do you know a bald man?" and he'd say, "No." It was as simple as that, and we got out of it. I thought, "Great," the next night would be cool. They spent all day refurnishing this place, putting in new French windows and everything. Come the evening, Keith comes up and says, "They done a great job," and immediately put an ashtray through the French windows. And off it goes again, furniture over the balcony again, see? We didn't get away with it again, not a chance. The second time it was like, "Oh, God, we can't get away with it," so instead, Keith put on his bravado, which was always funny to watch. We were drinking champagne, still celebrating 21, and the manager came up in his dressing gown. It was late, about three in the morning, and he said, "I know it was you this time. Who has done this?" And Keith put the manager's tie in his drink and said, "I did it." Like, whatcha gonna do about it? "Moon's the name." So I think he took most of the rap for that, which he should have done really.

The party got the army round. They sent the police in first day, and we got them drunk in the room listening to Booker T. We were wearing their helmets and still smashing the place up. So they brought the army in, and we had a man outside each door with a rifle! And if we opened the door, it was like "Get back in your room." And that was the story!

February 1968

1. Flight to Auckland, New Zealand.
10. Valentine Ball, Essex University Hexagon, Colchester.
11. Starlight Ballroom, Crawley, Sussex.
16. Sheffield University.
17. College of Technology, Manchester.
18. Recording in De Lane Lea Studios, London.
21. First date of US tour at Civic Auditorium, San José, California, supported by Blue Cheer and Sagittarius.
22. Fillmore Auditorium, San Francisco.
23. Winterland, San Francisco.
24. Winterland, San Francisco.
26. The Who record "Call Me Lightning" at Goldstar Studios, Los Angeles.

Pete Townshend: "Call Me Lightning" . . . was among the batch of songs that I submitted for The Who's first single. It tries to be a slightly surfy, Jan & Deany kind of song, to satisfy Keith Moon's and John Entwistle's then interest in surf music, which I thought was going to be a real problem. Being a trumped-up mod band was bad enough for us to handle, but trying to be a trumped-up mod band playing R&B but with surf overtones was almost impossible.

Anyway, I was trying to write this song which was all things to all men, with an accent on the men, and I came up with this kind of Shadow Morton backing track and then wrote the lyric for Roger. All of the lyrics are about things that I thought – it's like a double think – would help Roger to portray himself in the way he thought he should be portrayed. So this kind of braggadocio, grandiosity, aggression, flash, empty kind of figure is obviously what I took Roger to be at the time. When I wrote "Anyway, Anyhow, Anywhere" later, I realized how right I was [laughs].

What's really interesting for me about "Call Me Lightning" is realizing how hard from the very beginning it was, writing for Roger's voice – for the characteristics which Roger carried which I thought were lacking in me. I don't have what Roger has. I don't have his conviction that if he gets into a fight, he can win. I don't have his . . . well, not that I'd want his looks today, but when I was younger, I didn't have his looks, I didn't have his magnetism. I just had talent.

So what I was trying to do in a way, in the early days, was to get halfway to Roger and to bring Roger halfway to me. Me using Roger in the way I did always caused problems for us, and they perpetuate today [1994]. It's difficult for us both. It's an uneasy growth. Luckily, it's filled with great affection and love, but it's still fucking hard.

March 1968

1. Agrodome, Vancouver, British Columbia, Canada.

2. The band is thrown out of a bar in Edmonton, Alberta, Canada, after a gig at New Edmonton Gardens.

John Entwistle: We had pretty short hair and I was wearing a suit and a white shirt, but I still got thrown out for being a stinking hippie.

8. Bloomington, Minnesota.

9. Grande Ballroom, Dearborn, Michigan.

10. Youth Building, Exposition Gardens, Peoria, Illinois.
15. Municipal Auditorium, San Antonio, Texas.
16. "Call Me Lightning" is released as a single in the US, as the band play at the City Auditorium, Beaumont, Texas.
17. Music Hall, Houston, Texas.
22. Curtis Hixon Hall, Tampa, Florida.
23. Code 1, Fort Lauderdale, Florida.
24. Coliseum, Orlando, Florida.
27. The Forum, Montreal, Canada.
29. Baldwin Gymnasium, Drew University, Madison, New Jersey.
30. Westbury Music Fair, New York.
31. Constitution Hall, Washington, DC, supported by The Troggs.

Reg Presley (The Troggs): We toured with The Who when we first went over to the States . . . The Who were great, we got on with them really well.

Jim Hoagland (reviewer, *Washington Post*):

The Who have already established through their playing the abrasive nihilism that is the key to electronic rock . . . The Who's approach is a paradigm of the drug-state distorted music that dominates pop music today. This approach is tearing down the old linear concept of music.

April 1968

4. American civil rights leader Martin Luther King is assassinated.

John Morris (director, Fillmore East): I was with Peter Townshend the night Martin Luther King was killed. We had a Who concert the next night at Fillmore East and we had to make the decision whether or not to go ahead with it. We went back and forth and back and forth. Being supposedly the politically aware one back then, I said, "Look. There are going to be thousands of people out on the street waiting to get in. We've got to play." And Pete agreed. He was sitting in the office, talking about violence and how he hated it. How he didn't understand what was going on in the world. I mean, we literally talked for two or three hours. Even then, he was one of the most eloquent, intelligent human beings. He was a pleasure. We decided to go ahead and do it. A lot of people were against it. But we did it.

5. Fillmore East, New York.

Pete Townshend: Even in New York, where you knew that [promoter] Bill

[Graham] wasn't as in charge as he had been in San Francisco – it was in the papers all the time about local threats and stuff that was going on – you still felt you were going into his territory.

John Morris: Pete had been talking to me about peace and how he was never going to smash his amps again. He had been talking about how maybe he had been doing the wrong thing. Maybe he had been contributing to all this violence. He went on stage and he started to play. About halfway through the set, I was up on stage and I looked at him and I knew everything was about to change. Because up to that point, he had played this whole subdued physical thing.

Then he turned around and went at the amps. We had a screen behind them. While Townshend stabbed them, beat the shit out of them, and then smashed his guitar over them. At one point, he looked over and he saw me. And I went, "Whoops . . ." because I thought he was going to come over the top with a guitar and get me. He lost it. He had gotten into it so much that he had lost it and reverted. There was so much boiling up in him that the only way he could get it out was to do it that way.

Eric Rosen (audience): The Who were fantastic. I liked it when they busted everything up. Townshend walked to the tip of the stage, held his guitar like a lance, and ran into his amplifiers. It was unbelievable! He picked up the mike stand and rammed it across the guitar. It was the most incredible thing I had ever seen! Moon picked up his big bass drum and made believe he was going to throw it into the audience. They were wild then.

6. Fillmore East, New York.

Richard Kostelanetz (audience): Their final number was a rock improvisation, vaguely along the theme of "My Generation" . . . Townshend began to crash back into the speakers, which started to topple. This brought the group's factotum, seated on the edge of the stage, and even Bill Graham himself, on stage to hold the speakers up, even though Townshend slapped their hands away. He then started to bounce his guitar off the floor . . .

7. CNE Coliseum, Toronto, Ontario, Canada.

John Entwistle: The biggest gig of all was cancelled because Martin Luther King was assassinated, and we came back after 10 weeks with £300 each. There was a load of rubbish talked at the time about the grand job British groups were doing in earning all these dollars. Really, we were being milked dry by the

Americans. Why, I even remember one concert where the fellow actually fined us for playing too long.
23. Marquee, Soho, London.
25. Recording at Advision Studios, London.
27. Golden Rose Festival, Casino, Montreux, Switzerland.
29. Top Rank, Watford.

May 1968

3. Hull University.
4. Mountford Hall, Liverpool University. In the US, "Call Me Lightning" enters the Top 40 singles chart at its peak position, No. 40.
11. Strathclyde University, Scotland.
21. Pete Townshend marries Karen Astley, his clothes designer, at Didcot registry office, Berkshire.

Pete Townshend: I remember the first time I saw her back. It was in 1963. She sat in the booth beside me in Sid's Café by Ealing Art School. I thought she was a much younger girl because she hunched her shoulders up and, from behind, seemed so small. When she stood up and walked out, I realized she was actually very tall and graceful, her face stunningly beautiful.
22. "Dogs" is recorded at Advision Studios, London.
24. City University, Clerkenwell, London.
29. Recording "Melancholia" and "Fortune Teller" at Advision Studios, London.

June 1968

11. St John's College Ball, Cambridge.
15. The Who release their new single, "Dogs", in the UK.

Pete Townshend: My writing had gone apeshit. I was definitely coming out with some really weird stuff.
19. "Dogs" enters the UK singles chart, where it will peak at No. 25.
26. "Fire" by The Crazy World Of Arthur Brown, produced by Pete Townshend, enters the UK singles chart on its way to No. 1.

Arthur Brown: We didn't have much to do with the choosing of it. In fact, we did another song at that time called "Give Him A Flower" which was the one all the underground audiences joined in on. Lambert, Stamp and Townshend decided between them they wanted something a little harder. They even wanted me to leave the band so I could be a solo artist. They were trying to choose something that would project an image into the future, which is why "Fire" was chosen, because it had quite a good range of vocals.

28. US tour starts at the Shrine Auditorium, Los Angeles, California.

Roger Daltrey: You have to tour for at least six weeks over there. The first three weeks pays your fares and all the expenses. The fourth week pays for your road managers. The fifth pays for your manager. The sixth is profit for us . . .

29. Shrine Auditorium, Los Angeles, California.

Pete Johnson (reviewer, *Los Angeles Times*):

> They are great fun to watch, even aside from the widely publicized instrument-smashing ending of their act, which has become somewhat of a cliché. The three instruments and their four voices (they are capable of good harmonies) create an overwhelming feeling of excitement which more than makes up for their sometimes blurred lyrics.

30. The Who begin an eight-day break in Los Angeles, during which discussions are held with The Rolling Stones about the possibility of staging a Rock'n'Roll Circus.

Pete Townshend: This was an idea that three bands had almost simultaneously but separately – the Stones, The Small Faces and The Who. I was in LA, playing there with The Who, and I was summoned to see Mick and we had this open forum about the possibility of creating a travelling circus to tour the USA. Mick was deciding at that time whether or not The Small Faces and The Who would let their idea be co-opted and join in with it. I, being an absolute ass-licking Stones fan, agreed.

Chip Monck came up with this fabulous design for a tent based on the original Barnum & Bailey, where trains come up on tracks in the back of small towns and go round in a big circle and all these special carriages would spew out seats, the tent would go up around them and hey-ho, you'd have an instant circus. It all looked absolutely feasible.

About two weeks passed and I was very excited about it, and then I got a call from Mick to say that there was a problem. "Well, we've discovered that the track in America is so bad that in a lot of places the trains can only travel at four miles an hour. Which means that the tour would take something like twenty years . . ." But he'd kind of got the bug for it, as had we all.

July 1968

7. The Yardbirds break up, leaving guitarist Jimmy Page to fulfil upcoming concert obligations. He re-forms the group as The New Yardbirds, but when The Who's madcap drummer Keith Moon quips, "That'll probably go down like a lead zeppelin," Page's eyes light up.

8. Memorial Auditorium, Sacramento, California.

9. Exhibition Hall, Regina, Alberta, Canada.

10. Calgary Stampede Corral, Calgary, Alberta, Canada.

11. Saskatoon Arena, Saskatchewan, Canada.

Keith Moon: I get bored, you see. There was a time in Saskatoon, in Canada. It was another Holiday Inn and I was bored. Now, when I get bored, I rebel. I said, "Fuck it. Fuck the lot of you." And I took out me hatchet and chopped the hotel room to bits. The television, the chairs, the dresser, the cupboard doors, the bed . . . the lot of it.

Pete Townshend: Keith set the precedent, and once it was set, I fell into it, too. Like, I used to turn off the TV set with a glass ashtray. It was in the days before remote control, and I never bothered to get out of bed. I'd just hurl an ashtray and smash the television, which did the job.

Once, he was walking along with me on the second floor of a Holiday Inn, and he climbed up on the railing and said, "Bye, Pete!" and leapt off. There was a swimming pool down there, but it was at least five yards away. By some miracle he contorted himself and managed to barely squeeze into the pool. Then he got up and shouted "Voila!" I was the only person there, so who was he doing it for? It's ironic, since he and I had had several conversations about how we should behave – what was our responsibility and what was good publicity. In some ways he saw himself as The Who's publicity machine. If he could get a front-page story, he'd do it. And it was quite difficult for us because we didn't want to turn down the easy notoriety he gave us.

12. Indiana Beach Ballroom, Monticello, Indiana.

13. Grande Ballroom, Dearborn, Michigan.

14. Music Carnival, Cleveland, Ohio.

15. Memorial Centre, Kingston, Canada.

16. Civic Centre, Ottawa, Ontario, Canada, supported by The Troggs and Ohio Express.

17. Auto Stade, Montreal, Quebec, Canada.

18. Rhode Island Auditorium, Providence, Rhode Island, supported by Blood, Sweat & Tears.
20. Civic Center, Virginia Beach, Virginia.
21. Oakdale Music Theatre, Wallingford, Connecticut.
23. The Mosque, Richmond, Virginia.
26. Saint Bernard Civic Auditorium, Chalemette, Louisiana.
27. "Magic Bus" is released as a single in the US. That evening, The Who play at Orlando Sports Arena, Orlando, Florida.

Pete Townshend: A lot of demos have been so good, in fact, that it's scared us out of making recordings. "Magic Bus", we didn't want to do it. I listened to the demo and I thought the demo was good but that we're never gonna catch it on record. It's gonna bring us all down. Let's forget it, let's do something else. And Kit was going, "No, we're going to do it, you're going to learn every line, every little detail. Every precious thing in the demonstration record, you're gonna catch and you're gonna copy it if necessary."

In the end, we gave up and we thought, "Oh, we'll do it," and we went down and we did it completely differently, but it all came together and we went up and thanked him for making us do it.

John Entwistle: I played that on a Vox violin bass. Absolutely revolting thing that looked like a mint humbug. Vox gave us two guitars each. On stage, "Magic Bus" was always a complete bore for me. I'd be playing the same note, A, for six minutes. It wasn't so bad when we recorded it because that was only three minutes.

Pete Townshend: It was a gas to record and had a mystical quality to the sound. The words, however, are garbage, loaded with heavy drug references.

28. Marine Stadium, Miami, Florida.
29. Tamarack Lodge, Ellenville, New York.
31. The New Place, Algonquin, Illinois.

August 1968

1. Electric Theatre, Chicago, Illinois.
2. New York Rock Festival, Singer Bowl, Queens, New York. The Doors and The Who are on the same bill. Watching Jim Morrison perform inspires Townshend to write "Sally Simpson".

Pete Townshend: The Doors had become meteoric and Jim Morrison's Christ picture was all over fucking New York.

3. Majestic Hills, Lake Geneva, Wisconsin.

4. Melody Fair, North Tonawanda, New York.

6. Music Hall, Boston, Massachusetts.

7. Schaefer Music Festival, Wolman Skating Rink, Central Park, New York.

Robert Shelton (reviewer, *New York Times*):

A capacity audience watched and cheered as Peter Townshend broke up his electric guitar. Whether Mr Townshend was having a breakdown or being a showman was not discernible. Perhaps he thought, as have some other pop musicians recently, that the demolition of his instrument was making a statement. If so, it is the sort of statement that is populating our mental hospitals.

9. Cavalcade of Music, Illinois State Fairgrounds, Springfield, Illinois.

10. The Jaguar, St Charles, Illinois.

13–15. Three nights at the Fillmore West, San Francisco, California.

16. Selland Arena, Fresno, California, supported by Quicksilver Messenger Service.

17. Giants Stadium, Phoenix, Arizona, supported by Quicksilver Messenger Service.

18. Kelker Junction Concert Hall, Colorado Springs, Colorado.

22. Music Hall, Kansas City, Missouri.

23–24. Wedgewood Village Amusement Park, Oklahoma City, Oklahoma.

27. Community Concourse, San Diego, California.

28. Civic Auditorium, Santa Monica, California.

29. Earl Warren Showgrounds, Santa Barbara, California.

31. "Magic Bus" enters the US Top 40 singles chart.

Pete Townshend: "Magic Bus" was not really intended to be a throwback to an early R&B sound or anything, though it does sound a bit that way. It was written about the same time as "My Generation" – we listened to it then but didn't really think a lot of it. But we heard it again more recently and liked it, so we released it.

September 1968

18. "Magic Bus" is released as a single in the UK.

22. The first day of recording sessions for The Who's rock opera, *Tommy*, at IBC

Studios, Portland Place, London.

Pete Townshend: It was supposed to be a series of singles and any departure from that was introduced by Kit Lambert's coaching – "Keep that, write another tune, then repeat that." So I just wrote bits and stuck them into songs. It may appear to flow, but when I presented it to the band, it was simply a series of songs.

Roger Daltrey: It was really Kit Lambert's dream to do an Important Work in rock music – if there were ever any such thing. Kit had come from a classical background – his father, Constant Lambert, was founder of the English National Opera – and having his kind of education, it frustrated him that there were all these grand tales being told in classical music, so why couldn't rock address itself to something more serious than the three-minute soundbite?

It was a long way from what we'd been doing, but we'd have a go at anything. Only someone like Kit could have pulled *Tommy* off, though – all the hype that went with it. I mean the narrative is not particularly good, is it? Then again it does have a narrative, which is more than *Quadrophenia* had!

John Entwistle: We started out doing what was basically a single album, but it didn't make sense. We realized the only way to make it coherent was to make it a double album, because a lot more things happened to *Tommy* than could be put on one album.

Keith Moon: We wrote most of *Tommy* in a pub opposite the recording studio.

John Entwistle: It took us eight months altogether, six months recording, two months mixing. We had to do so many of the tracks again, because it took so long we had to keep going back and rejuvenating the numbers, that it just started to drive us mad, we were getting brainwashed by the whole thing, and I started to hate it.

Pete Townshend: [*Tommy*] was completely autobiographical. All I knew was that I spent time with a grandmother whom I didn't like very much. "See me, feel me, touch me." Where did that come from? It came from that little four-and-a-half-year-old boy in a fucking unlocked bedroom in a house with a madwoman. That's where it came from.

I was so earnestly trying to avoid writing something autobiographical. All of The Who's first work was about their early audience; we felt rock should be reflective of its audience. That was what was unique about rock'n'roll as an art form. I tended to write, if not my own biography, certainly an encapsulated biography assembled from bits of the audience. Yet *Tommy* felt to me – when I was writing it – to be the exception to that.

Roger Daltrey: Pete used to literally write his best stuff when he was writing about a character that he could see very, very clearly from outside himself. When he gets introspective it turns into melodramatic dross. And some of it's really good and I admire his courage for doing that. So, I'm not putting him down for that but he writes his best stuff when he's writing for a figure beyond himself. And I was that figure. And of course I personified Tommy. I was the guy who used to play the part. I played the damn part for five years. I slogged my balls off around the world sweating it out. People thought I was Tommy. I used to get called Tommy in the street.

John Entwistle: When we did *Tommy*, we had moved up to eight track, but we only recorded five. The last three were for the orchestration, but we couldn't afford it.

Roger Daltrey: Pete used to come in some days with just half a demo. We used to talk for hours, literally. We probably did as much talking as we did recording. Sorting out arrangements and things on *Tommy*.

Pete Townshend: I didn't write *Tommy* in any kind of chronological order. I already had some of the material – "Amazing Journey", "Sensation", "Welcome", "Sparks" and "Underture". "We're Not Gonna Take It" was a kind of anti-Fascist statement. The first rundown of the idea I put on a graph. It was intended to show Tommy from the outside and his impressions going on inside him.

John Entwistle: Pete suggested that I write two songs he felt he couldn't write.

Roger Daltrey: The most important songs in *Tommy*, which give it the kind of edge, are "Cousin Kevin" and "Uncle Ernie", which were written by John Entwistle, not by Pete.

John Entwistle: Basically, the brief I got was to write a song about a homosexual experience with a nasty uncle, and a bullying experience by . . . I don't know whether "cousin" was actually mentioned, but I figured it might well be the son of Uncle Ernie. I found it very easy. I'd written "Fiddle About", for the character of Uncle Ernie, by the time I'd got back to the room. If I've got the idea for a song, then it comes almost immediately.

Pete Townshend: I don't consider the album to be sick at all. In fact, what I was out to show is that someone who suffers terribly at the hands of society has the ability to turn all these experiences into a tremendous musical awareness. Sickness is in the mind of the listener and I don't give a damn what people think.

Roger Daltrey: *Tommy* came along at a time in our lives when everyone was searching for answers in their life. The ambiguity of *Tommy* allowed it to answer many things for many different people. But in fact it didn't really answer anything. That's the beauty of it.

Pete Townshend: There is no ending. What I was doing at the time was attending to the fact that in rock'n'roll what you don't do is make people's decisions for them. You share their ideas, difficulties and frustrations.

John Entwistle: I only ever played the record twice – ever. I don't think *Tommy* was all about [what] was on the record – I think it's on the stage. The message is much stronger on stage than on record.

Pete Townshend: I suppose the mistake I made in *Tommy* was instead of having the guts to take what Meher Baba said – which was "Don't worry, be happy, leave the results to God" – and repeating that to people, I decided the people weren't capable of hearing that directly. They've got to have it served in this entertainment package. And I gave them *Tommy* instead, in which some of Meher Baba's wonderfully explicit truths were presented to them half-baked in lyric form and diluted as a result. In fact, if there was any warning in *Tommy*, it was "Don't make any more records like that."

28. "Magic Bus" peaks at No. 25 in the US.

October 1968

2. Starting from BBC TV studios, Lime Grove, London, The Who tour London in a vintage French bus to promote the new single, "Magic Bus".

5. The Who begin a UK tour with an all-nighter at The Roundhouse in London, along with Joe Cocker, The Small Faces and The Crazy World Of Arthur Brown.

John Entwistle: We were recording [*Tommy*] during the day and playing concerts during the evening to pay for the next day in the studio. We knew it was going to be different because it was the first full concept thing that we had done.

Roger Daltrey: Please don't think we've forgotten about Britain. We all love working here, but what is the point with the tax we pay? It's stupid. We pay 18s 3d in the pound so it's hardly worth working.

7. Recording "Beat Club" at Radio Bremen Studios, Bremen, Germany.

11. UK TV show "How It Is", presented by Peter Asher of Peter And Gordon, features The Who, Spooky Tooth, David Ackles. That night The Who play at York University.

12. The compilation *Direct Hits* is released in the UK. That night The Who play at Sheffield University.

18. The Lyceum, London, supported by The Crazy World Of Arthur Brown, Alan Bown, Elmer Gantry and Skip Bifferty.

Chris Welch (reviewer, *Melody Maker*):

> Playing like men possessed, they are more together than during their entire career. Roger Daltrey looking splendid in a fringed jacket, naked chest and glittering cross, has perfected his microphone swinging stage movements and sang better than I have ever heard him.

19. California Ballroom, Dunstable.

21. Recording sessions begin for Tommy at IBC Studios, London.

23. "Magic Bus" enters the UK singles chart, where it will peak at No. 26.

25. Granby Halls, Leicester, supported by Joe Cocker and Family.

30. Eel Pie Island, Twickenham.

November 1968

8. The Who begin their last theatre tour at the Granada Theatre, Walthamstow, London.

9. Adelphi Cinema, Slough.

10. Colston Hall, Bristol.

15. An all-night extravaganza at The Roundhouse, Chalk Farm in London features Joe Cocker, The Small Faces, The Crazy World Of Arthur Brown, The Mindbenders, Yes and The Who.

16. Another all-night extravaganza at The Roundhouse, Chalk Farm in London features The Who and The Mindbenders.

17. Birmingham Theatre.

18. City Hall, Newcastle.

19. Paisley Ice Rink, Paisley, Scotland.

20. Empire Theatre, Liverpool, with The Small Faces, The Crazy World Of Arthur Brown, Joe Cocker, The Mindbenders.

21. Recording UK TV show "Crackerjack" at Golders Green Theatre, London.

22. City Hall, St Albans.

26. Southampton University.
30. The Who have their first US album chart entry with the US-only release *Magic Bus – The Who On Tour*. It will peak at No. 39.

December 1968

10. The Who are among the rock superstars present when The Rolling Stones begin filming their TV special, "Rock'n'Roll Circus", at Intertel Studios, Wembley, London. Other guests include John and Yoko, Eric Clapton, Taj Mahal, Jethro Tull, Marianne Faithfull and Mitch Mitchell.

Pete Townshend: When I saw Keith for the first discussion, which was at the Hilton Hotel, he walked into the breakfast bar there and he was literally yellow, like he had hepatitis. I remember thinking, "This isn't going to happen. They're just all too sick."

David Stark (audience): It was December, and pretty cold in a cavernous studio. There were a lot of circus acts interspersed throughout the whole thing . . . endless retakes which bored the pants off everybody . . . but it was great . . . everyone was just hanging around . . . the artists were not far away from the audience and just chatting. A nice sociable atmosphere. At one point I went to the loo and walked past a group of four guys having a chat – Lennon, Jagger, Townshend and Clapton.

Pete Townshend: Anita Pallenberg was extremely wired up and angry with everybody and not in very good shape. I said hello to Anita and bumped her arm in a rather boyish way, as you sometimes do when you say hello to someone; it obviously hurt her a lot, like she was completely wracked in some kind of pain. She was obviously withdrawing or something.

Brian was deeply, deeply tragic but he was always very, very sweet to me. I have fantastic affection for Brian; he was an extraordinary guy. I won't say intelligent, but he was very dilettantish and refreshing and accepting and open. He would have made a good critic, in many ways; he was articulate and eager.

I found the whole day really quite sad because it was clear that he was going to go. At the time the word was that he was very happy: he was going to go off and make his eclectic world music records – he had a kind of Peter Gabrielesque vision. I don't think any of the people around him could help him and it was extremely tough to see Anita – she'd already completely abandoned him. They'd been a couple and she was certainly very much like him: they were both very beautiful, very self-destructive but also very passionate and well-read and artistic and literary. They were fucking great company, I must say; I suppose they were just both smashed by the drugs that they were taking, which, thank God, I didn't use at the time. So it was a sad day for me because of that.

It is possible that Marianne Faithfull was pregnant; certainly she was shining like a fucking star all night, in contrast to the greyness and darkness of the Stones on that occasion. I remember being really quite obsessed – there's a few embarrassing pictures of me just gawping at her. She was very fanciable, of course, but there was something very magic about her on that occasion. Later on one saw the other side – she came and sat in the crowd and got drunk and larked about and had fun. She was great. I'm always grateful to see that she survived.

Michael Lindsay-Hogg (director): It was always Mick's idea to have a supergroup . . . We talked about Paul McCartney doing it and then Mick thought that John would be the right person to approach. He had enthusiasm for projects like that. John said sure and, as he was very close to Eric Clapton at the time, John got Eric involved, and then Keith did bass, and that's how Dirty Mac evolved.

Pete Townshend: I remember feeling that you couldn't put a band of more impenetrable beings on the stage. Eric was in a very impenetrable stage, Lennon was really the most impenetrable being – much more impenetrable than Noel Gallagher: he was completely inaccessible emotionally; he was very funny and witty, but it masked an inner silence.

The Stones are capable of doing extraordinary stuff live . . . that didn't happen on this occasion; there's no question about that. They weren't just usurped by The Who, they were also usurped by Taj Mahal who was just, as always, extraordinary.

11. Further filming for The Rolling Stones' "Rock'n'Roll Circus", at Wembley, London.

12. Reading University.

14. Bubbles Club, Brentwood, Essex.

17. The Who's Christmas Party, Marquee Club, Soho, London, supported by Yes.

19. The Pier, Worthing.

21. *NME* reviews the album *S.F. Sorrow*, a "rock opera" by The Pretty Things, declaring, "They have improved out of all recognition and produced an album which should rate as one of the best of 1968."

Dick Taylor (guitarist, Pretty Things): It took us well over a year to record *S.F. Sorrow*, and when it was released, we learned that Pete Townshend had heard it at a party with Kit Lambert, and he became quite fascinated by it, played it several times.

Phil May (vocalist, Pretty Things): We weren't thinking of "rock opera" when we did *S.F. Sorrow*, but it was a rock album with a complete story following a central character through his life.

Dick Taylor: If you listen to the track "Balloon Burning" on *S.F. Sorrow*, and then listen to "Pinball Wizard" on *Tommy*, you'll notice quite a similarity in the rhythmic riff that opens them both. I suspect that if Townshend did lift something from us, he probably did it unconsciously.

Phil May: In so many write-ups, he always said that *S.F. Sorrow* influenced *Tommy*. Just recently, Townshend's been denying any knowledge. It almost sounded like a lawyer's statement – "we want to categorically deny we never heard any copy of *S.F. Sorrow*." You know, there's room for *Tommy* and *S.F. Sorrow*.

1969

January 1969

17. The Who play their first gig of the year at the Great Hall, King's College, London.

19. Mothers Club, Erdington, Birmingham.

24. Roger Daltrey is fined £11 in Luton for minor traffic offences. Gig at Civic Hall, Wolverhampton.

25. Middlesex Borough College, Isleworth, Middlesex.

31. Meher Baba, guru by appointment to Pete Townshend, Ronnie Lane, Melanie and other rock luminaries, moves on to a higher spiritual plane.

February 1969

1. Union Ballroom, Newcastle.

Pete Townshend: I heard that Baba's word has been spoken, probably about the time of his death. I was suffering from a bout of flu when Baba was about to drop his earthly body. We were playing Newcastle the day he died, and when I got home the news was broken to me. I felt as if I had betrayed myself. I felt as if I hadn't had enough time to really make myself ready, to learn to love Baba and hang tightly to his apron strings as the whirlwind of spiritual events around the closing of his manifestation speeded up.

Today I understand a little better. I am not the spiritually advanced seeker I imagined myself to be. Reading too much Herman Hesse and Idries Shah can be a bad thing in that respect. One builds a sort of hero worship for the "Seeker" in the same way one would a film star. It's only recently I've begun to see that Baba's word is an eternal word. Its impact reaches well into the past and the future. The wave of spiritual fervour and obsession that sweeps youth today is a reflection of the force of that word, that expression of his almighty loneliness . . .

Baba washed the religious preconceptions from my heart with my own tears. I love Jesus far more now than I ever did at infant school as I sang, "Yes, Jesus loves me." Now I know he really was the Christ.

2. Cothams Hotel, Redcar.

7. Recording "Pinball Wizard" at Morgan Studios, London.

Pete Townshend: I knocked it off. I thought, "Oh my God, this is awful, the most clumsy piece of writing I've ever done . . . Oh my God, I'm embarrassed. This sounds like a music hall song." . . . I scribbled it out and all the verses were the same length and there was no middle eight. It was going to be a complete dud, but I carried on. I attempted the same mock-baroque guitar beginning that is on "I'm A Boy", and then a bit of vigorous kind of flamenco guitar. I was just grabbing at ideas. I knocked a demo together, and took it to the studio and everyone loved it. Damon Lyon-Shaw [engineer] said, "Pete, that's a hit." Everybody was really excited and I suddenly thought, "Have I written a hit?"

8. Central London Polytechnic, London.

14. Lanchester College, Coventry.

15. Dreamland, Margate.

21. Birmingham University.

22. Liverpool University.

23. The Who top the bill at an eight-hour benefit for the London School of Economics in The Roundhouse, London, also featuring Cat Stevens, Third Ear Band, Circus and Pete Brown's Battered Ornaments.

John Burgoyne (audience): I wasn't a huge Who fan but this seemed like a good gig to go to with my girlfriend. All I really remember is that they served blue cake in the café and that they were so incredibly loud that my ears were still ringing when I went to work on Monday and for days after.

March 1969

1. On the occasion of Roger Daltrey's 25th birthday, The Who play a gig at Mothers Club, Birmingham.

John Woffinden (audience): We queued and grabbed the best two seats in the house. It was an incredible show. We were so close, we were literally dodging Roger's microphone when he twirled it . . . Keith Moon kept coming round the drums between numbers to scrounge cigarettes. He made a few disparaging remarks about the fact we could only afford Player's No. 6, but he still had them.

It was, of course, Roger's birthday, and he actually started the wrecking when his microphone packed up. He smashed it with the mike stand and threw it at Bob Pridden, who seemed used to such things. Townshend soon followed, rocking the stacks until the top one fell down and his guitar and feet went through it. And we all know, when Roger and Pete started wrecking things, Keith could become very careless . . . This gig was the nearest I ever came to seeing The Who on auto-destruction and it was just about the most wonderfully exciting thing I've ever seen on stage.

7. The Who release a new single, "Pinball Wizard", in the UK.

Pete Townshend: I got very into Baroque music with people like Purcell, and I started to be interested in the fact that they used melodic transitions very rarely and there would always be suspensions and tension and it would be another level of tension and it would drop. This was mainly Purcell who was an English composer and I was deeply influenced by him. In fact the beginning of "Pinball Wizard", on the demo, that chord sequence runs for about 15 minutes. It's just an exploration of how many chords I could make with a running B: the B was in every chord. It went through about 30 or 40 chords very slowly and then into the song. "I'm A Boy" did that as well in the solo.

14. Corn Exchange, Cambridge.

19. "Pinball Wizard" enters the UK singles chart.

22. "Pinball Wizard" is released as a single in the US.

28. A daughter, Emma, is born to Pete and Karen Townshend, now living at their 1745 Georgian town house in Twickenham, Middlesex.

April 1969

2. Pavilion Ballroom, Bournemouth, supported by Third Ear Band.

10. The Who are seen performing "Pinball Wizard" on "Top Of The Pops".

11. Pete Townshend is interviewed by BBC radio about the album *Tommy*, in Studio 2, Kensington House, Richmond Way, West London.
18. UK TV appearance on ATV show "This Is Tom Jones".
22. The Who perform parts of *Tommy* for the first time at the Institute of Technology, Bolton.
24. Mayfair Ballroom, Newcastle.
25. Strathclyde University, Glasgow, Scotland.
26. Community Centre, Auchinleck, Scotland. "Pinball Wizard" peaks at No. 4 in the UK.
27. Kinema Ballroom, Dunfermline, Scotland.

John M. Millar (audience): I had a beer with all four members of The Who in the bar beforehand. They played most of *Tommy* as well as all the major hits: "I'm A Boy", "I Can See For Miles", "Pictures Of Lily", "Happy Jack". Townshend demolished a Rickenbacker at the end of the performance and Moon put his foot through the bass drum. Support band was called The Shadettes, a local band who shortly thereafter renamed themselves Nazareth and became minor heavy metal celebrities in their own right . . . Roger Daltrey drove away from the venue in a Corvette Stingray with custom exhaust pipes down the side – at that time completely unseen outside the US.

28. Bay Hotel, Whitburn, Sunderland.

May 1969

2. The Who preview their new rock opera, *Tommy*, for the press at Ronnie Scott's Jazz Club in London.
3. "Pinball Wizard" enters the US Top 40 singles chart.
9. The Who take *Tommy* on the road for the first time, with a US tour opening at the Grande Ballroom, Dearborn, Michigan.

Roger Daltrey: Everybody is Tommy, that's why it took off. The people made *Tommy*. They found something they believed in, something they could identify with *en masse*. The Who took it on the road and got something back from the people and it built from there.

John Entwistle: At first, people were going, "Yeah, too much," mostly because it was such a mammoth. But as we got on with the tour, it started to mean something to everybody, it started to work.

10-11. Grande Ballroom, Dearborn, Michigan.

13-15. Boston Tea Party, Boston, Massachusetts.

16-18. Three nights at the Fillmore East, New York. On the first night, Townshend is arrested and briefly incarcerated after kicking New York undercover cop Daniel Mulhearn off the stage.

Posey Rosenbloom (audience): The concert was the night before *Tommy* was out in the shops but the radio had been playing it. We had first row seats the night of the Fillmore fire.

Alan Arkush (audience): I got to Fillmore East and everyone was really psyched. Because we loved The Who and we had heard "Pinball Wizard" and we knew we were going to see *Tommy*. They launched into it, and it was awe-inspiring. Naturally, towards the end of the explosively pyrotechnic show, when smoke started to drift across the auditorium, most of the audience assumed it was all part of the entertainment. It wasn't.

Posey Rosenbloom: I glanced over my shoulder once and saw smoke but didn't think anything of it.

Pete Townshend: There's a lot of rumours about that too, some say it was a firebomb that was aimed at the Fillmore, whereas Bill Graham says without a doubt, he knows the history of the whole thing, that it was a protection thing for the store . . .

Bill Graham (Fillmore owner): Someone threw a Molotov cocktail in a grocery store next door because the owner refused to pay protection money.

Pete Townshend: . . . and he let them blow the place up and collect on the insurance, right? Basically, that's the story of that one.

Frank Barsalona (booking agent): They had all these special policemen down there that night. Ones who looked like hippies with beards and earrings.

Bill Graham: Smoke was coming into the house now and the audience was in hysterics. They were convinced that we had hired these guys as part of the show. After all, this was The Who. They had destroyed amplifiers and turned over trucks and what not. So it could have been part of the set.

Posey Rosenbloom: Then this cop [plain-clothes officer Daniel Mulhearn of the Tactical Police Force], we didn't even know he was a cop then, jumped on stage in the middle of "Summertime Blues". He ran over to Daltrey, trying to grab the mike but Daltrey wouldn't let him have it, then Townshend ran over and kicked the guy in the balls . . .

Frank Barsalona: Without missing a lick, Townshend squared off and kicked this guy right off the stage.

Posey Rosenbloom: . . . and Entwistle slammed him over the neck with his bass. Then the Fillmore ushers grabbed the guy. They finished "Summertime Blues" and then Bill Graham came on stage and said there was a fire.

Bill Graham: The firemen were telling me, "We have to evacuate this building now!" I went into the wings and I waved to the band and I said, "There's a fire next door." "Is it real?" they asked. "Yes," I told them. So they finished their song and walked off. I went on stage and I grabbed the mike. I remember thinking how I would react if I were sitting in the audience and someone started talking to me about a fire.

So I said, "Will you listen please? Across the street. Across the street, there is a fire. We're being asked by the Fire Department to please slowly and quietly evacuate the building. For safety reasons. There is no problem." All I kept saying to them was, "Across the street." Because I didn't want them to know that it was right next door.

Alan Arkush: That drove the audience wild. They were standing up by now because it was after *Tommy* and "Summertime Blues". When the guy got kicked off the stage, it was as high as an audience could ever possibly get. They were all standing on the seats screaming and we were thinking, "How the hell are we going to get all these people out of a building that's on fire?"

Bill Graham: All the fire marshal wanted to know was, "Where the hell is that guy who threw me off the stage?" The minute the show was over, The Who were sitting in their dressing room. They knew what had gone on. That they had kicked some guy off the stage. I grabbed the group and I took them out the side door. We went around the block all the way down to First Avenue and then around to 71 East Seventh, where I stuck them away in my apartment. The police were already holding Frank Barsalona, who was trying to get hold of their lawyer. There was no second show that night and we refunded all the money. The next afternoon, Daltrey and Townshend surrendered at the police precinct.

Frank Barsalona (owner, Premier Talent): I was the only one at the police station that night. I don't think Kit Lambert or Chris Stamp was there. I tried to get the police not to arrest them. I told them it was a mistake. I mean, how the fuck could they tell these were police? They looked like guys coming out of the audience. I didn't want them arrested. For all the regular reasons, and because it might affect their getting back into the country the next time, if in fact the arrest held up.

So we were talking and the cops were really angry. I went and got a lawyer to fight it and I was there all night. They finally arrested Pete and Daltrey, I think.

Jane Gerachty, controller, Fillmore East: What happened was that the fire was during the early show and of course we had people outside lining up for the late show. We had like twenty-four hundred people waiting to come into the building. We had to get everybody out who was already in and then they cordoned off the street so they could fight the fire.

Then we had to find money to bail Townshend and Daltrey out. We had to take all our little concession money and count our ones and fives and pennies and nickels. Because the fire ruined the weekend, I think Bill called Frank and asked him if at the end of their tour, they would come and replay the date. We advertised it as "The Triumphant Return of The Who". It really broke them. They were enormous. From all of that.

Bill Graham: Before they were released, there was an agreement made that no charges would be brought. That it had all been just a misunderstanding. That The Who had thought it was all just part of the show. I told them to say, "We thought Bill hired those guys. All just part of Bill's madness, only good fun, and we apologize." The next day, Townshend and Daltrey were let go at like a quarter to seven at night. At 7.30, they walked out on stage at Fillmore East and played.

18. Jimi Hendrix is in the audience when The Who play their final night at Fillmore East, New York.

19. Rockpile, Toronto, Ontario, Canada.

21. Capitol Theatre, Ottawa, Ontario, Canada.

23. The Who release their rock opera album, *Tommy*, in the UK. That night they play at the Electric Factory, Philadelphia, Pennsylvania.

Leonard Bernstein (composer/conductor): Pete Townshend of rock's toughest and most innovative group, has made the dream a reality with *Tommy*, a full-length rock opera that for sheer power, invention and brilliance of performance, outstrips anything that has ever come out of a recording studio.

Pete Townshend: We joked as a group about *Tommy* being true opera (which it isn't) but The Who's audience and many of the rock press took it very seriously. It was this seriousness that ultimately turned *Tommy* into light entertainment.

Roger Daltrey: In fact, the *Tommy* album was not a particularly big success. It got into the charts but then it quite rapidly disappeared again. It was only after us flogging it on the road for three years, doing Woodstock and things like that,

that it got back in the charts. Then it stayed there for a year, and took on a life of its own. We were flat broke and busted before *Tommy*, and for the three years afterwards until it caught on. But when it did, it totally made our fortunes.

Pete Townshend: We went from the ridiculous to the sublime – being told we were musical geniuses when really we were just a bunch of scumbags.

24. Electric Factory, Philadelphia, Pennsylvania. "Pinball Wizard" peaks at No. 19 in the US chart.

25. Merriweather Post Pavilion, Columbia, Maryland, supported by Led Zeppelin.

Charles E. Brault (audience): The warmup band was pretty unknown at that time. I don't think their first album was even out yet, and they sounded like they hadn't played together much.

27. Roger Daltrey and Pete Townshend plead not guilty in Manhattan Criminal Court to a charge of kicking a policeman in an onstage scuffle during a Fillmore East concert. They are released on bail.

29-31. The Who play three nights at the Kinetic Playground, Chicago, Illinois.

31. *Tommy* is released in the US.

June 1969

5-6. Fillmore East, New York, supported by Chuck Berry.

John Ford Noonan (director, Fillmore East): When Chuck Berry was opening for The Who, we had already put the pinball machine from *Tommy* in the star dressing room. Peter said, "No, no. We can't have that as our dressing room. It must be for Chuck." So we moved the pinball machine upstairs, and Chuck had the star dressing room.

Peter would come in the theatre and there was a Spanish or a Puerto Rican or a Cuban guy who washed the stage or worked as a custodian. Peter would say, "Your accent's a lot better, man. You're getting to know a lot more English." He would remember people from one time to the next.

Peter wouldn't let anyone in the band use anything before they went on. I remember one time Keith Moon was really drunk and they sobered him up before they went out to play. Peter was the most focused and professional and I think it showed in his work.

Richard Kostelanetz (audience): Chuck Berry got such a good hand from this audience – at least two standing ovations – that The Who hurried on stage and quickly did three loud songs in a row. Even though their amplifiers conked out at one point, they still transcended the aura left behind by Berry. However, before long the unrelenting decibels and the repetitiousness of their songs became more than a bit maddening . . . I would have left well before the end but my date wanted to see Townshend crack up his guitar; but just as it appeared he would begin that notorious act, at the end of the song "My Generation", he pulled out the plug connecting his guitar to its amplifier and simply walked off stage, disappointing us all . . .

John Ford Noonan: After one show, we had a party for the band at Max's Kansas City and it lasted 17 minutes. They walked in there, Keith Moon picked up a bottle and smashed the mirror, and they threw them all out. They said, "Hey, we're The Who." And they said, "We don't care who you are. You're fucking out!" I was on my way to it but the party was over before I could get there. They were pretty nuts but Townshend was definitely the most interesting guy.

7. As the band play at Majestic Hills Theater, Lake Geneva, Wisconsin, *Tommy* enters the Billboard album chart at No. 96. It also enters the UK chart, where it will peak at No. 2.

8. Guthrie Theater, Minneapolis, Minnesota.

Tom Farmer (audience): The shows were mindblowers. Daltrey's voice was shot, and so Pete had to sing nearly all of the songs, which was actually a very rare and cool experience. Poor Roger mainly twirled his microphone the whole night and looked miserable. Keith's drum kit was set up over the Guthrie trap door and so, periodically, he (and his drums) would move below, and above, the stage.

13. Hollywood Palladium, Los Angeles, supported by Bonzo Dog Doo Dah Band and Poco.

14. *Tommy* enters the US album charts, where it will peak at No. 4, giving The Who their first American Top 10 entry.

17-18. Fillmore West, San Francisco.

19. Fillmore West, San Francisco.

Allan McDougall (reviewer, *Melody Maker*):

The Who gave perhaps the performance of their lives . . .

20. After an overnight flight to New York, Townshend is fined $75 for kicking a police officer at the Fillmore East on 16 May.

July 1969

2. "Something In The Air" by Thunderclap Newman, produced by Pete Townshend, reaches No. 1 in the UK singles chart.

Andy "Thunderclap" Newman: A friend called Rick Seaman went to Ealing Technical College. One day he heard me playing the piano and asked me to do some tapes. He took them to the college and some got to Townshend's ears, way before he formed The Who.

Jimmy McCullough (guitarist, Thunderclap Newman): I met Pete in Denmark Street one day and got talking to him. Pete was going to put me out playing guitar and singing on my own. I had just packed up with my old band when I met Speedy [Keene].

Andy Newman: Townshend phoned me in November [1968] and said he would like me to come and play with some other boys and make some film music. Later, he sent a letter about forming the group permanently. He said, "I'm gonna make you a star," and I thought, "Oh yes, I've heard that one before."

3. Townshend's friend Brian Jones of The Rolling Stones is found dead at his home, Cotchford Farm.

Pete Townshend: Brian should have been put in a straitjacket and treated. I used to know Brian quite well. The Stones have always been a group I really dug. Dug all the dodgy aspects of them as well, and Brian Jones has always been what I've regarded as one of the dodgy aspects. The way he fitted in and the way he didn't was one of the strong dynamics of the group. When he stopped playing with them, I thought that dynamic was going to be missing, but it still seems to be there. Perhaps the fact that he's dead has made that dynamic kind of permanent. A little bit of love might have sorted him out. I don't think his death was necessarily a bad thing for Brian. I think he'll do better next time. I believe in reincarnation.

5. When Chuck Berry and The Who perform on the final night of the Pop Proms, Royal Albert Hall, London, the audience storms the stage. As a result, rock music is banned at the prestigious venue.

John Entwistle: I've seen him [Roger] knock someone out for throwing pennies at him. We did a gig with Chuck Berry and there were a whole bunch of rockers there making a lot of noise because we had actually pulled the plug on Chuck Berry because he was running over time. We were contracted to play an hour and a half, and we only had an hour and five minutes left. But we kept playing until they pulled the plug on us, and this guy was throwing pennies, and Roger saw the guy throw it when one hit him on the head. So Roger just pointed to the guy, aimed, and . . . phwump!

6–8. IBC Studios, London. Townshend acts as producer on Thunderclap Newman's album *Hollywood Dream.*

16–17. IBC Studios, London. Townshend does further production work on Thunderclap Newman's album *Hollywood Dream.*

19. Mothers Club, Erdington, Birmingham.

20. Pier Ballroom, Hastings.

27. Cothams Hotel, Redcar.

28. Bay Hotel, Whitburn, Sunderland.

August 1969

2. Winter Gardens, Eastbourne.

3. Cosmopolitan Ballroom, Carlisle.

4. Pavilion, Bath.

7. Assembly Hall, Worthing.

9. The Who headline the second day of the 9th National Jazz & Blues Festival, Plumpton Racecourse, Sussex. Other acts on the bill include Chicken Shack, Fat Mattress, John Surman, Aynsley Dunbar, Yes, John Morgan, King Crimson, Groundhogs, Dry Ice, Wallace Collection.

12. Tanglewood Music Shed, Lenox, Massachusetts, supporting Jefferson Airplane.

John Morris (production co-ordinator, Woodstock): I booked a lot with [Frank Barsalona's] Premier Talent, because I knew them very well. And we needed one more key act. To get The Who for Woodstock, Frank and I had Peter Townshend to dinner at Frank Barsalona's house. Frank's an insomniac, and I was pretty good at staying awake in those days because I was almost as much of an insomniac. And we wore Peter down to the point where he agreed to do it. Finally. This is after him saying for hours and hours and hours, "No, no, no, I'm not going to do it, I'm not going to do it." Because they didn't want to stay in the US that long. They wanted to get back to their families. Or he wanted to. And Frank and I finally wore him to the nubbin that he was at that point. He was sitting in a corner and finally he said, "OK, all right. But it will have to be fifteen thousand."

And I had to look him straight in the face at six o'clock in the morning and say, "We only have $11,000 left. That's all that's left in the budget." And I thought he was going to kill me, but he was just too tired. He just said, "Oh, all right, if you let me go to bed. Whatever you say."

17. The third day of the Woodstock Festival features Iron Butterfly, The Moody Blues, Johnny Winter, The Band, Jeff Beck Group, Blood, Sweat & Tears, Joe Cocker, Crosby, Stills & Nash, The Who, Jimi Hendrix.

Pete Townshend: I was nervous because we didn't go there by helicopter. We went by road. We got as far as the car could go in the mud and it got stuck. It became the hundred and ninety-fifth limo to get stuck. We got out and landed in mud and that was it. There was nowhere to go. There were no dressing rooms because they had all been turned into hospitals. There was nowhere to eat. Somebody came out of the canteen, which was where we had been naturally gravitating towards in order to sit down and eat because we were told that we wouldn't be on for 15 hours.

To get us there in the first place, the production assistant in the limo had told us we were on in 15 minutes. Then when we got there, they said, "Oh, sorry. We meant fifteen hours." As we were going towards the canteen, somebody came out saying that the tea and coffee had got acid in them and all the water was polluted with acid. I spent a bit of time on the stage but everybody was very freaked. I would find a nice place to sit and listen to somebody like Jefferson Airplane and then some lunatic would come up to me like Abbie Hoffman or some stagehand and go, "Ahhhhhhh! Aaaaaaah! Buuuuuuuupw!"

It was very, very frightening. Somebody else would come up to me and go, "Isn't this just fantastic! Isn't it wonderful!" They would go over the hump of their cheap acid and into dreamland. People kept talking about America. It was most unfortunate. They kept talking about the American Dream and the New Albion. All kind of hippie-esque stuff was coming out and I kept thinking to myself, "This can't be true. This can't be what's happening to America. We're just arriving here. We're just about to break big and the whole thing's turning into raspberry Jell-O. I don't believe it."

Roger Daltrey: Everybody was spiked, and we were there for like 10 hours before we went on stage and you had to drink something in 10 hours.

John Entwistle: I had my own bottle of bourbon, my own bottle of Grandad, and I walked around the audience and I met this friend of mine who was at this big tent that was pitched up and I went in there and had the bourbon and he had some Coca-Cola. Poured one out and I drank it and went, "This is great, where'd you get the ice?" And he said, "Oh we stole it from backstage." And I went, "Aw, fuck!" And that's what the acid was in. I felt an acid trip coming on so I went back to the dressing room, drank the rest of the bourbon, and passed out. When I came around I was almost okay.

Joel Rosenman (co-producer, Woodstock): The Grateful Dead and The Who spring to mind as acts who were just not going to play unless they were paid in cash.

Bill Belmont (artist co-ordinator, Woodstock): A few of them had curious requests. The Who always got paid in cash in $100 bills before the first foot hit the stage.

Roger Daltrey: The only reason it was a miserable experience as far as I was concerned was, to be honest, being an artist you always want to give your best. By the time we got on the stage we were in no condition whatsoever to play a show.

Henry Diltz (photographer): On Saturday, The Who was absolutely fantastic. Just Roger Daltrey up there with his cape flying around, the fringe of his cape flapping in the wind, and he'd twirl that microphone around. He really had that down, where he'd twirl it around and just miss the floor and it would come arcing through the air and he'd grab it just in time to get into "Talking 'bout my generation."

Michael Lang (co-producer, Woodstock): The Who was the high point of the day for me. And I was sitting with [political activist] Abbie Hoffman on stage, watching The Who . . . I think he had taken a little too much acid.

John Morris (production co-ordinator, Woodstock): He decided in the middle of The Who set that he had to tell the world about [anarchist revolutionary] John Sinclair being held prisoner in Wisconsin or Michigan or wherever he was, and free him.

Roger Daltrey: In the middle of my singing *Tommy*, Abbie Hoffman came up on stage and started doing this big political speech about John Sinclair. Pete just kicked him up the arse, kicked him off the stage, I think quite rightly. If you want to make political speeches, go to a political rally or do it in between the bands, don't do it while the band's on stage. We've got our agenda.

John Morris: He came up from behind Townshend and Townshend didn't know who the hell he was, and Townshend laid him one upside the head with a guitar and Abbie went off the front of the stage and just kept going till he got to New York City.

Pete Townshend: Abbie Hoffman said on the stage of Woodstock that John Sinclair was in jail for one lousy joint, and I kicked him off the stage. I deeply regret that. If I was given the opportunity again, I would stop the show. Because I don't think rock'n'roll is that important. Then I did. The show had to go on.

Henry Diltz: I remember seeing all that happen. It was electrifying. I was very close, maybe 20 feet, something like that. It was almost like a ringing in my ears. I remember it as quite an intense moment and I remember being very shocked by this. And then things just kept on going and the show went on. The Who went on and nothing happened and no one said a word and it just passed. The Who went on and played this great show.

Bill Graham: The Who were brilliant.

Roger Daltrey: It was the worst performance we ever did.

Pete Townshend: All these hippies wandering about, thinking the world was going to be different from that day on. As a cynical English arsehole, I wandered through it all and felt like spitting on the lot of them and shaking them, trying to make them realize that nothing had changed and nothing was going to change. Not only that, what they thought was an alternative society was basically a field full of six-foot-deep mud laced with LSD. If that was the world they wanted to live in, then fuck the lot of them.

Roger Daltrey: But let's be honest. Woodstock did our career an immense amount of good. And the fact that the sun came up on the "See Me, Feel Me" bit was extraordinary. It really was like a gift from God.

18. *Tommy* is certified as a gold album in the US.

22. Music Hall, Shrewsbury.

Pete Townshend: Just after Woodstock, The Who had a big revival of interest in *Tommy*. A lot of people used to come and see us and in Britain it was, "You are our favourite group with Deep Purple," and I used to go, "Huh?" And over here it used to be, "You are our favourite group with Ten Years After." And both groups I hate! I admit that all the people in the bands are very good friends of mine but I hated their music. And it was very hard to live with in a way that we were being lumped in with these very heavy metal bands. I think it was because Richie Blackmore used to sort of bash his guitar on his head and smoke a cigarette through his teeth and play a mouth organ back to front. And of course with The Who it was smashing up, pyrotechnics, and with Ten Years After it was that backwards-tape Chinese guitar playing.

23. Festival Marquee, Grays, Essex. Single "I'm Free" peaks at No. 37 in the US on its week of entry.

29. Pavilion, Bournemouth.

31. Isle of Wight Festival. Bob Dylan is the headliner.

Rikki Farr (promoter): The first significant Isle of Wight was 1969 with Dylan and The Who. The PA system was 2,000 watts, huge for the time, so as well as being heard by the audience, the music was clearly audible to the inmates of Parkhurst jail and the monks in Quarr monastery, who hadn't heard live music since the Second World War.

Pete Townshend: Our manager hired a nice helicopter for us to ride in, and when it landed, it did something terrible to its rear end. My faith in the aeronautic world rapidly dwindled.

September 1969

6. Kinema Ballroom, Dunfermline, Scotland.

7. Cosmopolitan Club, Carlisle.

13. The Belfry, Sutton Coldfield.

John Woffinden (audience): The Herd were on the same bill . . . and when they'd finished my mate and I decided to go for a walk and get some fresh air. We stepped outside and were run into by Keith Moon. The Who were coming straight back on, and we finished up next to Pete's speaker stack. Deafened for a week but a great view.

21. Fairfield Halls, Croydon.

Tony Smith (concert promoter): The first really major thing I did in the rock scene was *Tommy.* I'd heard the album, which completely blew me away, and I went to Kit Lambert and suggested they did it all in one evening. We chose the Fairfield Hall in Croydon and used colour slides and lights for the first time.

It was such a success, the first time The Who had done the concert straight through all on their own. It lasted two hours with no interval and everybody was really wary at first because they didn't know what was going to happen.

Elton John (diary entry): Going to see The Who at Croydon – took Catherine – they were excellent.

Pete Townshend: The best [*Tommy*] performance of all was at Croydon, Fairfield Hall. It was the first time we played it including "Sally Simpson" and a few other things we did specially. The sound in that place – oh, Croydon, I could bloody play there all night . . . It is just a good acoustic.

Alan Lewis (*Melody Maker*): The Who are now the band against which the rest of rock must be judged . . . a shattering tour-de-force. It was exciting, moving, frightening – and musically brilliant.

27. German TV show "Beat Club" devoted to The Who.

29. Concertgebouw, Amsterdam, Netherlands.

October 1969

5. Taping an appearance on UK TV show "This Is Tom Jones" at ATV Studios, Elstree, UK.

10. US tour kicks off at Commonwealth Armory, Boston, Massachusetts.

11. Grande Ballroom, Dearborn, Michigan.

14. CNE Coliseum, Toronto, Ontario, Canada.

15. Capitol Theatre, Ottawa, Ontario, Canada.

17. Holy Cross College Gymnasium, Worcester, Massachusetts.

18. State University of New York Gymnasium, Stonybrook, New York.

19. Electric Factory, Philadelphia, Pennsylvania.

20–25. Six nights at the Fillmore East, New York.

26. Syria Mosque, Pittsburgh, Pennsylvania, supported by The James Gang.

27. Townshend flies to Florida for a four-day break.

31. Kinetic Playground, Chicago, Illinois, supported by The Kinks and Liverpool Scene.

Pete Townshend: In the old days, we used to dream about opening for The Kinks.

November 1969

1. Veterans Memorial Auditorium, Columbus, Ohio. Townshend's song "Put The Money Down" was inspired by this gig.

2. McDonough Gymnasium, Georgetown University, Washington, DC.

3. Westchester County Center, White Plains, New York.

4. Bushnell Auditorium, Hartford, Connecticut.

6. Raccoon Creek Rock Festival, Livingstone Gymnasium, Denison University,

Granville, Ohio.
7. State University, Athens, Ohio.
8. Keil Opera House, St Louis, Missouri.
10. Palace Theatre, Albany, New York.
11-12. Boston Tea Party, Boston, Massachusetts.
13. State University Gymnasium, New Paltz, New York.
14. Public Music Hall, Cleveland, Ohio.
15. Kleinhans Music Hall, Buffalo, New York.
16. War Memorial Auditorium, Syracuse, New York.

December 1969
4. Hippodrome, Bristol.
5. The Palace, Manchester.
9-11. Three-day visit to Paris, France, for TV promotion.
12. Empire Theatre, Liverpool.
14. *Tommy* is performed at the Coliseum, Covent Garden, London.
15. Keith Moon joins in on drums when John Lennon's Plastic Ono Band makes its UK debut at the Lyceum, London.

Roger St Pierre (PR man): When promoting Black Velvet's "Peace And Love Is The Message" at Christmas 1969 with a charity concert in aid of UNICEF at London's Lyceum, we sat in the office one dark, dank evening, wondering who we could get to top the bill. The Beatles had just broken up and, tongue in cheek, someone suggested we ask one of them, as they weren't doing anything.

"Good idea," I responded, and next morning we rang Mike Berry at Apple. "I'll find out and let you know," he replied. We put the phone down and forgot about it until the next day when the phone rang and a scouse accent inquired, "If I do it, can I bring some of my friends along?" The caller was John Lennon, the friends were Yoko Ono, Eric Clapton, Klaus Voorman, Keith Moon, Billy Preston, Delaney & Bonnie and Alan White of Yes.

Alan White (drummer): I think contractually, he'd got himself into a position where he had to do it and he said, "Let's round the boys up." I went down there in my little Mini and went on stage at the Lyceum. Just prior to the Plastic Ono Band going on stage, up turns Eric Clapton with the whole Delaney & Bonnie band, so we had to hustle another couple of drum kits. Then Keith Moon joins me on stage playing my big 16-inch tom-tom. It was a thing where somebody would hit one chord and it was a jam forever. Through experience of the previous jams I'd been in, when we'd already been playing the song for over half an hour, the best way of getting out is just to speed the number up until nobody can play the thing any more. So I just gradually started picking the tempo up and up and up.

19. City Hall, Newcastle.

31. BBC TV Centre, London. The Who open a 75-minute TV special, "Pop Go The Sixties", also featuring The Rolling Stones, Dusty Springfield, Sandie Shaw, Lulu, The Hollies, The Kinks, The Tremeloes, Cilla Black, Helen Shapiro, Adam Faith and others.

1970

January 1970

4. After Keith Moon opens a disco in Hatfield, his chauffeur, Neil Boland, is run over and killed.

"Legs" Larry Smith (friend of Keith Moon): Keith and I had gone to quite a large pub and discotheque in North London, in the suburbs really. Not particularly wonderful, but Keith always accepted invitations. It was about half past ten and this place was going to close about eleven, and things started to get a bit crazy. Keith was looping about with the boys, but I had an odd sense of the evening, I felt we should get the hell out and beat closing time, but Keith said, "No, no, dear boy, I'm going to have another dance." And he waltzed out into the crowd again.

Ten minutes later, Keith and eight thousand people came tumbling out of the pub, the driver Neil behind him, and suddenly all the rabble realized that they were going to have to wait in a bus queue for 20 minutes, and we were going to go gliding in the comfort of a pink Rolls Royce [actually a Bentley]. They snapped, started emptying their pockets, and we were being rained upon by small change. Because Neil was so proud of the Bentley, he got out and started to run at them, which was even crazier. Neil had put the car in drive, and it was crawling forward. Suddenly, we found ourselves rolling toward the main road with no one driving the damn thing. Keith slid over to the driver's seat, not being able to drive, of course – Keith couldn't do things like that.

At this point, people had surrounded the car and were raining down fists, kicking, smashing the windows. Neil was out having a bash with them. I leaned up over the back seat, put my arms over Keith, and started to steer. People were screaming, getting hysterical. When we turned on to the main street, Neil was running alongside the car, still fending off these attackers, and he must have tripped and fallen under the car, so we actually must have run over Neil.

The car rolled on and on, and Keith finally stopped it somehow. We didn't feel anything, we were carrying right on, we didn't know that Neil's body must have been in the middle of the road.

The police came, the reporters came, we were holed up in Keith's house for two weeks not answering the phone.

16–17. European tour begins with two nights at the Champs Elysées Theatre, Paris, France.

26. Stadt Opera House, Cologne, Germany.

27. Stadt Opera House, Hamburg, Germany.

28. Deutschland Stadt Opera House, Berlin, Germany.

30. Concertgebouw, Amsterdam, Netherlands.

February 1970

14. A live concert at the Refectory, Leeds University is recorded for future release as an album.

Pete Townshend: We recorded all the shows on the American tour thinking that would be where we would get the best material. When we got back we had 80 hours of tape and, well, we couldn't sort that lot out, so we booked the Pye mobile studio and took it to Leeds.

Chris McCourt (photographer): I was booked into the same hotels as the band, two nights, Leeds, then Hull. Terrified, crapping myself really. My image of them was of these loonies with a reputation for smashing up hotels, but they seemed to be trying to be more serious. Pete said they were frightened by the kids at the front, fighting, the mods. You wouldn't imagine they had a conscience. He seemed really considerate and intelligent, nothing like the lout I imagined. Entwistle was never around – permanently asleep, apparently. Daltrey was very preoccupied with the sound and practising flinging his mike at the soundcheck. Interesting to photograph, actually, because of his American Indian suede fringe jacket thing with the tassles, plenty of movement.

Kit Lambert made various provisos which made it really difficult. You're not allowed on stage, so I had to photograph from the pit, you know, up their nostrils. You've got to get all four in each picture – again impossible. Photos backstage were completely off the menu. You can't use flash.

Patrick Dean (reviewer, *Yorkshire Evening Post*):

Students packed the refectory to see and hear The Who roar through over two hours of the best music I have heard . . .

Bob Pridden (concert recording engineer): It was a bloody great gig. They were being serious about recording, and I think they got the nervousness over recording out in the States so that it made no difference to them at all.

Pete Townshend: It just happened to be a good show, and it just happened to be one of the greatest audiences we've ever played to in our whole career, just by chance. They were incredible, and although you can't hear a lot of the kind of shouting and screaming in the background, they're civilized but they're crazy.

Bob Pridden: The leakage is terrible, but when it all comes together, it's like the teeth of a comb. Bear in mind, they were very loud, and there were real problems with separation – but it made them sound bigger. It breathed. If you set a mic in front of an amp, it doesn't sound like that. Basically, the sound on Leeds is a freak.

15. City Hall, Hull.

Chris McCourt: Townshend asked me to sit with him at Sunday lunchtime. I was pretty scared, to be honest. He talked about how they'd stopped smashing their guitars on stage, and how he was now into white jumpsuit leaping mode, and I asked him how he managed to jump so high.

March 1970

21. "The Seeker" is released as a single in the UK.

John Entwistle: I never liked that song. I hated playing it on stage. It's very . . . "The Seeker" and "Relay" are two of my least favourite songs. They rely entirely on feel, which is awkward. I don't think we ever got the feel on record or on stage. It was there on the demos. They should have stayed demos. I didn't like them as songs, and I was never sure what Pete was trying to do on them.

Roger Daltrey: I've always found it a bit ploddy. It's a real late sixties rhythm. I don't like it that much.

Pete Townshend: Daltrey often sang songs I'd written that he didn't care for with complete commitment, and I took him for granted. I said what I wanted to say, often ignoring or being terribly patronizing about the rest of the group's suggestions, then sulked when they didn't worship me for making life financially viable.

April 1970

While Eric Clapton is recording at Olympic Studios, Barnes, London, he and Pete Townshend renew their friendship.

Pete Townshend: It was strange. He obviously had some cash-flow problem, because he was selling guitars. Actually selling guitars to people who would buy them. Then I heard why, from Bob Pridden, The Who's senior sound man, whose wife went to school with [Clapton's girlfriend] Alice Ormsby-Gore.

Bob said Eric had a drug problem. That's why he was selling guitars, to raise ready cash to buy dope.

4. "The Seeker" enters the UK singles chart.

13. Working at IBC Studios, London on "Heaven And Hell", "Substitute", "Pinball Wizard", "Shakin' All Over"/"Spoonful", "I'm Free", "The Seeker".

John Entwistle: I basically wanted to write a song with a big subject, an important subject rather than spiders or drunks. The original version of "Heaven And Hell" had a different chorus. It was basically I'd much rather stay in the middle with my friends because I don't like the sound of either of them. I still don't. I don't fancy hell or heaven. I said before maybe there is an in-between place.

18. Leicester University, Leicester.

25. Nottingham University.

27. Civic Hall, Dunstable.

May 1970

1. Great Hall, Exeter University.

2. Sheffield University.

8. Liverpool University.

9. Manchester University.

15. Lancaster University.

16. "The Seeker" peaks at No. 19 in the UK on the same day that the album *Live At Leeds* is released in the US.

23. "The Seeker" peaks at No. 44 in the US on the same day that *Live At Leeds* is released in the UK.

June 1970

1. The *Woodstock* triple album is released in the UK, featuring live tracks ecorded by The Who and other artists at the festival.

6. *Live at Leeds* enters the UK album chart, where it will peak at No. 3. On the same day, it enters the US chart, where it will peak at No. 4.

Roger Daltrey: *Live at Leeds* is the end of a two-and-three-quarter-hour show. It's just the jamming bit at the end [laughs]. The whole rest of the show is hardly there.

Pete Townshend: There was some nice stuff [guitar playing] there. I don't know what possessed me to actually start to play like that. I suppose it just must have been the influence of Hendrix. Because up to that point I just wasn't interested in single-note work. It seemed mad for me to even try to compete with the likes of Beck and Clapton and Jimmy Page. I first saw Jimmy Page when I was 14 or 15 and he was already in a professional band. He was one year older than me and he was in a professional band at 16 and he was earning £30 a week when I was just still in school. He was playing really fast stuff and Richie Blackmore was in a heavy pop band like a Ventures-type outfit. You would just listen to records like that open-mouthed at the time. But at one particular time after Hendrix I decided it was worth trying to express myself through single-note work.

John Entwistle: On *Live at Leeds* we were shit-hot. We'd done a whole bunch of touring, and we were extremely confident and our sound was perfected and everything was real smooth – we could do a great show every time.

7. *Tommy* is performed at the Metropolitan Opera House, New York.

Peter Rudge (Who staffer): It was 1970. The Who had just made *Tommy.* Kit Lambert, another great genius, another of my true idols, sent me over to New York for reasons known only to himself. He said, "The Who have made this rock opera. Go there and find somewhere for The Who to play. Why don't you get the Metropolitan Opera House?"

So I walked into the Metropolitan Opera House. Sir Rudolf Bing, a countryman of mine, was there. For some reason, I got an appointment with him. It may have been the beginning of him completely flipping but, to cut a long story short, he agreed to let us have the hall.

Bill [Graham] sensed something historic was about to take place. He said, "You need the Fillmore East family." Right? You need.

I went for it. I said, "Nice touch." The Who at the Met with the Fillmore East. Everyone was happy. Only Bill wanted his name in bigger letters than anyone else on the poster. Basically, Bill did it because he wanted to help. Not for money.

Pete Townshend: It seemed to me to be a very mature and sensible gesture that we and our fans should be invited to a place like the Met. It's a wonderful notion, the idea of a snotty pop group playing opera houses. But we actually did it . . . We shit in their toilet.

Binky Philips: It was the best show I had ever seen. Pete came out there and showed everyone he didn't give a shit for the opera. They were so violent and vicious. They sounded like the old Who.

Pete Townshend: The Met had that feeling of being full of dead ideas, dead people, and too much fucking reverence.

Binky Philips: That was the night I caught Townshend's guitar which was the culmination of everything for me. I went to the concert with a girl I had been infatuated with for years. Townshend walked to the tip of the stage with his busted guitar and looked at me as if to say "Are you ready?" I stood up and all my friends stood back. They all wanted the guitar as badly as I did but they stepped back. It was like a Joe Namath pass over the 30-foot orchestra pit. It just fell right into me. I was looking at Townshend as he walked off stage and he was dragging the guitar by the strings like he was walking a dog.

Roger Daltrey: It was just another gig to me. That was how I used to feel about everything. I never used to be impressed with any of that shit. It's a hole with a stage! So it had chandeliers, so what!

Keith Moon: It was rather like playing to an oil painting.

15-16. *Tommy* is performed for two nights at the Berkeley Community Theater, Berkeley, California.

Pete Townshend: The show at Berkeley was the best we did in the States on that tour. The sound was great, if a little loud for such a small place, and the crowd just super-aware and alive. I could smell a lot of dope, but I think a good many people are beginning to realize that it is a bit of a risk getting high to watch The Who. Keith Moon might do something terrible . . .

Peter Rudge: We played in the Berkeley Community Theater with the Jefferson Airplane sitting in the fourth row. It was Bill Graham's idea to put these big spotlights behind The Who and shine them into the house. We paid for it but it was Bill's idea and The Who took it with them when they left.

Pete Townshend: Bill did that thing with the Super Troopers for *Tommy* when we played for him in the Berkeley Community Theater. Fucking great sounding hall. It's very interesting from my point of view. I remember three details of that evening. One of which was that backstage, I got my fresh supply of Dr Wong Tea. Bill got one of his guys to pick it up for me. 'Cause I used to get the concentrate which was never as good as the straight stuff from Dr Wong. It was an herbal remedy. Dr Wong had more Mercedes than I'll ever own. He was a rich man. The stuff cost $200 a month and he had half of the San Francisco Sufi movement drinking this tea. Powerful stuff. Extraordinary stuff. Among other things, it had ginseng in it.

The second thing was that I remember that somehow Bill had sorted out all the important people. I had left no list at all on the back gate. Absolutely true. Nothing. And he had let in all the people that I wanted to see and none of the people that I didn't want to see.

The third thing was that he had two dressing rooms. That was quite unique at the time. It was the first hospitality room I had ever come across outside of a festival. In which there were fondues. There was a meat fondue and a cheese one. What's great before you go on to give a concert is to have some very quick-acting protein. Raw steak or pasta is good and they were both there. These three details were more important to me than when we went out and suddenly the curtain rose and there was 4,000 watts of light on the band. Of course, we picked up that technique and we've used it ever since.

20. After a show at Hofheinz Pavilion, University of Houston, Texas, John Entwistle is inspired to write a song.

John Entwistle: On "What Are We Doing Here" the words were written in the States, they're very homesick words. We were stuck in Houston, Texas, the television had finished, there was no booze, we'd done a terrible show and I'd been away for four weeks and was starting to get a bit homesick so I wrote those words. I wrote part of the tune when I got back, then I finally finished it when we were actually recording the album.

22. The Who board an Eastern Airlines flight from Memphis to Atlanta, where they will play in the Municipal Auditorium.

John Entwistle: We were waiting to take off for a long time. The pilot had switched on the intercom to announce the delay, then had left it on and you could hear him whistling for 45 minutes. We were really drunk and the whistling was driving us crazy so, all of a sudden, Townshend jumps up and shouts "All right, all right, I'll tell you where the bomb is." The stewardess overheard him and the plane was delayed. They took us out, searched all our luggage, and detained him for questioning.

July 1970

1. US tour continues at the Auditorium Theatre, Chicago, Illinois.

4. The movie of the Woodstock festival is premiered.

Roger Daltrey: I think *Woodstock* was groundbreaking, because I think *Woodstock* really captured the whole event. What I get from *Woodstock*, maybe because I was one of the people on the stage, and obviously one of the main reasons that film put bums on seats, is that the message of the film is that the star of the show was the whole Woodstock community. All the bands were just a catalyst. The Who got very good press from it.

Unfortunately, with the passage of time, people kind of reflect on Woodstock now and just think it was the bands that made Woodstock great. They forget that it wasn't that at all. It was the Woodstock community that made Woodstock the great event that it was.

I must say when I did see what they had done with our performance, with the split screen, I just thought it was mesmeric. It was hypnotic. It was wonderful.

10. Release of a new single, a cover of Eddie Cochran's "Summertime Blues", in the UK, backed with "Heaven And Hell".

John Entwistle: I got the idea [for "Heaven And Hell"] from listening to "Tubby The Tuba", and somehow the Tubby tune ended up as the beginning of "Heaven And Hell". It was one of those songs that was more popular on stage; it never got on to an LP. I remember bringing along the demo I'd made of the song and the band particularly liked the chord sequence. It was probably the first time that that chord sequence had been played in rock, and it was great to jam to. It was a good song to tune up to as well, a lot of open strings, which is why we always started the act with it. A lot of Who fans will remember that as the opening song of our set. Well, that's partly why we used to play it first, to tune up.

11. "Summertime Blues" is released in the US.

25. Civic Hall, Dunstable.

August 1970

1. "Summertime Blues" enters the US Top 40 singles chart.
6. *Live At Leeds* is certified a gold album in the US.
8. "Summertime Blues" enters the UK singles chart.
15. "Summertime Blues" peaks at No. 38 in the UK and No. 27 in the US.
24. Civic Hall, Wolverhampton.
30. Isle Of Wight Festival, East Afton Farm, Isle Of Wight.

Nick Richards (audience): I couldn't really say there was a lot of trouble there. There was one stage when a couple of rockers or Angels decided they had had enough of being shut out of the arena. I think some of them were French. They attacked the steel fences with pickaxe handles, chains, you name it. Broke their way through the first and second fences. Security guards and dogs just scattered because there were so many. It was quite violent although I don't think anyone actually got hurt. From then on it was free for all.

Pete Townshend: Hendrix was a psychological mess of a man. Nobody cared. People thought, "He can play such great guitar, so he's obviously okay." What made me work so hard was seeing the condition Jimi was in. He was in such tragically bad condition physically, and I remember thanking God as I walked on stage that I was healthy.

September 1970

12. European tour begins at the Munsterlundhalle, Munster, Germany.
13. Orberrheinhalle, Offenbach, Germany.
16. De Doehen Halle, Rotterdam, Netherlands.
17. Concertgebouw, Amsterdam, Netherlands.
18. De Doehen Halle, Rotterdam, Netherlands.
20. Falkoner Center, Copenhagen, Denmark.
21. Vejlby Rissov Hallen, Aarhus, Denmark.

October 1970

6. UK tour begins at Sophia Gardens, Cardiff, Wales.

Pete Townshend: The crowd were incredible. It was the first airing of the now shortened *Tommy* in Wales, and we enjoyed the show as much as we have ever. We have deliberately cut down our act to leave us more energy to cope with the important part of the show – the finale. It doesn't matter how well you play, if you don't leave on the right foot you may as well not bother.

Neil Hughes (reviewer, *South Wales Echo*):

Daltrey cavorted about on stage, swinging his mike through the air like a lasso, and even doing something resembling a backward roll across the stage into an amplifier . . . Townshend provided choreographic balance to Daltrey's gymnastics, performing little ballet-like leaps all the time while beating hell out of his guitar.

7. Free Trade Hall, Manchester.

Pete Townshend: The show went so well at the Free Trade Hall that night. The James Gang played a superb set . . . We can tell how the band before us go down by the audience response to our own opening. At Manchester, it was just as exhilarating as Cardiff to feel the wave of familiarity and warmth from the crowd as we began.

8. Orchid Ballroom, Purley.

Pete Townshend: As we walked through the audience to the stage, surrounded by bouncers, I heard elderly mods asking for "Can't Explain" and "Substitute" with such zest that I began to believe they were new releases. From the stage, however, the feeling was not one of nostalgia.

Caroline Boucher (reviewer, *Disc & Music Echo*):

They're exciting visually, exciting musically – and don't quit as soon as 45 minutes are up. The Who play for nearly an hour and a half.

10. "See Me, Feel Me" is released as a single in the UK. When The Who play that night at the University of Sussex, Brighton, they are joined on stage during "Magic Bus" by John Sebastian of The Lovin' Spoonful.

Michael Watts (reviewer, *Melody Maker*):

There are no highs or lows in their current performances – just a general level of all-round competence, which ultimately has a slightly unsatisfying feeling about it. They neither take you to the heights, or plunge you in the depths, of emotional strata . . . It was hot stuff, but they never got it on properly.

17. "See Me, Feel Me" enters the US Top 40 singles chart.

23. The Who play at Green's Playhouse, Glasgow.

Steven Lyall (fan): Apart from it being a generally outstanding show, I remember two things in particular. The first was perhaps 20 or so Glasgow policemen marching in to line the stage just as "Listening To You" was getting under way at the end of the *Tommy* set. This was probably because the 3,000-

strong crowd were all going bananas at the time. Far from being in any way threatening, the effect of seeing the uniforms between us and the stage just added to the excitement and overall dramatic effect of the music, the mic swinging, the sweeping searchlights, etc.

The second exceptional thing I remember was that the crowd simply wouldn't stop at the apparent end of the show. The band had been off stage for a while, the house lights were up and the road crew had even removed the HiWatt amps. The applause, stamping and whistling remained as intense as ever. Finally, and I don't recall anything like it at any of their subsequent shows, the roadies actually wheeled the amps back on and reconnected them. On came the band, the lights went down and an explosive "Twist'n'Shout" was the crowd's reward for their persistence.

27. Hammersmith Palais, London.

Chris Charlesworth (reviewer, *Melody Maker*): I gave them a great write-up after the show I saw at Dunstable . . . Much to my surprise Keith rang me up a week later to thank me . . . Keith said the next time The Who played in London, I could be his guest at the show so we went to the Hammersmith Palais together in his lilac Rolls-Royce.

The Palais was absolutely heaving and what today would be called a mosh-pit had assembled on the ballroom floor at the front of the stage. It was another great show and, at the end, Pete threw his guitar high into the air, almost hitting the lighting rig. It broke into two parts and he threw them into the crowd. There was a fight over them. Someone had hold of the body and someone the neck, but the strings held them together. It was very frightening.

November 1970

7. An EP version of *Tommy* is released in the UK. On the same day, an album of John Entwistle's songs for The Who is released as *Backtrack 14 – The Ox.*

John Entwistle: Ah, he's a miserable bastard, John Entwistle. I always wore black clothes, and I was supposed to be, like, the strong, silent bass player. When I was writing songs, I started off writing . . . sort of horror stories, horror songs for children . . . I've always found it very difficult to write love songs. To be that cliché all the time.

21. Leeds University.

28. "See Me, Feel Me" peaks at No. 12 in the US singles chart as the band play a disastrous gig at Lanchester Polytechnic, Coventry.

Pete Townshend: We never got an encore. It was pretty bad and when it was over, we just sat in the dressing room. It was the first bad gig for at least a year.

December 1970

Townshend is working on demos for a new project, *Lifehouse*, at Eel Pie Studios, London.

Pete Townshend: I wrote a story called "The Lifehouse", which explored the Sufic notion that all life and all nature – especially anything expressed, received, or imparted – is based on harmony or disharmony of a very physical variety. In other words, if you are in harmony with the people around you, and in harmony with life, your body has become more attuned to certain rhythms and frequencies. And when you attain higher levels of spiritual equipoise through meditation, biofeedback, or other methods, what you are really doing is exposing yourself to elevated and hopefully longer-lasting rhythms and frequencies of brainwaves, breathing, heartbeat, pulse rate, and so on.

While I was working on the *Lifehouse* script I actually did a lot of experiments with sounds that were produced from natural body rhythms. I was working with the musical bursar of Cambridge University at the time. What we did was ask some individuals a lot of questions about themselves and then subject them to the sort of test a GP might undertake. We measured their heartbeat and the alpha and beta rhythms of the brain; we even took down astrological details and other kinds of shit. Then we took all the data we'd collected on paper or charts and converted them into music, and the end result was sometimes quite amazing. In fact, one of the pulse-modulated frequencies we generated was eventually used as the background beat to "Won't Get Fooled Again". Later I used another one of these pulse-modulated frequencies as the foundation for "Baba O'Riley".

15. Fillmore North, Mayfair Ballroom, Newcastle.

Pete Townshend: We walked off, and I couldn't remember who I was – I swear it. I wandered out into the audience. I didn't go back into the dressing room, and I got into a fight. Somebody started making remarks and I didn't know what they were talking about and I got into a fight with this guy and he started to beat the living daylights out of me, and I sort of came to get up, and I started to do lots of showy things, pieced myself together again, went back to the dressing room and got a drink. And then I drove all the way home at 120 miles per hour. And, by the time I got home I was me again. It was an amazing thing.

16. The Futurist Theatre, Scarborough.

20. The Who and Elton John play at The Roundhouse, Chalk Farm, London.

30. The Who appear on a "Top Of The Pops" New Year special edition.

Keith Moon: I broke me collarbone once. That was in me own 'otel, the one I own, one Christmas. I collapsed in front of the fire at four o'clock one morning and some friends of mine decided to put me to bed, and they were in as bad a state as I was, but they were still on their feet. Just about. One of them got 'old of me 'ead, the other got 'old of me feet and they attempted to drag me up the stairs.

They got me up two flights and then promptly dropped me down both of them, breaking me collarbone, y'see. But I didn't know this until I woke up in the morning and tried to put me fucking shirt on. I went through the fucking roof.

Now . . . I was supposed to do a television show, the "Top Of The Pops" New Year's Eve special, and two days before I 'ave me arm all strapped up so I can't drum. I went to me doctor, dear Dr Robert, and he gave me a shot on the day of the gig so I wouldn't feel anything. I put a shirt over the cast, fastened the drumstick to my wrist with sticking plaster, sat down behind the drum kit, and got Mr Vivian Stanshall to tie a rope around me wrist. We then threw the rope over the lighting pipe overhead, the one that holds the floods and all, and I kept an eye on the television monitor; every time I was on camera, I'd give the signal to Viv, and he'd give a pull on the rope, which caused me right arm to shoot up and then come crashing down on the cymbal. AH-HAHAHAHAHAHAHA!

These farcical situations . . . I'm always tied up in them. They're always as if they could be a Laurel and Hardy sketch. And they always 'appen to me. AH-HAHAHAHAHAHA! I think unconsciously I want them to 'appen, and they do.

I suppose to most people I'm probably seen as an amiable idiot . . . a genial twit. I think I must be a victim of circumstance, really. Most of it's me own doing. I'm a victim of me own practical jokes. I suppose that reflects a rather selfish attitude. I like to be the recipient of me own doings. Nine times out of ten I am. I set traps and fall into them. OH-HAHAHAHAHAHA! Of course the biggest danger is becoming a parody.

1971

January 1971

4. Young Vic Theatre, Waterloo, London.

13. Townshend reveals his plans for the *Lifehouse* project to a specially invited audience at the Young Vic Theatre, Waterloo, London.

Pete Townshend: It was terrible. I suddenly realized that all these smart journalists thought I was completely mad. I was so relieved that the guys from the band weren't there. They were very supportive about Lifehouse, but they didn't quite understand what I was going on about and . . . I suppose it was a bit art school.

John Entwistle: Originally [*Who's Next*] was going to be called *Lifehouse* and incorporate film footage. Basically the project centred around The Who living with its audience. We did a couple of experimental things down at the Young Vic and then the whole thing fell through.

Pete Townshend: The idea was to perform the songs over a period of two weeks. We were going to have an open-door policy. The band was gonna do this long, long concert with the doors open all the time.

Frank Dunlop (director, Young Vic): We threw the doors open and let anyone come who wanted to. Even the police came and wanted to dance to the music.

John Entwistle: We actually sort of tried inviting an audience in off the street at the Young Vic a couple of times and it just didn't work. We figured if that didn't work, I don't think *Lifehouse* is going to work. The whole idea of living with the audience; we were wondering if we would be allowed home at night to visit our wives.

Pete Townshend: *Lifehouse* started with my feeling that stadium rock was going to kill us all. Because I knew as an artist that I was completely powerless. I couldn't stop The Who performing in football stadiums, and I absolutely hated it.

February 1971

1. Frank Zappa begins filming his movie, *200 Motels*, at Pinewood Studios, London. Keith Moon shows up during the week, and is cast as a nun.

14-15. Two shows at the Young Vic Theatre, London, are filmed for a proposed movie of The Who in concert.

Pete Townshend: "Baba O'Riley" was originally 30 minutes long and the way you hear it now is all the high points just shoved together. [It] was a number I wrote while I was doing these experiments with tapes on the synthesizer. Among my plans for the concert at the Young Vic was to take a person out of the audience and feed information – height, weight, astrological details, beliefs and behaviour etc. – about that person into the synthesizer. The synthesizer would then select notes from the pattern of that person. It would be like translating a person into music. On this particular track, I programmed details about the life of Meher Baba, and that provides the backing for the number.

Roger Daltrey: The fucking synthesizer used to drive me fucking nuts!

John Entwistle: When we started, *Lifehouse* was to be a double album. Half of it ended up on [*Who's Next*] and another four tracks are on *Odds'n'Sods.*

Roger Daltrey: The whole problem with *Lifehouse* was that the concept was too ethereal. Music-wise it was some of the best songs Pete's ever written. But the narrative, again, wasn't very strong. We would have needed another three years working on it before recording it to make it complete.

22. Another open-door concert at the Young Vic, London.

Pete Townshend: All we got were freaks and 13-year-old skinheads. If we had advertised the thing as a Who concert, we could have packed the place for a year. But we were just opening the doors and playing, waiting to see who came in.

March 1971

With Universal having picked up the *Lifehouse* movie option for $2m, Townshend flies to New York to seek Kit Lambert's help in getting it off the ground.

Pete Townshend: I had lost [contact with] Kit Lambert somewhere in the writing of *Lifehouse.* I don't quite know what happened, but I put together the retrospective picture of him drifting into drugs and stuff, which may or may not be true. He was certainly using drugs at the time, but whether or not that is why we drifted apart, I don't know.

I thought, "Kit's going to save me, now it's going to happen." Then, as I walked up to his office door, I heard him say to Angie Butler, his secretary, "If Townshend thinks he's going to walk all over my *Tommy* project . . ." I was so naive, but it was hearing him call me "Townshend" that did it. I got a panic attack. I sat in there thinking, "He's calling me Townshend. There's nobody calling me Pete any more. I'm Townshend. I can't live like this."

I looked round, and Kit and the other people in the room became frogs. I stood up and walked towards an open window until Angie grabbed me. She said it was obvious I was going to jump out of the window . . .

. . . and then I kind of came to and looked at Kit and he looked at me. And I think from then on what actually happened was – I just gave up. I completely gave up. I now realize that that kind of surrender was a very, very valuable and useful response. I just gave up and thought, "Screw it. I'm just gonna let this go and we'll do whatever happens next." So we did that, and I just let *Lifehouse* go.

Although he was in terrible shape, he [Lambert] did actually rescue the project and help us get to the point where we created a record from it in *Who's Next*, which Glyn Johns then picked up.

16. "Won't Get Fooled Again" is recorded at Record Plant, New York, with Kit Lambert as producer, but the results are unsatisfactory.

Jack Douglas (sound engineer): There was an engineer there, Jack Adams. He was doing the Who sessions for what would be *Who's Next.* He did the R&B that came into the place and didn't like rock, no matter who the artist was. So we get the room set up and he says to me, "I hate this rock shit. I don't care about any of it."

Now, Jack lived on a houseboat on the 79th Street boat basin. So he tells me to go into the other room and call him on the phone, and say his houseboat is on fire. He was like a method actor – he needed motivation to lie. So I'm 12 feet away and I can hear him screaming, telling Kit Lambert and Pete Townshend that his boat's on fire. It's sinking in the boat basin. He tells them that I'm not the assistant but the other engineer on the session, and that I'll be doing the sessions. Up till then, I had only done some jingle dates and one record session with Patti LaBelle, during which I had set the old Datamix console on fire by knocking someone's beer on to the transformers. So I was a little nervous. Everything was set up. The first song was "Won't Get Fooled Again".

Pete Townshend: "Won't Get Fooled Again" I wrote at a time when I was getting barraged by people at the Eel Pie Island commune. They lived opposite me. There was like a love affair going on between me and them. They dug me because I was like a figurehead . . . in a group . . . and I dug them because I could see what was going on over there. At one point there was an amazing scene where the commune was really working, but then the acid started flowing and I got on the end of some psychotic conversations. And I just thought, "Oh, fuck it."

17. "Pure And Easy" and "Love Ain't For Keeping" are recorded at Record Plant, New York.
18. "Behind Blue Eyes" is recorded at Record Plant, New York.

April 1971

"Won't Get Fooled Again" is re-recorded at Stargroves, Berkshire. Glyn Johns is now in the producer's chair.

Glyn Johns: I worked with them up until "My Generation", and prior to that, we'd always been very good mates, because we knew each other from way back, when they were called The High Numbers. I used to manage this band when I was a kid, and we were on the same circuit for a while, and we used to go to watch each other play, so we knew each other well, really. Then, when I started engineering seriously, they got a deal and started making records, and I happened to be their engineer, up through "My Generation", the whole Shel Talmy period. Then they broke from Shel, and there was a court case in which I was a witness for him and, obviously as a result of that, we didn't work together for a long time. They went off and did *Tommy* and so on, and then they asked me to do *Who's Next*, which was probably five or six years after the last time I'd worked with them. They'd obviously decided they wouldn't work with Kit Lambert any more for some reason.

We went to Stargroves, which was Mick Jagger's house in the country in those days, a huge old Victorian mansion. "Won't Get Fooled Again" was one of the first things we recorded, and it had been very much a question of seeing how it went – I said, "I'll come and work with you for a week, and we'll see how we get on, and if it doesn't work out, you can have whatever we've done as a prezzy, and we'll call it quits." But it worked really well, so we carried on.

John Entwistle: I guess the time that this was recorded was the time we were happiest. We'd sorted out most of our problems by then and we were still being very creative. "Won't Get Fooled Again" was recorded at Stargroves, Mick Jagger's house. We used his hall as the studio floor and used the Stones' mobile outside. There were further overdubs at Olympic Studios. It's always been one of my favourite songs of The Who, mainly because I got a chance to mess around in the middle of it while the synthesizer's playing.

Glyn Johns: Pete came up with synthesizer basics for the tracks which were just unbelievable. Nobody had done it that way before and it was amazing to work with.

Pete Townshend: I like synthesizers because they bring into my hands things that aren't in my hands – the sound of the orchestra, French horns, strings. There are gadgets on synthesizers which enable one to become a virtuoso of the keyboard. You can play something slowly, and you press a switch and it plays it back at double speed.

Glyn Johns: Jagger had got into them and bought himself one, a vast great thing, which he never figured out how to play, so we didn't use it. But Townshend is the only musician I've met before or since who really knows how to work one, really knows it. He's really got it down. I know keyboard players now who are really into it, but still not to the same extent Pete is. Pete's so innovative, and that album was so early – 1971. That says it all, doesn't it? And it wasn't a matter of trial and error. He really knows what he's doing with those things and how they work. It's like the demos he makes, which are invariably better than anything that's ever done afterwards, records that are released. And he's a brilliant engineer too, amazing.

Roger Daltrey: It was good because we were kind of hanging out. What's great about *Who's Next* is that it was the only album where we played all those songs over and over again. They were our songs. They weren't just Pete's songs. That's the difference with *Who's Next*. We had that freedom to do that. We were never allowed that freedom after that.

12. "Too Much Of Anything" and "Time Is Passing" are completed at Olympic Studios, Barnes, London.

23. Mixing session at Olympic Studios, for "Behind Blue Eyes" and "Getting In Tune".

26. Young Vic Theatre, Waterloo, London.

May 1971

2. Young Vic Theatre, Waterloo, London.

7. The Who begin a UK tour at the Top Rank, Sunderland.

Roger Daltrey: When we first went back on the road, after the project, they were the best gigs we've ever played, ever. Everybody really played well. Then, I dunno . . .

11. Recording "The Song Is Over" at Olympic Studios, Barnes, London.

13. Kinetic Circus, Birmingham.

Nick Cavalier (reviewer, *Disc & Music Echo*):

It all added up to a wild night, and The Who proved what a fine, exciting band they really are. Roger Daltrey's vibrant vocals had everyone yelling for more . . . After 90 minutes exhilarating guitar-work by Pete on lead and John Entwistle on bass, plus the usual inimitable display on skins by Keith Moon, The Who called it a day much to the disappointment of the fans, whose stomping and cries for more carried on for a full half-hour after they had left the stage.

14. Liverpool University.

Peter Leay (reviewer, *Melody Maker*):

The group's dynamics have matured and they have them off to a fine art . . . This has obviously evolved with them not having any personnel changes since the beginning.

23. Caird Hall, Dundee, Scotland.

24. A second daughter, Aminta, is born to Pete and Karen Townshend.

June 1971

5. Mixing session at Olympic Studios, Barnes, London for "Bargain".

7. Recording is completed on "Naked Eye", "Getting In Tune" and "When I Was A Boy", at Olympic Studios, Barnes, London.

18. Mixing session at Olympic Studios for "The Song Is Over".

19. Recording of "Bargain" is completed at Olympic.

20. Final mixing session for "Let's See Action" at Olympic.

25. "Won't Get Fooled Again" is released as a single in the UK.

Pete Townshend: It was an irresponsible song. It was quite clear during that period that rock musicians had the ear of the people. And people were saying to me then, "Pete, you've got to use The Who. You've got to get this message across . . ."

But it was a valuable lesson for me today, looking back on the political relevance – or irrelevance – of a song like "Won't Get Fooled Again". I greatly regret that it's one of the most powerful songs that I've ever written. The Labour party asked me if they could use it in their election campaign. And I said, "Yeah, but please let me rewrite the verses."

July 1971

1. Assembly Hall, Worthing.

3. City Hall, Sheffield.
4. De Montfort Hall, Leicester.
8. Pavilion, Bath.
10. "Won't Get Fooled Again" enters the UK singles chart. That night The Who play at the Civic Hall, Dunstable.
12. Winter Gardens, Eastbourne.
14. The album *Who's Next* is officially launched with a party at Keith Moon's home, Tara, in Chertsey.
15. Town Hall, Watford.
17. "Won't Get Fooled Again" is released as a single in the US.
29. The Who begin a US tour at Forest Hills Tennis Stadium, Flushing, New York, in support of the album *Who's Next.* Keith Moon is wearing headphones to be able to hear a backing tape used during "Won't Get Fooled Again".

Roger Daltrey: We had to put all those sounds on tapes and again I used to hate it. Once you were playing with a tape that's when it started to die for me. You were no longer free to do what you felt like doing. You'd be stuck into this thing. It worked for the sound. It made the sound bigger and we were still a four-piece but it didn't work creatively for me at all.

Keith Moon: I play with the tape. If the tape isn't there, none of us are there. So we got the earphone idea, we were playin' some theatres where the monitors just couldn't be heard at all. It happened that first night at Forest Hills.

I had a couple of pairs catch fire. I was wearing them and Bob came rushing over halfway through "Won't Get Fooled Again" with a bucket of water. He looked as if he was gonna throw it at me. So I started to move around, turned me head and there was smoke pouring off my headphones, and the bloody thing was alight. That's what I call pyrotechnics . . .

John Entwistle: I didn't have a guitar stand on stage, so I just leaned it against the amplifier and Keith tripped over it and knocked the head off. So I smashed the rest of it. Pretty clumsy guy.

Pete Townshend: The way we've gone around arriving at a stage act from *Who's Next* is very much the way we used to – we've taken the numbers that are practically possible on the stage, the best and most adventurous being "Won't Get Fooled Again" and that, really, is the feather in my cap at the moment, that's what I'm really relying on because that was the basis, that was the first number that we did. But it has to be transcended though, right? "Won't Get Fooled

Again" is great because it's the kind of stabbing rhythm that you can play to.
31. George Byrington, a security guard, is stabbed to death during the second of two concerts at Forest Hills Tennis Stadium, Flushing, New York.

August 1971

2. US tour continues at the Performing Arts Center, Saratoga Springs, New York.
3. The Spectrum, Philadelphia, Pennsylvania.
4-7. Four nights at the Music Hall, Boston, Massachusetts.
7. "Won't Get Fooled Again" enters the US Top 40 singles chart, where it will peak at No. 15.
9. War Memorial Auditorium, Rochester, New York.
10. Civic Arena, Pittsburgh, Pennsylvania.
12. Public Hall, Cleveland, Ohio.
13. Hara Arena, Dayton, Ohio.
14. "Won't Get Fooled Again" peaks at No. 9 in the UK, and the album *Who's Next* is released in the US. On the same night, The Who play at Cobo Arena, Detroit, Michigan.

Roger Daltrey: The front cover is a composite with the background put on. The big concrete block photo was taken just outside of Sheffield. I don't think it's there any more. They used to pick these big blocks to hold slag heaps from mine shafts. They used to put these big concrete blocks in there to stop them from slipping. It was just there on this big black mountain of slag. There was this big white concrete block sticking out.

15. Metropolitan Sports Center, Minneapolis, Minnesota.
16. Southern Illinois University, Edwardsville, Illinois.
17-19. US tour ends with three nights at The Auditorium Theater, Chicago, Illinois.
21. *Who's Next* enters the US album chart.

Pete Townshend: We did initial recording for *Who's Next* in New York with Kit Lambert who had produced all our stuff up until then, and Kit was getting a bit sick and I was kind of sick – both of us were suffering from mental and physical exhaustion – and Glyn [Johns] was brought in at the last minute to help out. He was brought in to remix the stuff we had done in New York and do overdubs. And he listened to it and said it was great. It was good, but if we started again I could do a lot better. And Glyn was really pitching to do this standout album and we knew all the material so it was just a simple matter of going in and playin'. And every time we went back in we were just getting astounded at the sounds he was producing.

The stuff on the album is quite unadventurous, and I mean they're not pure electric sounds, they're musical sounds, they're rock sounds which celestially work on you. We were gonna do a whole thing, then we figured it would be far better, much more solid to just pick the best stuff out and make it a good, hard, rock-solid album because we were very, very afraid of doin' what The Beatles did, just layin' ourselves wide open like they did with their double albums and making it so that it was too much, too many unlinked ideas which to the public would look like untogetherness, despite the fact that it's always there in the background.

We decided on a single album because really it was the straightest thing to do, basically every angle, every tangent that we went off on we eventually arrived back, if you like, to where the group used to be. The more times this happened the more times it reinforced Roger's stand, which was that the group was perfectly all right as it was and that basically I shouldn't tamper with it.

September 1971

11. *Who's Next* enters the UK album chart.

16. *Who's Next*, engineered by Glyn Johns, is certified as a gold album in the US.

John Entwistle: Glyn Johns was very good at convincing us to take stuff out. He was great at getting sounds, although we always disagreed about the sound of my bass. I've yet to find a producer I agree with on that. There's never any argument about the melodic content of what I play. It's about the sound, because I use a lot of top, trebly sounds.

18. *Who's Next* reaches No. 1 in the UK, and peaks at No. 4 in the US. On the same day The Who take part in the Goodbye Summer event at The Oval Cricket Ground, Kennington, London. Other acts on the bill include The Faces, Atomic Rooster, America, Mott The Hoople, Quintessence, Lindisfarne, The Grease Band and Cochise.

Bill McAllister (reviewer, *Record Mirror*):

> The Who were amazing ... they had all the punch and fire and professionalism that the Faces lacked.

28. Free Trade Hall, Manchester.

October 1971

John Entwistle's first solo album, *Smash Your Head Against The Wall*, enters the US album charts at No. 126.

John Entwistle: I'd been putting off booking time for the album for quite some time 'cause I didn't feel that I had enough numbers to complete the album, so I kept hanging back and waiting to compose the rest of the material. And I went down to the office and Cyrano, the guitarist, works at Track because he's too lazy to join a group, and he decided to give me a push to do the album while I was there. We were looking for a drummer but we just couldn't find one . . . and he was pretty friendly with Jerry Shirley so we got hold of Jerry. He sounds a bit like Townshend. He plays that way because he's seen him so many times.

The actual shape of the album, when the numbers are associated with each other, that doesn't begin until "Heaven And Hell". The rest are just some of the recent things I wrote.

On "What Kind Of People Are They", the first thing I wrote was the brass section, the beginning, and then I'd written this song about people in uniforms because they always get so officious. Waiters and policemen, you know, I've been turned out of so many restaurants because I didn't have a tie on. I've got so many parking tickets, I could wallpaper a room with them . . . traffic wardens. In every traffic jam in England, when you get to the front of it there's a policeman sort of directing things but he ends up causing a backup himself. So I had those three things in mind and I joined them together in different verses.

Roger Daltrey: I love his voice. I love all his songs. I think one of the sad things about John's writing is his best work was done on *Smash Your Head Against The Wall*, which I think he should re-record. And if he does I'd like to sing some of it.

John Entwistle: After my first solo album, I really didn't think of any of my songs as Who songs. The only songs that they used of mine since my solo albums started have been "My Wife" and "When I Was A Boy". I started realizing there was no outlet for my songs, because The Who were more or less based on Pete's style of writing and Roger sang Pete's compositions best. I'd written my music for me to sing, really. I couldn't see Roger singing them. So I realized it was a choice – I was getting so frustrated that it was either leave the band or do a solo album.

2. Reading University.

9. Surrey University Gymnasium, Guildford, Surrey.

Chris Charlesworth (journalist, *Melody Maker*): Keith invited me along to this gig but I was sworn to secrecy. Entry was restricted to university students only, and advertised only 24 hours in advance. Around 600 tickets were available, making this one of the smallest venues The Who ever played during the seventies. The temporary stage in the gym was only a couple of feet off the ground. It didn't seem overcrowded but the crowd could almost touch the band. John Sebastian, who with his wife was Keith's house guest at the time, came along and jammed on harmonica at the end of the set.

10. Elliot Masters House, Kent University, Canterbury.

15. A new single, "Let's See Action", is released in the UK.

18. A UK tour, supported by Quiver, begins at the Guild Hall, Southampton.

20. Odeon Cinema, Birmingham.

21. Green's Playhouse, Glasgow, Scotland.

Tim Renwick (guitarist, Quiver): After the soundcheck at five o'clock, everyone stood around waiting for the show to begin. Townshend was leaning against a wall getting more bored by the minute. There were crates of miniature bottles of mixers and he stood there lobbing bottle after bottle of ginger ale against the wall.

John "Willie" Wilson (drummer, Quiver): The dressing rooms at Green's Playhouse were underneath the stage and our dressing room was right underneath the bit where Pete stood. We knew when he came on stage because he took this flying leap from the wings in his Doc Martens and came crashing down right over our heads. We all thought the stage was going to cave in.

22. Opera House, Blackpool.

23. "Let's See Action" enters the UK singles chart. That night The Who play at Liverpool University.

28. Odeon Cinema, Manchester.

29. ABC Cinema, Hull.

30. Compilation album *Meaty, Beaty, Big And Bouncy* is released in the US. That night, The Who play at the Odeon Cinema, Newcastle.

November 1971

4. The Who inaugurate a new London venue, The Rainbow, Finsbury Park.

6. The single "Behind Blue Eyes" is released in the US.

9. Green's Playhouse, Glasgow, Scotland.

20. As a US tour begins at the Coliseum, Charlotte, North Carolina, the compilation *Meaty, Beaty, Big And Bouncy* enters the US album chart, where it will peak at No. 11.

Chris Charlesworth (reviewer, *Melody Maker*): While The Who were waiting to go on stage, Keith and I went for a stroll along the backstage corridors of the Coliseum where, in a storeroom, we discovered a hollow wooden egg, large enough to conceal a man, and a four-wheeled cart on which it could be mounted and transported. Keith concealed himself inside the egg and I towed him towards The Who's dressing room where he intended to leap out and surprise everyone. Indeed, he was hatching a plot to be wheeled on stage in this contraption.

Unfortunately, en route to the dressing room, there was a steeply sloping downhill curve, and I lost control of the vehicle, causing it to crash, the egg to topple over and break, and the world's greatest rock drummer to come tumbling out head first amid the wreckage.

Keith and I narrowly avoided being ejected from the premises by a security guard who heard the crash and thought we were a couple of vandals.

Skeet Betts (audience): The Who was the first sold-out rock show Charlotte had. When they came on stage a near riot ensued and I was actually pushed to the front. The police were tossing people over the barrier in front of the stage, and I remember seeing a cop swing one unlucky long-haired fan round and round by his hair.

Townshend leaned over the stage with his hands extended with a "stop" gesture after the opening number of "I Can't Explain" until the cops quit pushing people around and the crowd settled down. After that the band seemed to enjoy themselves.

It was the first stop of their autumn of '71 North American tour. Moon commented on the size of the crowd, saying, "It's nice to see so many people in Charlotte. I didn't know there WAS this many people in Charlotte." They played some of their old standards in addition to "Explain" such as "Summertime Blues", "Baby Don't You Do It", and "Magic Bus". Most of the concert revolved around *Who's Next* and *Tommy*, and ended with an extended "My Generation" that included "Naked Eye". Something pissed Townshend off during "Magic Bus" and he almost jerked sound man Bobby Pridden over an amplifier, and then tossed his guitar in the air at the end of the song, letting it crash to the stage. It was by far the best rock concert I have ever seen.

22. University of Alabama Memorial Coliseum, Tuscaloosa, Alabama.
23. Municipal Auditorium, Atlanta, Georgia.
28. Mid-South Coliseum, Memphis, Tennessee.
29-30. The Warehouse, New Orleans, Louisiana.

December 1971

1. Sam Houston Coliseum, Houston, Texas.
2. Memorial Auditorium, Dallas, Texas.
3. Compilation album *Meaty, Beaty, Big And Bouncy* is released in the UK.
4. "Behind Blue Eyes" enters the US Top 40 singles chart.
7. Veterans Memorial Coliseum, Phoenix, Arizona. The same night, The Who play the first of two nights at Denver Coliseum, Denver, Colorado.
8. Sports Arena, San Diego, California.

Robert Hillburn (reviewer, *Los Angeles Times*):

> See rock'n'roll at its most powerful. See young minds twisted before your very eyes by the evil powers of this music. See four musicians in this group from over the seas manipulate their audience in an irresistible combination of showmanship and music . . .

Pete Townshend: That rather camp and glossy show-business side of rock was something that the audience wanted. And it was something that was necessary for a technical reason, which a lot of people overlook. The halls were getting bigger. So the staging had to be grander. You couldn't rely on facial expression and sheer volume and body movement. And that did lead to theatrical pomposity. It was out of scale. It had to be larger than life because the audience was larger than life.

9. The Forum, Los Angeles, California.

Nat Freedland (reviewer, *Billboard*):

> I have never had very strong feelings about The Who one way or another . . . I enjoyed Peter Townshend's spectacular standing-split leaps and Roger Daltrey's twirling his hand-mike . . . I still find the bulk of their music rather monotonous and the lyrics hard to hear.

10. Long Beach Arena, Long Beach, California.
11. "Let's See Action" peaks at No. 16 in the UK singles chart.
12-13. Civic Auditorium, San Francisco, California.
15. Seattle Center Coliseum, Seattle, Washington.

John Entwistle: We've always worked best in the States. Work's more concentrated there. There's no home life to distract you. When you're here [in the UK], you have to take care of bills, and go to the office between gigs. There, you're just the group, and that's all that matters.

18. "Behind Blue Eyes" peaks at No. 34 in the US Top 40 singles chart, as *Meaty, Beaty, Big And Bouncy* enters the UK album chart, where it will peak at No. 9.

28. When Keith Moon comperes a live show starring American rock'n'roll revival band Sha Na Na, he wears a gold lamé suit, specially made for the event.

1972

January 1972

The Who begin a six-month break from working, their first extended holiday since they started having hits in 1965.

February 1972

Pete Townshend visits Arangaon, India, to visit the tomb of Meher Baba.

Pete Townshend: It felt like home.

March 1972

19. The Who are featured on the cover of the *Observer* Sunday magazine.

May 1972

2. Townshend completes a demo of "Long Live Rock" at Olympic Studios, Barnes, London.

13. The album *Tommy Part 1* is released in the UK.

22. "Join Together" is recorded at Olympic Studios, Barnes.

26. "Relay" is recorded at Olympic.

Summer 1972

Pete Townshend continues to aid Eric Clapton in his fight against heroin addiction.

Pete Townshend: I was having to answer hysterical phone calls from [Clapton's girlfriend] Alice Ormsby-Gore practically every night. She always wanted me to go over there. It was an hour and a half's drive, and always at awkward hours of the night.

Alice Ormsby-Gore: Pete was one of the most extraordinary, intuitive and intellectual people around. I needed him so that someone besides me could see what Eric was like in his attitude towards me.

Pete Townshend: When I got there, usually she just wanted to explain what was happening. Eric would be asleep somewhere and she would be running around hysterically. What was worrying her, what she needed to talk about, was that she was giving Eric all of her heroin supply, most unselfishly. And then she was having to deal with Eric's extremely selfish outbursts accusing her of doing the reverse.

It was a typical junkie scene. It was despicable. But even through all that, you know, I got to like and love them both very much. It was the first encounter I'd had with heroin addicts. I wasn't prepared for the lies, I wasn't prepared for the duplicity.

June 1972

3. At Crystal Palace, London, Keith Moon and Elton John jam with The Beach Boys.
5. Final version of "Long Live Rock" is recorded at Olympic Studios, Barnes, London.
6. "Put The Money Down" is recorded at Olympic.
17. The new single, "Join Together", is released in the UK.
21. Keith Moon goes to see Sha Na Na at The Speakeasy.
24. The album *Tommy Part 2* is released in the UK.

July 1972

8. The single "Join Together" is released in the US.
22. "Join Together" peaks at No. 9 in the UK.

August 1972

Eric Clapton asks Pete Townshend to help him out with some Derek & The Dominoes tapes.

Pete Townshend: They'd done four or five tracks, which we sat and played through, but they weren't quite *there*. My job was to try to revive his interest, engineer, produce, finish the records off. But by the time I got there, he was very, very unwilling. He vacillated tremendously. He gave me all sorts of excuses. He sent me off to write lyrics for the songs, look for new material – anything to stop me doing what he knew should be done.

Then he took me into the little sub-sitting-room, the room where he used to listen to short-wave radio all night and where I'd sat with him on many occasions for hours and hours, talking.

Finally, in that little room, he announced it to me, "Look, I'm a junkie. That's why I'm having such difficulty."

I answered: "Look, I *know*" – and Eric was flabbergasted. "God, did you *know*?"

"I know," I replied. "That's why I came down here so often – to try and help you get active again."

"Oh God," said Eric, "I thought I was hiding it really well."

5. "Join Together" enters the US Top 40 singles chart.

11. The Who return to live work with a European tour, kicking off at the Festhalle, Frankfurt, Germany.

12. Ernst-Merck Halle, Hamburg, Germany.

16. Foret Nationale, Brussels, Belgium.

17. Oude Rai Auditorium, Amsterdam, Netherlands.

21. KB Hallen, Copenhagen, Denmark.

23. Kungliga Tennishallen, Stockholm, Sweden.

Bjorn Lanner (audience): The concert started in the usual manner, very loud, very fast tempo, which seemed to increase from the very beginning. Tennishallen is, of course, built for tennis and not for rock concerts, so they had built a temporary stage just for this occasion. Halfway through the show, the stage started moving and swinging. A concert is usually stopped on these occasions. But to stop The Who was impossible, now they were getting warmed up. Then, a little man appeared at the edge of the stage. He crawled up on stage and started to hit with a hammer. The show continued with Pete Townshend and Roger Daltrey looking notably thrilled by this little happening. It all ended with smoke and thunder, the way it should. We left Tennishallen with a memory for life.

24. Scandinavium, Gothenburg, Sweden.

25. KB Hallen, Copenhagen, Denmark.

30. Deutschlandhalle, Berlin, Germany.

31. Grugahalle, Essen, Germany.

September 1972

2. The European tour continues at the Wienerstadthalle, Vienna, Austria.
4. Deutsches Muzeum, Munich, Germany.
5. Mehrzeckhalle, Wetzikon, Zurich, Switzerland.
8. Ahoy Halle, Rotterdam, Netherlands.
9. "Join Together" peaks at No. 17 in the US singles chart. When The Who play at the Fete de L'Humanité, Paris, France, Eric Clapton flies out to see the show.
10. Palais Des Sports, Lyons, France.
14. European tour ends at The Palaeur, Rome, Italy.
18. The Who top the bill of the open-air gig Rock At The Oval, Kennington Oval, London. Supporting acts include The Faces, Mott The Hoople, Atomic Rooster and Quintessence.

October 1972

21. Pete Townshend's first solo album *Who Came First* enters the UK albums chart at its peak position, No. 30.

Pete Townshend: *Who Came First* wasn't really a solo album. In a sense, I don't think I've ever made one. *Quadrophenia*, if you like, was my solo album.
23. The rock movie *That'll Be The Day*, with Moon featured as drummer J.D. Clover, goes into production on the Isle Of Wight.
28. "Join Together" is adopted as the anthem of the United States Council for World Affairs.

November 1972

John Entwistle's second solo album, *Whistle Rymes*, peaks at No. 138 in the US.
25. The Who's new single, "The Relay", is released in the US. (In the UK it will be known simply as "Relay".)

December 1972

9. An all-star fully orchestrated version of *Tommy* is presented at The Rainbow, London. Rod Stewart, Steve Winwood and Peter Sellers are in pivotal roles, with Daltrey as Tommy.
23. New single "Relay" is released in the UK.

1973

January 1973

6. The Who perform "Relay" on UK London Weekend Television show "Russell Harty Plus".

Pete Townshend: In 1973 and '74 I was the ageing daddy of punk. I was bearing a standard I could barely hold up any more. My cheeks were stuffed, not with cotton wool in the Brando-Mafioso image, but with scores of uppers I had taken with a sneer and failed to swallow.

Tony Bramwell (Beatles aide): You'd bump into them in town, and they'd be totally under the influence of everything. They'd look like they were 60 . . . they were old men in their twenties.

Pete Townshend: Paranoia does not adequately describe my feelings, though I suppose all of The Who were to a degree paranoid towards one another. But my trouble was also manifestly spiritual. I felt I had let myself down morally and artistically. I felt quite genuinely a hypocrite. I complained a lot about things I felt I was doing from the goodness of my heart but wasn't receiving enough credit for.

13. "Relay" enters the UK singles chart, where it will peak at No. 21. On the same day, it peaks at No. 39 in the US. That night, Pete Townshend takes part in Eric Clapton's comeback concert at The Rainbow, London.

Glyn Johns (producer): Up to then I'd never been a great fan of Eric's. Pete had told me of the situation, and I readily offered my services when he told me that the idea was to encourage Eric to start playing again, because he was in dire need of being dragged out of his house, which everyone agreed with, whether you liked him or disliked him or whatever else.

Eric Clapton: I did that very much against my will. It was purely Townshend's idea. I'm indebted to him.

Pete Townshend: I had to prop him up and teach him how to play again. The guy had shut himself away for the better part of 22 years. Me and the father of the girl Eric was living with at the time [Alice Ormsby-Gore] organized this concert and bullied him into doing it. He didn't want to do it.

Eric Clapton: He really took a lot of time to help out because he thought I was worth it when I didn't think I was. He gave me faith in myself again.

Glyn Johns: I think Townshend's amazing – apart from being the great musician he is and all the rest of it, for anyone to take that much interest and actually do it, as opposed to the talking about it that you often hear, he should really take all the glory. Because it was easy for everyone else – all we had to do, the rest of us, was just turn up, but Townshend put the rhythm section together. Woody [Ron Wood] offered his house for rehearsal, which I thought was very sweet, and I went along to the rehearsal. I didn't produce, because it's a live album after all, I was just there at the rehearsals, and I don't remember saying very much – what do you say to Eric Clapton? I said I'd do it and remain involved with it as long as Eric proved to be interested, and the minute he didn't turn up, or started pulling any nonsense like being four hours late, I'd be long gone, because I couldn't be bothered with all that, and that was the arrangement.

Eric turned up at the gig and he was very nervous. He played the gig, but not terribly well, although no one expected him to be brilliant. The net result was that we had a tape that wasn't particularly amazing, which in my view, in the interests of the artists, shouldn't have been released as it was.

Pete Townshend: My wife measured it against time spent with her . . . There's no point pretending that it is possible to help bring a man off heroin while you're doing a nine-to-five job. Tea and the wife don't mix with 3 a.m. phone calls and Rainbow reunion rehearsals that actually start at six in the morning.

27. "Relay" peaks at No. 21 in the UK singles chart.

29. The Who record live versions of "Relay" and "Long Live Rock" at Presentation Studio B, Television Centre, Wood Lane, London for BBC TV show "The Old Grey Whistle Test".

February 1973

Eric Clapton and Pete Townshend begin work on unreleased Derek & The Dominoes material for possible release.

Eric Clapton: Pete's an important influence on the life of anyone who's ever met him or heard him. Once you've got him as a friend, he's there. That's it. He's probably the kind of friend that you sometimes really don't want to have, because he's the most honest man you'll ever meet, and he'll tell you stuff you don't want to hear. But in the long run, it's good for you. So you have to value it.

10. In a *Melody Maker* interview, Townshend defends his low-profile policy for The Who.

Pete Townshend: I've got to get a new act together for The Who. And I don't care if it takes me two years before you see The Who again. We've got to get something fresh . . . we've tried going through all the old hits, basing our show on that, but that doesn't work. It's all in the past now. People don't want to sit and listen to all our past.

March 1973

10. Sporthall De Vliegermolen, Voorburg, Netherlands.
13. Roger Daltrey appears on BBC TV show "The Old Grey Whistle Test" to promote his solo album, *Daltrey*.
17. Roger Daltrey appears on UK TV show "Russell Harty Plus".
29. Roger Daltrey appears on "Top Of The Pops", performing his single "Giving It All Away".
31. Keith Moon opens in a stage version of *Tommy* at the Myer Music Bowl, Sydney, Australia.

Keith Moon: I went over there and generally intimidated the Australian cast. Graham Bell [vocalist] came over with me. It was a good idea, really, because any experience we'd got from the London show, we were able to help the others because we'd seen how it had worked in London.

April 1973

Roger Daltrey opens his own studio. Daltrey's discovery Leo Sayer is among the first clients.
12. Roger Daltrey's debut solo single, "Giving It All Away", enters the UK singles chart.
13. Roger Daltrey releases his first solo album, *Daltrey*.

Roger Daltrey: I was really pleased with the way the first solo album went. I didn't want to do a heavy album; I wanted to do some easy-going songs, not saying anything really heavy, but there again with some sort of quality. I think it had that. And it was really nice to sing other people's material. I've only sung Townshend for the last 10 years and you start becoming narrow-minded, but experimenting can be very good; it gives me another breath coming back into singing for The Who. I'll probably do another one. I really like working with orchestras, I'd like to try that out a lot more. There's no reason why an orchestra can't come out having as much bollocks as The Who. They're all musicians, playing instruments; it's just a matter of what they put into it.
24. *Daltrey* peaks at No. 45 in the US.

May 1973

5. Troubled UK folk singer Sandy Denny begins a three-day session at A&M Studios, Los Angeles, during which she will record a song called "Friends", about her unhappy relationship with Pete Townshend.

Pete Townshend: I liked her tremendously. She was, to my eyes, very pretty and compactly voluptuous. I was very attracted to her. Adding fire to this chemistry was the fact that I found her intelligent and assertive as a writer. When she sat to play the piano . . . she had a strident, purposeful attitude.

One night we nearly slept together. She had come several times to the Who studios and I ran her home in my chauffeured Mercedes 600 stretch limousine. The driver sat in the street while we talked. She had been crying at the studio. I had no idea about what. I had some notion that she had parted company with her man . . . She had a lovely flat in Parsons Green with a huge grand piano and an even larger double bed with lace and linen sheets. I kissed her, but she insisted that I should stay all night, otherwise I could not touch her. I took my driver's presence as an excuse and left. I was married, and very rarely unfaithful to my wife at the time. I remember Sandy and I were both drinking a lot, but she seemed, like me, able to handle it physically.

I feel very dim not to have realized that she was reaching out to me so urgently, in need not only of some physical love, but also some . . . of my spiritual strength perhaps . . . She later rang and told me she'd written me a song.

12. Daltrey's single, "Giving It All Away", peaks at No. 5 in the UK.

26. The album, *Daltrey*, debuts at its UK peak of No. 6.

June 1973

John Entwistle's third solo album, Rigor Mortis Sets In, limps to No. 174 in the US.

8. "Love Reign O'er Me" is completed at The Kitchen, Battersea, London.

Glyn Johns (producer): I did four or five things on that [*Quadrophenia*], and one was "Love Reign O'er Me", I think. Because *Tommy* had been so successful, which had been done with Kit Lambert, I think Pete felt that he needed to work with Kit again on *Quadrophenia*, because that was a concept thing as well. Funnily enough, Kit didn't even turn up on many of the sessions, so I think they ended up without him, but I don't remember why I did those sessions or even at what stage I did them. I just remember doing them, and it was all very amicable

– there was no problem about me not doing the whole album or anything like that, because I can remember Pete ringing up and telling me he needed Kit, and I understood. Kit and I never got on either, as it happens.

Ken Russell (film director): We were there the night they recorded a number called "Reign" and there was a cloudburst and they wanted a stereo rain effect. We were in this caravan outside and bit by bit the playing stopped except for the piano, and I went in and the floor and the roof had caved in as they were singing and the rain had really deluged them. They were soaking wet and there were firemen with a hose pumping it out except for the actual man in the cubicle playing the piano, and he was gamely playing on and he was up to his neck in water and when they opened the door it poured like a waterfall, which was very funny.

27. During the recording of "5:15" at The Kitchen Studio, Battersea, London, Townshend and Daltrey become involved in a fight.

Roger Daltrey: We got along very well. Everybody talks about this big fight. It wasn't a big fight. We were rehearsing *Quadrophenia* and we had a film crew to film the rehearsal. We'd played almost the whole of *Quadrophenia* and this film crew were all sitting on their trunks watching the show without a camera turning! So I just said, "For fuck's sake, when are you lot gonna start filming? You're waiting for me to wear my voice out so you can film me when I'm flogged out! *Quadrophenia* is a hard piece of work to sing, I don't want to sing it twice!"

And Pete came over to me and started poking me: "You do as you're fucking told." He was on his brandy and he started poking me in the chest. And the roadies, 'cause they know what I'm like – if I ever get rolling I'm a little tiger – they all jumped on me! They're holding me down [laughs]. Pete hits me with his Gibson across the shoulder while I'm being held and then he starts spitting at me, calling me "a little cunt". And then he says, "Let the little cunt go, I'll fucking kill him."

And then he threw two punches, which I ducked and I still didn't want to fight him . . . it was just silly. But then he threw these two punches – one went to one side and one went the other. And I thought, "Oh, fuck this, this has gone far enough." He was completely off balance, and he was trying to punch me, and I ducked it to the left, and came up with an uppercut. I was going forward. It was all off balance – and it just so happened it was the sweet spot. No one felt worse than me after I did it.

John was like, "What are they doing?" I've never felt great about it. I felt immediately dreadful – I thought I'd killed him. Our manager, who saw the whole thing, said his feet went six inches off the floor. But it frightened the life out of me. And the next thing I know, I've got his head in my lap, cradling him, yelling for someone to call for an ambulance. I was in tears. I mean, I just didn't want to be there. I didn't want to be doing that. And I hated myself, because it's the first time I'd lashed out at anyone in such a long time. I used to have a terrible temper, and this was not done in temper at all. I used to have a dark and the most violent temper – violent. I would pick up anything and hit you with it.

John Entwistle: Around *Quadrophenia* was when I changed to Gibson Thunderbird basses. Either Thunderbird or Fender/Thunderbird hybrids. I had bodies made with the Thunderbird pickup and bridge. The bridge is positioned a sixteenth of an inch forward of where it is on the stock Thunderbird. And I put Fender necks on because Thunderbird necks were too thin on top.

July 1973

3. Keith Moon attends a star-studded post-show gathering for David Bowie at the Café Royal, Regent Street, London. Other guests include Paul McCartney and Ringo Starr, Mick Jagger, Lou Reed, Jeff Beck and Lulu. Music is supplied by Dr John.

4. Roger Daltrey's single "I'm Free" enters the UK singles chart.

August 1973

25. Keith Moon hangs out at the Reading Festival where Rod Stewart & The Faces are playing. Other backstage liggers include Eric Clapton, Donovan, George Harrison and Peter Frampton.

September 1973

15. Daltrey's solo single "I'm Free" peaks at No. 13 in the UK, giving him his last Top 20 entry. A new Who single, "5:15", is released in the UK on the same day.

October 1973

Keith Moon's long-suffering wife Kim finally leaves him.

Kim Moon: We led separate lives under the same roof. He'll get up in the morning and decide to be Hitler for a day, and he is Hitler.

13. "5:15" enters the UK singles chart.

20. "5:15" peaks at No. 20 in the UK singles chart.

27. "Love Reign O'er Me" is released as a single in the US.

28. *Quadrophenia*, requiring a crew of 30 and 20 tons of equipment, is performed live for the first time at Trentham Gardens, Stoke-on-Trent. Five numbers have to be cut because of technical problems.

John Entwistle: It's not so much that we found it difficult to play on stage. Once we devised a way of keeping the band in time with the tapes that we were playing, the only way we could do that was put it on a four-track and Keith would have a click track in his cans plus his own little voiced instructions, like, "Middle eight coming up, 1-2-3-4." It came through the PA once. It was quite funny.

29. Based on advance sales, *Quadrophenia* is certified as a gold album in the US.

Pete Townshend: *Quadrophenia* was actually a simple idea made complicated. It was my readdressing the original Who audience.

I felt that when I came to *Quadrophenia*, I had to get back on track, go back to the original brief. The continuum of The Who had been that we had carried a group of people with us, they'd grown with us and we'd grown with them, and somehow, in the American experience that accompanied *Tommy*, and the subsequent growth of the band on the road with electric theatre, like the Fillmore and the Chicago Factory, we'd actually lost our English roots.

Quadrophenia was a story about a day, or a couple of days, in the life of a boy who has been abandoned by everybody – his parents, his girlfriend, his hero and his favourite pop band. It's a simple story about a mod and his relationship to his group, who go off into celestial territory, and yet take with them the four mirrors, if you like, of his character; they take with them his very soul, they steal him, and leave him with an empty husk. So it's also about the same thing that underlies *Iron Man*, *Psychoderelict*, *Tommy* – what happens in the world of rock celebrity as opposed to any other kind of celebrity. A celebrity in rock is charged by the audience with a function, like "You stand there and we will know ourselves", not "You stand there and we will pay you loads of money to keep us entertained while we eat oysters." It's a much more profound thing, but it's also much more functional. It's also, "When we're finished with you, you can go and we'll replace you with somebody else."

What's interesting about the song "The Real Me" is again the way a spiritual *cri de coeur* is tied up with anthemic power. This song exemplifies it. You have the big, big, big bass of John Entwistle, the big, big drums of Keith Moon, the power chords, the huge voice of Roger Daltrey, and what they're actually saying is "I'm a pathetic little wimp." I was able to offer essentially frail material to this incredibly powerful elemental machine and I had to allow for that in my writing. I had to know that however delicately I wrote, however poignantly I put the thing together, however direct, however right, however honest and true it was, I then had to hand it to this fucking war machine and it would be churned out like Wall's pork sausages. Every single track on *Quadrophenia* sounds like a bunch of Rwandans trying to terrorize the natives, doesn't it? "Helpless Dancer" – the very title, it's supposed to be something that's helpless, but Roger sings it like it's a war cry. I'm not saying that I didn't want it to be that way at the time, but I was very good at acceptance and I had to accept the tools I'd been given to do the job. No wonder it stopped working. No wonder I couldn't do it in the end.

John Entwistle: The best thing Wagner ever wrote. I like the album. I like the songs. I like my performance on it. I was playing in a completely different way on *Quadrophenia* because I'd got stuck in one of my bass ruts and changed equipment and I was finding a new me.

November 1973

1-2. King's Hall, Belle Vue, Manchester.

3. The new album, *Quadrophenia*, is released in the US.

5-7. A performance of *Quadrophenia* has to be abandoned on the first of three nights at the Odeon Cinema, Newcastle, when a 15-second delay in the backing tapes throws the band completely out of time. Townshend storms off stage, but returns 10 minutes later to lead the band through a set of old Who hits. The remaining two nights proceed without problems.

10. *Quadrophenia* enters the US album chart, where it will peak at No. 2.

11-13. Lyceum, Strand, London.

16. *Quadrophenia* is released in the UK.

Pete Townshend: We failed with *Quadrophenia*. It wasn't just the failure of the album, which in fact did quite well in the UK at least, but it was the failure of the relationship. Roger blamed me for its failure. He said that I'd taken too much control, that I'd done it all single-handedly and that I'd mixed him down in the mix and it didn't sound right and it didn't work and I was so hurt by that that I hit him . . .

17. *Quadrophenia* enters the UK album chart, where it will peak at No. 2.

Roger Daltrey: I love the album but I still think *Quadrophenia* should be remixed. I've never heard a good mix of it. It's incredibly weak, it's thin. I've heard what's on the tapes. It lacks the real power that I know is there from hearing it in the studio. I always remember when I first heard the record I thought, "Oh, dear, maybe I should have another listen to it." I think a lot of the vocals are very low.

20. After taking an overdose of animal tranquillizer, Keith Moon collapses on stage at the Cow Palace, San Francisco. The night is saved when audience member Scott Halpin stands in for him.

Pete Townshend: When Keith collapsed, it was a shame. I had just been getting warmed up at that point. I'd felt closed up, like I couldn't lay anything out. I didn't want to stop playing. It was also a shame for all the people who'd waited in line for eight hours.

Roger Daltrey: What do you do when your drummer is passed out on literally the third song in the show? You're just about to premiere your new work, *Quadrophenia*, which is a difficult piece anyway. There you are and you have 14,000 raving fans. We weren't quitters. So I stood at the front and said, "Is there a drummer in the audience?" Simple as that. And they all lined up and we picked one out . . .

Scott Halpin: It all happened really quick. I didn't have time to think about it and get nervous.

Roger Daltrey: . . . and we basically had a jam session. The audience was happy. Keith was happy, he was out of his brain. John was unhappy because Keith smashed his French horn.

Scott Halpin: Most of the stuff was four-four. There was only one six-eight. But it was easy to follow because Pete signals when to end it by jumping up and down. I really admired their stamina. I only played three numbers and I was dead.

Roger Daltrey: We had to deal with these problems when Keith took the overdose of the monkey tranquillizer in San Francisco and we seriously had to consider what we could do. We had this whole tour booked, can we do it? Keith couldn't even walk for three days then. We did seriously consider getting another drummer in to get us through. You do those things to keep together as a band but you never, ever talk about getting rid of the bloke. I mean, The Who without Keith Moon? Who do they think we are, fucking mad? There's no truth in that at all. But I will admit to saying that we might have to get another drummer in to finish this record.

22-23. The Forum, Los Angeles, California.

Robert Hillburn (reviewer, *Los Angeles Times*):

The Who showed much of the power, precision and desire that made it one of rock's most rewarding and influential bands. But even the improved performance Friday didn't erase the troubling impression that the group's momentum – and therefore importance – is waning.

25. Memorial Auditorium, Dallas, Texas.

27. The Omni, Atlanta, Georgia.

28. St Louis Arena, St Louis, Missouri.

Ken Barnes (reviewer, *Phonograph Record*):

For the most part The Who again proved peerless hard-rockers . . . abetted by a much better sound than on the last tour.

29. International Amphitheater, Chicago, Illinois.

Lynn Van Matre (reviewer, *Chicago Tribune*):

The Who arrived on stage in the usual way, lead singer Roger Daltrey's legs chugging like pistons, microphone twirling, Peter Townshend's guitar arm windmilling, Keith Moon manic on drums and John Entwistle minding his business on bass. The din from the stage was incredible; the din from the audience matching that and then some . . . they are in the final analysis, pure, raw energy – which is, after all, what rock'n'roll's always been about.

30. Cobo Hall, Detroit, Michigan.

December 1973

2. After wrecking a hotel suite, The Who are arrested in Montreal, Canada. The management decides not to press charges when the group agrees to pay £1,400 in compensation.

3. Boston Garden, Boston, Massachusetts.

4. The Spectrum, Philadelphia, Pennsylvania.

6. US tour ends at The Capital Center, Largo, Maryland.

13. *Tommy* is presented again at The Rainbow Theatre, Finsbury Park, London, with an all-star cast.

22. The Sundown, Edmonton – the third night of a four-night stand, billed as The Who Christmas Party.

John Einarson (audience): As the group took the stage, Townshend heaved bottles of cognac into the audience, Moon did a somersault before mounting his kit to proclaim "It's great to be back in Cleveland," and with that The Who were off and running and never looked back for the next two and a half hours. With a set boasting much of *Quadrophenia* peppered with the odd Who chestnut, it was a rousing evening of fun with the four (plus keyboard player "Rabbit" Bundrick) obviously in high spirits throughout. At one point Townshend called to the audience for requests and was met with a hail of Who favourites. As the group closed out with a tumultuous "Won't Get Fooled Again", thousands of balloons were released from the ceiling cascading over the crowd, capping off a memorable Christmas party indeed.

29. "Love Reign O'er Me" peaks at No. 76 in the US singles chart.

1974

January 1974

1. Work begins on the soundtrack for the film version of *Tommy* at Ramport Studios, Battersea, London.

Pete Townshend: We spent about six weeks preparing the tracks before shooting began in April 1974.

Richard Barnes: Because the music had to fit the film, it had to be timed to tenths of seconds but the director, Ken Russell, would keep changing things and so Townshend was forever having to re-record the tracks, which made him quite livid at times. He was not in a good mood.

Ken Russell: The first time I went into the recording studios someone [Keith Moon] was six hours late, and I got very impatient and I phoned Townshend up the next day and said I was very upset this person didn't turn up and, you know, any other director would have walked out for good. He said, "I'm sorry, he's like that." And then I realized that obviously they had been waiting for this chap on and off for eight years and he's always been six hours late. Townshend said, "Well, he sometimes might be five hours late, and sometimes actually, once in a blue moon, might come on time."

12. A new single, "The Real Me", is released in the US.

February 1974

Pete Townshend: At the end of one recording session, which I had gotten through by pulling incessantly at a total of about 20 cans of coke, I wished everyone goodnight, walked up to a makeshift bar, and drank a bottle of vodka . . . getting drunk, having a good time and screwing birds . . . I was waking up in bed with somebody and not knowing what had led up to that particular point. Then I was going home and trying to face me old lady.

8. French tour begins at Lille.

Pete Townshend: I was thoroughly depressed. I honestly felt The Who were going on stage every night and, for the sake of the diehard fans, copying what The Who used to be.

9. Palais Des Grottes, Cambrai, France. "The Real Me" peaks at No. 92 on the US singles chart.

10. Palais Des Expositions, Paris, France.

11. Compilation *Odds'n'Sods* enters the US album chart, where it will peak at No. 15.

John Entwistle: It became my project. I think the idea was to try and release everything possible, to stop the bootlegs. We were probably one of the worst bootlegged acts of all time. I mean, in 1975 there were about 250.

14. Keith Moon plays drums in Roy Harper's all-star band at The Rainbow, London. His band-mates include Ronnie Lane, John Bonham and Jimmy Page.

15. Les Arenas, Poitiers, France.

17. Toulouse, France.

22. Palais Des Expositions, Nancy, France.

24. Palais Des Sports, Lyons, France.

Late February 1974

Keith Moon begins filming for *Stardust.*

March 1974

After a recording session for Clapton's part in *Tommy*, at Ramport Studios, Townshend helps Clapton get Patti away from George Harrison.

April 1974

1. Keith Moon is in Los Angeles, jamming with Paul McCartney and Harry

Nilsson at McCartney's beach house.
2. Keith Moon and Harry Nilsson visit Paul McCartney's Los Angeles beach house again.
14. Townshend appears solo with Tim Hardin, Byzantium and Coast Road Drive at The Roundhouse, London, in a fundraiser to provide cash for the purchase of a bus for the Camden Square Community.

Pete Townshend: I did that after the *Tommy* film recording sessions so I was still pretty shattered. I'd just over-committed myself again. I'd said to Lisa Strike, one of the singers on the *Tommy* film, "Oh yeah, I'll do The Roundhouse for you," and thought it was going to be a very small thing but it turned out to be bloody massive.

People were ringing me up and saying, "I hear you're doing a solo gig at The Roundhouse," and I thought, "Hold on, this is getting out of control." I started to work seven days a week before the gig trying to get material together to make it better, so that by the time I came to do the gig, I'd actually been doing it for about a week before up in my studio.
22. Ken Russell's film of *Tommy* goes into production.

Pete Townshend: I tell you one of the problems, in fact our biggest problem, is that our managers desperately want to make that movie, and they're very disorganized people. They started with The Who for the sole purpose of making a movie. And it's something that I think Kit Lambert desperately wants to do before he's ready to die, I think this is probably what keeps him alive. When I suggested to him (in 1971) that we might have another bash at talking about a movie of *Tommy*, he literally jumped for joy and leapt around the room and kissed me and hugged me and took me out to dinner and started to talk to me again, y'know [laughter]. I mean, when I said that it might be good if he directed it, he gave up everything he owned and gave it to me, brought it round in a big truck and dumped it on me doorstep and said that he'd be my servant for life. That's how much Kit wants to make a movie.

Richard Barnes: Pete Townshend is an old friend of mine, and before filming started, he asked me to write a book about the making of the film, so I was taking photographs and making notes almost the whole time. It took ages to get the film financed. Kit Lambert, the Who's original manager, tried and tried to raise the money, and Pete had endless meetings with movie people.

Pete Townshend: What we were really after was a deal which would enable us

Townshend and Moon charming the ladies in the mid-70s.
PeteTownshend: **"Keith was killing himself in front of everybody's eyes. I was also drinking a lot, huge amounts by this time, and my drinking was affecting my personal behaviour."**

The Who at their moddest, mid-1965.
Roger Daltrey: **"Before that, you never saw a Union Jack anywhere, except up a bloody flag-pole. After we did that, Union Jacks were on everything."**

Keith Moon with Paul and Linda McCartney in the late 70s.
Roy Carr (journalist, friend): **"Keith looked like a caricature of himself. He was crying – you don't know if he'd put it on or if he was just over-emotional."**

That deaf, dumb and blind kid sure plays a mean pinball…
Roger Daltrey: **"I played the damn part for five years. I slogged my balls off around the world sweating it out. People thought I was Tommy. I used to get called Tommy in the street."**

The loudest band in the world.
Lynn Van Matre (reviewer): "**...Roger Daltrey's legs chugging like pistons, microphone twirling, Peter Townshend's guitar arm windmilling, Keith Moon manic on drums and John Entwistle minding his business.**"

Townshend takes off.
John Wilson (drummer, Quiver): **"Townshend took this flying leap from the wings and came crashing down. We all thought the stage was going to cave in."**

The legendary Maximum R&B poster.
Keith Altham (journalist/publicist): **"I first saw them at The Marquee on one of the Maximum R&B nights … it sounded like somebody chain-sawing a dustbin in half."**

Elder statesmen of rock.
Pete Townshend: **"The unfinished business of The Who is the friendship. I know that sounds a bit cheesy, but it's true."**

to control the film. But we could never get close to that. Film companies always wanted somebody else to control it.

Richard Barnes: It was Robert Stigwood in the end who put up about $3.5 million and organized a deal with Columbia.

Elton John: Originally, when the *Tommy* film was discussed . . . Rod [Stewart] approached me and said, "They're going to do a film of *Tommy*." And I said, "Oh no, not a film now. Bloody hell, what are they going to do next? It'll be a cartoon series soon."

Rod told me they wanted him as the Pinball Wizard and I said, "I should knock it on the head if I was you." So a year went by and they were trying to get the world and his mother to do it. I was offered loads of parts in it and I always said no. Then I found out Ken Russell was doing it, and I spoke to Pete about it, and became quite enthusiastic about the idea. To cut a long story short, I ended up doing the Pinball Wizard and, of course, Stewart, when he found out, couldn't believe it! "You bastard!"

Richard Barnes: One of the first things was that Moonie's part was dramatically cut down, because Russell realized he couldn't act. He was always over-acting, very clumsy in front of the camera.

Richard Barnes: Ann-Margret and Ollie Reed were on set most of the time, because they were the parents, but mostly the Hollywood people, like Jack Nicholson, would come in for maybe three days, do their bit and go off again.

Clapton was filmed and recorded, I think, in a big church at Hayling Island in Hampshire, around April. Pete originally wanted Arthur Brown to play the preacher, but Eric was of course much better known and Stigwood was his manager, so there were connections there.

Eric Clapton: I think Pete chose me . . . I think it was the song he thought fitted me because it's the only one he didn't write, and it's written by Sonny Boy Williamson. It's a blues, you know. I think he just thought that I could do that better than anything else, and I think he wanted me to be in it as a mate because he wanted all his mates to do it.

Richard Barnes: This wasn't long after Eric had got off heroin. He was in a pretty bad way with the boozing, and he couldn't cope with the hanging around. They deliberately scheduled his main day to be a Sunday, when there were no off-licences open. There was a strict ban on booze on the set, but I remember, in the make-up room, he opened up a vacuum flask, like you'd keep tea in, but it was full of vodka.

Eric Clapton: The filming bit is really strange because they call you so early in the morning just in case something might happen spontaneously but, of course, you're still there at ten o'clock at night waiting for them to get the spots lined up.

Richard Barnes: Usually by the time they were ready to film him, he'd be drunk. They had to put off doing his close-ups till later. They rebuilt his pulpit in Shepperton and he came back to do it then.

Eric Clapton: He [Russell] gets very carried away. He has to have this guy on the set who keeps telling him to stop. A supervisor character telling him, "No we can't do that, it's too much." . . . A reality supervisor!

Richard Barnes: Ken really doesn't direct actors. He's more interested in how the yellow is going to clash with the red. For example, there was a scene where Roger Daltrey had to run through a field. It's in the film for just a few seconds but it took a whole day to shoot, because Ken got obsessed with it, so he just kept filming and ordering retakes.

There was another sequence, in a scrapyard in Portsmouth, where Roger had to run through a hundred-yard corridor of fire, made with hidden gas jets, which was very dangerous, and Russell had him doing that several times. They had fire engines standing by the whole time. He actually got burned doing that. But Roger would do anything to get in the film.

Roger Daltrey: *Tommy* was fabulous to do. I'd had no acting training – I was turned down for the school play – so the fact that he was deaf, dumb and blind was a godsend.

I became kind of almost deaf, dumb and blind through the whole fuckin' film, you know. I kind of shut down to anyone. It was weird. The only person I talked to was Ken Russell.

Richard Barnes: Elton's section, where he sings "Pinball Wizard", was done at the King's Theatre in Portsmouth live in front of 1,500 students from Portsmouth College. Musically, it was probably the most exciting bit of filming we did, but Elton had to wear these ridiculously high-heeled platform boots. He had to climb a stepladder to be strapped into them, and it took ages, so whenever his feet weren't actually in shot, he'd stand on a cardboard box instead to get the height right for the camera angle.

There was an accident too, when Townshend threw his guitar in the air as the kids were rushing the stage and it came down and hit this girl on the head.

Roger Daltrey: It was complete chaos . . . we used students as extras, and of course they were all huge rock fans. And after being there filming all day, since seven o'clock in the morning, they were still there at seven o'clock at night. We had been doing bits of the song all day, never actually completing the whole of the song. And doing that to rock fans is a kind of weird thing to do, you know? So at the end of the day we played the whole damn thing, and it was a riot.

They really did go wild; in the film, you can see them going nuts. If you look at the faces of the people, they really are going for it.

Richard Barnes: Pete bought a boat, a 50-foot cruiser, and he had it brought down to Hayling Island, so we all went out on it. There was me, Pete, Keith Moon, his minder, Dougal, and Oliver Reed, and three girls. At one point, we went on deck and Moonie's clothes were scattered around, and the rowing boat was gone. So it looked like he'd jumped overboard. Then we discovered that the rowing boat, our only way of getting back to shore, was missing. So we were marooned out there, in a state of panic, sending an SOS. Of course, it turned out Keith was hiding, stark naked somewhere, and he'd deliberately untied the rowing boat.

In the end, Moonie and Reed did jump overboard and swam back to shore to find us a dinghy that we could get back to land with.

Ken Russell: *Tommy* fell nicely into my scheme of things and I was able to slip in a couple of scenes that I'd been trying to get into films for years. One being the Marilyn Monroe shrine, and another was the TV set vomiting baked beans and shit.

Richard Barnes: During the vomiting TV scene, Ann-Margret throws a bottle of champagne and smashes the TV, then she's writhing around in all this stuff and she gashed herself badly on the glass. They were terrified that she might sue them but she was lovely about it. They then had to reschedule all the filming, because she had her arm in a sling for quite a while.

Roger Daltrey: Ann-Margret . . . was a sweetheart. Beautiful.

Keith Moon: A lovely girl with great huge tits . . .

Richard Barnes: All sorts of people were considered for the Acid Queen. Pete wanted Tiny Tim to do it, and then Little Richard, Mick Jagger, David Bowie . . . but Tina Turner was perfect. She flew into England one day and recorded her song at Ramport Studios the next. She then filmed for four more days, before returning to America for a concert.

Tina Turner: Ken Russell wasn't too sure about me at first. He said, "I didn't know you had that much hair. And I thought you were taller." I mean, what was I supposed to do – grow? He said he wanted me in black, so I came in wearing this nice Yves St Laurent skirt, which came to about mid-calf. He said, "No, no, no, no."

So they went out and got this horrible little short skirt and these awful platform shoes, which made me instantly tall, and then I figured we might as well go all the way, so I dug out these old fishnet stockings I had worn years before, and bright red nail polish and lipstick. But Ken Russell was still sort of pessimistic. Then I started making this madwoman face – I was trying to look like Vincent Price, with the bulging eyes and the quivering head, you know? – and Ken started getting real excited. He said, "Yes, yes! More! More!"

Then we came to my big scene, and this pair of twins walked in with a pink pillow – and there's this huge hypodermic needle on it! I was shocked – I didn't know anything about this. I said right out loud, "My God, is this movie promoting drugs?" I don't know why I'm so naive about those things. I mean, even the name of my character – the Acid Queen – hadn't tipped me off. Ken Russell just laughed, though.

I became so involved with it that when I had to drag Roger Daltrey up some stairs, I literally dragged his ass up those steps. I really became a madwoman. I think I scared him.

Richard Barnes: The final scenes were shot in the Lake District, always a favourite location for Russell.

Pete Townshend: The result was a much more literal film than I expected. It's an exaggeration in some ways, almost burlesque at times.

May 1974

10. All 80,000 seats for The Who's upcoming shows at Madison Square Garden, New York, sell out in eight hours.

18. Charlton Athletic Football Ground, Charlton, London.

Pete Townshend: At Charlton, I got completely pissed . . . I was so happy to get out of it. For Madison Square Garden we had to fight and snatch the time off from the film and, consequently, when we got there it wasn't really that wonderful from our point of view . . . I felt really guilty I couldn't explode into the exuberant and happy energy our fans did. I screwed up every inch of energy doing it, then would be brought down by a monitor whistling or something, and I'd have to work myself up again.

Ossie Clark (fashion designer, diary entry): We had fish and chips on the way and lots of hassle to get in, despite hand-written notes. The Who are really on form – and who wouldn't be with 60,000 faces out front. And lots of madness on stage . . .

20. It is reported that Roger Daltrey has been offered the lead role in Ken Russell's biopic on the life of Franz Liszt.

22. Guildhall, Portsmouth. Special concert for Polytechnic students who'd appeared in the film of *Tommy.*

Pete Townshend: . . . at the "thank you" concert we gave in Portsmouth, England, for the extras in the *Tommy* film, I signed several managerial and recording contracts in a complete fog. The only event I remember is quietly screaming for help deep inside, as I asked John Entwistle if it had ever happened to him. The fact that I'd signed the contracts didn't come home to me until we were actually in the middle of a legal wrangle some months later.

June 1974

Townshend and co. sue Lambert and Stamp because half a million of publishing money has gone astray . . . Bill Curbishley takes over as manager.

10. Start of a four-night stand at Madison Square Garden, New York.

Pete Townshend: In all the years I'd been with The Who I'd never had to force myself. All the leaping about and guitar smashing, even though I'd done it a thousand times, it was always totally natural. And then, on the first night at the Garden, I suddenly lost it. I didn't know what I was doing there, stuck up on stage in front of all these people! I had no instinct left; I had to do it from memory. So I looked down into the front row and all these kids were squealing, "Jump! Jump! Jump!" And I panicked. I was lost.

It was the most incredible feeling. After half my lifetime to suddenly go blank. The other three shows I was terrified. I got smashed or I couldn't have gone on.

Chris Charlesworth (journalist, *Melody Maker*): There was a terrible atmosphere backstage after the opening concert. The Who were screaming at each other behind a locked dressing room door. Kit Lambert, who wasn't often seen at Who concerts in those days, had turned up unexpected, drunk as a lord, and demanding to mix the onstage PA in future, a ludicrous suggestion, and that didn't help matters at all.

11. Madison Square Garden, New York.

Pete Townshend: I felt acute shades of nostalgia. All the Who freaks had crowded around the front of the stage and when I gazed out into the audience, all I could see were those very same sad faces I'd seen at every New York Who gig . . . It was like some bicentennial celebration and they were there to share in the glory of it all. They hadn't come to watch The Who, but to let everyone know they were just original Who fans. It was dreadful. They were telling us what to play. Every time I tried to make an announcement, they all yelled out, "Shurrup Townshend and let Entwistle play 'Boris The Spider' . . ."

12. Madison Square Garden, New York.

13. Madison Square Garden, New York.

Roger Daltrey: We could have done Madison Square Garden with our eyes closed, only the group was running on three cylinders, especially the last night . . . It was because Townshend was in a bad frame of mind about what he wanted to do. And he didn't play well.

July 1974

Pete Townshend: I got very scared by memory blackouts, as scared as I had ever been on bad LSD trips eight years before. Once in July 1974 – just after the *Tommy* filming – I sort of "came to" in the back of my own car. Keith and John were with me (we were probably going to a club), but although I knew who they were, I didn't recognize either my car or my driver, who had been working for me for about two months. The shock that hit me as the pieces fell into place was even more frightening than the black holes in my head as the memory lapses began. Eight drug-free years and still this mental demise.

27. Townshend attends a party thrown by Mick Jagger, along with Rod Stewart, Debbie Reynolds, Mama Cass and Bryan Ferry.

August 1974

2. When Eric Clapton plays at the Coliseum, Greensboro, North Carolina, he is unexpectedly joined by Pete Townshend and Keith Moon.

Skeet Betts (audience): This was Clapton's first major tour after his famous heroin addiction. Pete Townshend had helped Clapton with his recovery, and apparently thought it would be a good idea if he accompanied Clapton on part of this tour. The first hint that Townshend was there came when Keith Moon came charging on stage and smashed a toy guitar filled with what looked like hamburger meat over Clapton's head. The meat – probably pilfered from the backstage food table – covered the stage, so Moon shot backstage and re-emerged swinging a broom and swept up the mess.

By the time the concert was almost over, most of us down front knew Pete Townshend was there because he had spent a good bit of the show standing off to the left of the stage watching his friend. When Clapton returned for the encore, he introduced Townshend to thunderous applause, and then Townshend ripped off the intro to "Layla" and the place went completely nuts. Townshend was not particularly animated during the song, possibly due to concentrating on the intricate guitar demands of "Layla", and also possibly in an attempt to not upstage Clapton. At any rate, Townshend did do one of his famous back-to-the-audience split/leaps to end the song and the show.

October 1974

26. The compilation *Odds'n'Sods* enters the UK album chart, where it will peak at No. 10.

Roger Daltrey: I like *Odds'n'Sods* . . . I loved "Put The Money Down" . . . I think there's some really great tracks on that album. "Dreaming From The Waist" is a great track. "How Many Friends". I love "Blue, Red And Grey", that's one of my favourite tracks.

We really used to let John choose the songs he wanted to do. The trouble is, when John wanted to do his songs, John had to sing them and unfortunately John has this habit of singing incredibly out of tune.

Sometimes he sings all right but if you notice, I'm singing behind him shadowing him every way. He's just gone deaf. He's a good singer, John, I love his voice.

5. The Who's recent Charlton Football Ground concert is transmitted on BBC2 TV in the UK.

December 1974

8. The Ox, the band headed by John Entwistle, begins a UK tour at City Hall, Newcastle Upon Tyne, attended by only 300 people.

1975

February 1975

21. In Sacramento, California, John Entwistle embarks on a five-week US tour with his band The Ox.
22. *Tommy – The Original Soundtrack* is released in the US.

March 1975

At his studio in Goring-on-Thames, Berkshire, Townshend begins demoing songs that will become the album *The Who By Numbers*.

Pete Townshend: They were written with me stoned out of my brain in my living room, crying my eyes out. All the songs were different, some more aggressive than others, but they were all somehow negative in direction. I felt detached from my own work and from the whole project . . . I felt empty.
18. The film version of *Tommy* premieres in New York, and is presented in something dubbed "quintophonic sound".

Roger Daltrey: I think it's a milestone in film-making. Ken Russell put a completely new slant on the musical film. He was doing it on TV six or seven years before it started. And I think there are some extremely great performances; Ann-Margret, I think, is tremendous in the film.

What's amazing about *Tommy* is you don't seem to notice that everything is sung. It's an extraordinary piece of work in that sense. But it suffers from the same weakness that Tommy always suffered from, in the narrative, especially towards the end. Tommy is a bit too good for my liking, as a character. To me, though, the film stands up today, and I think it always will. I think it is a classic, there is no doubt about it.
26. The Who's rock opera movie *Tommy* is premiered in London.

April 1975

Following Keith Moon's year-long affair with Swedish model Annette Walter-Lax, Kim Moon is granted a decree nisi in the London Divorce Court, in the Strand, London.

Keith Moon: The pressures on us have been tremendous because of the nature of my work. I have been away from home for long periods. And my wife has been subjected to all kinds of verbal and physical abuse – even having eggs thrown at her.

Annette Walter-Lax: Keith mentioned to me once that he broke her nose with his head. And I think if you do that to your wife, you can't blame her if she doesn't want to stick around. He wasn't proud of it but, on the other hand, he wasn't exactly shy about talking about it either. So maybe inside, he felt that it was terrible, maybe he needed to talk about it because he regretted it so much.

7. Townshend records a demo of "Squeeze Box" at his home studio, Goring-on-Thames, Berkshire.

May 1975

Keith Moon releases his only solo album, *Two Sides Of The Moon.*

Roger Daltrey: Only Moon would have the balls as a drummer to make an album where he sings! And I love it for that. And I love "Don't Worry Baby". He loved The Beach Boys . . . That's all he ever wanted to do, was be in The Beach Boys. He never wanted to be in the fucking Who, we played rubbish! So we used to do "Barbara Ann" to keep him happy. "Moon's in a mood, quick, play 'Barbara Ann'." And "Bucket-T", that was another one that would keep him happy for six months.

27-30. Recording sessions for *The Who By Numbers* at Shepperton Studios Sound Stage, London.

Pete Townshend: I forced the band into a corner with that material. When I first played the demos, Keith burst into tears. He came and put his arms around me. I suppose he was thinking, "Poor Pete," but that was the kind of material I was dishing up. The group recoiled from the stuff.

Roger Daltrey: There was a breakthrough on the side of the musical content because we had a serious discussion about how The Who had worked itself into a niche, hence there's a lot of different feels on the album. That's cool. I know it's only my personal opinion, but if Pete would explain things like "They're All In Love" then I think it would help for a better understanding.

Pete Townshend: What the lines are about is that we went in to sue Kit Lambert. It's not really what it seems to be about. Punks didn't mean what it does today. Punks is what I used to call the New York fans who used to try and get you by the ears and pin you down and take you home in a cardboard box. The song was about what the band had become. It was about money, about law courts, about lawyers and accountants. Those things had never mattered, and the band had a backlog of tax problems and unpaid royalties. We had to deal with it.

I really felt like crawling off and dying.

Roger Daltrey: Truthfully that's one song that I really didn't wanna sing until Pete clarified certain aspects. I knew what the first two verses were about but the last one had me completely baffled. "Goodbye all you punks" is a goodbye to all you nostalgic bastards who are still living on the nostalgic part of The Who because nostalgia just ain't no good to us. We're not past it, we're just different.

June 1975

Pete Townshend and his family spend 10 days at the Meher Center, Myrtle Beach, South Carolina.

Pete Townshend: My family, particularly of course my wife (who, as a matter of personal policy, tries to avoid aspects of the music world that I still find exciting), had suffered a lot from my pathetic behaviour of the previous year, but they would naturally be by my side on any trip other than Who tours. So they came with me, or rather I went with them, to Myrtle Beach.

We were all staggered by the impact of the love that literally filled the air.

July 1975

26. Roger Daltrey's second solo album, *Ride A Rock Horse*, enters the UK album chart.

August 1975

The Ken Russell film *Lisztomania* premieres, with Roger Daltrey in the title role.
14. Daltrey's album, *Ride A Rock Horse*, peaks at No. 14 in the UK.
23. The soundtrack to the film version of *Tommy* enters the UK album chart, where it will peak at No. 2.
30. Daltrey's solo album, *Ride A Rock Horse*, enters the US chart, where it will peak at No. 28.

October 1975

3-4. When the Back To Basics tour of the UK begins at New Bingley Hall, Staffordshire, the band is playing with much energy but no guitar smashing.

Pete Townshend: I think it was the healthiest period for The Who, even though a lot of people look back and say, "What a pointless waste of energy, what a foolish thing to have done." But in a way it got rid of some of the anger, the vengeance, and allowed us to concentrate on what really mattered, which, at the time, was probably strictly entertainment.

6-7. Belle Vue, Manchester.

15-16. Apollo, Glasgow, Scotland.

18-19. Granby Halls, Leicester.

18. *The Who By Numbers* is released and enters the UK album chart, where it will peak at No. 7.

Pete Townshend: *Who By Numbers* was revealing, I suppose, because it was all I had left at the time. I just thought, "What am I gonna do, because I'm fucked up, not writing anything?" There was one little chink in the armour, and that's the ukelele track ["Blue, Red And Grey"].

John Entwistle: The cover drawing only took me an hour, but the dots took about three hours. I took it down to the studio while we were mixing and got the worst artist in the room to fill it in. Discovered I'd left two inside legs out.

We were taking it in turns to do the covers. It was Pete's turn before me and he did the *Quadrophenia* cover, which cost about the same as a small house back then, about £16,000. My cover cost £32.

21. Wembley Arena, London.

23-24. Wembley Arena, London.

25. *The Who By Numbers* is released in the US.

27. Brief European tour begins at Sportpalais Ahoy Halle, Rotterdam, Netherlands.

28. Stadthalle, Vienna, Austria.

29. Stadthalle, Bremen, Germany.

30-31. Phillipshalle, Düsseldorf, Germany.

November 1975

1. *The Who By Numbers* enters the US album chart, where it will peak at No. 8.

2-3. Messehalle, Sindelfingen, Germany.

4. Keith Moon reportedly attends a party in honour of Andy Warhol, thrown at the Regent's Park home of Lord and Lady Lambton. If so, he must have flown back in the gap between German gigs.

6-7. German tour ends with two nights at Friedrich Ebert Halle, Ludwigshafen.

20. The Who launch a US tour at the Summit, Houston, Texas. Keith Moon is arrested for disorderly conduct at the after-concert party.

21. Assembly Center, State University, Baton Rouge, Louisiana.
22. A new single, "Squeeze Box", is released in the US.
23. Mid-South Coliseum, Memphis, Tennessee.
24. The Omni, Atlanta, Georgia.
25. MTSU Murphy Center, Murfreesboro, Tennessee.
27. Hampton Coliseum, Hampton Roads, Virginia.
28. Memorial Coliseum, Greensboro, North Carolina.
30. Assembly Hall, Indiana University, Bloomington, Indiana.

December 1975

1. North American tour continues at Kemper Arena, Kansas City, Missouri.
2. Veterans Memorial Auditorium, Des Moines, Iowa.
4-5. Chicago Stadium, Chicago, Illinois.
6. Metropolitan Stadium, Pontiac, Michigan.
8. Riverfront Coliseum, Cincinnati, Ohio.
9. Richfield Coliseum, Cleveland, Ohio.
10. *The Who By Numbers* is certified gold in the US. On the same day, the band plays at Memorial Auditorium, Buffalo, New York.
11. Maple Leaf Gardens, Toronto, Ontario, Canada.
13. Civic Center, Providence, Rhode Island.
14. Civic Center, Springfield, Massachusetts.
15. US tour ends at The Spectrum, Philadelphia, Pennsylvania.

Mark Voger (reviewer, *Astbury Park Press*): The Who show was the hottest ticket in the area at that time. Everybody but everybody wanted to go to that show. Our tickets, which we were very grateful to get, were stamped "Obstructed View". This meant we were behind the stage looking at the backs of The Who's heads. But actually, it was a pretty cool perspective. I'll never forget seeing the dark silhouettes of Daltrey, Townshend, Entwistle and Moon running from backstage up the steps behind the stage, being blasted by flash-cubes. Nor will I forget the sight of Roger Daltrey singing "Listenin' To You" . . . with all of the house lights on, his hair flowing, while thousands of people stood in front of him rocking out.

After the first song, Moonie called down to some roadies and had them move some huge equipment that was behind him (cabinets, possibly?) so that all of the people behind the stage could get a better look at him. Then he waved to all of us. We cheered him, of course.

I also remember that Townshend busted one guitar unceremoniously on the second or third song – just a quick slam to the ground, nothing theatrical. Kind of warm-up, you might say. But at the end of the show, Townshend and Moonie made a huge pile with Townshend's guitar and Moonie's drums. It was pandemonium. Entwistle played through the whole thing.

21-23. The Who Christmas Show is staged at Hammersmith Odeon, London.

1976

January 1976

3. "Squeeze Box" enters the US Top 40 singles chart.

24. "Squeeze Box" is released in the UK and enters the singles chart.

February 1976

14. "Squeeze Box" peaks at No. 16 in the US singles chart.

Pete Townshend: I wrote this song called "Squeeze Box". I went out and bought an accordion and learned to play it in about 10 minutes, so it's a devastatingly simple song.

John Entwistle: That was just a kind of fun thing. We all knew it was about tits. I thought Joe Walsh's "I Like Big Tits" was more to the point.

27. A brief European tour begins at Hallenstadion, Zurich, Switzerland.

28. "Squeeze Box" peaks at No. 10 in the UK singles chart. On the same day, The Who play at the Olympiahalle, Munich, Germany.

March 1976

1-2. European tour concludes at the Pavilion De Paris, Paris, France.

9. Having taken a handful of downers, Moon collapses during the first show of a US tour at the Boston Garden, Boston, Massachusetts, requiring that the ensuing tour be postponed.

John McCabe (*Generations* magazine): My first impression of the group was one of incredible power and energy as the first chords rang out. But, as the song progressed, I sensed that something was wrong. The drumming was sluggish, almost as if Keith Moon was being left behind the rest of the band.

They finished that song and went right into "Substitute". I was using binoculars to get close-up views of the band and when I focussed on the drum set, there was no one behind it. The song stopped immediately after that and the house lights came on. Townshend and Daltrey talked to the crowd, trying to buy some time while they assessed the situation.

The situation was not good. The audience was worked into a frenzy by this point. They expected to see The Who and were not about to settle for anything less. Once the decision was made that Moon could not continue and the concert would have to be cancelled, Townshend and Daltrey did their best to soothe the audience with promises of a make-up concert. Unfortunately, this was not very effective. Their announcements were met with screams of protest.

When Townshend and Daltrey left the stage, the crowd went wild. After about 15 minutes of shouting, people realized that there would be no further show and began to leave the Garden with lots of pushing and shoving and general mayhem.

On our way out, we noticed that several large glass windows in the lobby were smashed.

10. Moon spends the day incarcerated in his suite at the Navarro Hotel, New York, to prevent him socializing or taking any more pills. Instead, he destroys the room and cuts himself.

Bill Curbishley (manager, Who): There was more fucking blood than you ever saw in your life. It was a light-coloured carpet, and the blood was black, really deep. I went down the hallway of the suite, and there was blood all the way down into the living room. I went into the bathroom, and Keith was lying there, and I couldn't immediately get it together, and then I noticed the blood was coming from his foot, and it wasn't that big a cut, but very deep, right on the instep, right into the vein, and with every beat of his heart, it was pouring out. He was so fucking drunk, he didn't know. And he'd been walking around the apartment with it pumping out of his foot until he was so weak he passed out.

11. Miraculously, Moon has recovered sufficiently to play at Madison Square Garden, New York.

John Rockwell (*New York Times*):

> What remains incontrovertible is the sheer excitement of the playing. In concert even more than on records, The Who sticks to the rock'n'roll basics, and executes them with an angry passion that nobody has matched.

Chris Charlesworth: I went back to the Navarro after this show to have a drink with the band and I was told that Keith was locked in his room with a

security guard outside to stop him from getting out. They didn't want him going out and getting drunk and staying up all night and collapsing at any more shows.
13. Dane County Coliseum, Madison, Wisconsin.
14. Civic Center Arena, St Paul, Minnesota.
15. Myriad Gardens Convention Center, Oklahoma City.

Wayne Coyne (audience member, later to play with Flaming Lips): I had older brothers who were into drugs and great music and they would take me to shows when I was pretty young. I saw The Who when Keith Moon was still playing. It was a good time for that big rock show bullshit and that's impressive when you're young, to go to a stadium full of people who go crazy and your brothers are on drugs.

Keith Moon just beat everything in sight, Pete Townshend jumped around and Daltrey hit everyone with his microphone. I didn't know anything about their music, but I was just looking at those guys wrecking the shit up there. They'd do those triumphant songs and it was a powerful experience. I walked away going, "Gosh, why doesn't every band play like that, where they're so into it?" The mayhem of that was so awesome.
16. Tarrant County Convention Center, Fort Worth, Texas.
18. The Salt Palace, Salt Lake City, Utah.
19. McNicholls Arena, Denver, Colorado.
21. Anaheim Stadium, Anaheim, California.
24. Memorial Coliseum, Portland, Oregon.
25. Seattle Center Coliseum, Seattle, Washington.
27-28. Winterland, San Francisco, California.
30. McNicholls Arena, Denver, Colorado.

April 1976

1. The Who end their US tour with a rescheduled date at the Boston Garden, Boston, Massachusetts, to make up for the earlier show at which Keith Moon had collapsed.

John McCabe (*Generations* magazine): Keith Moon made his entrance on stage ahead of the others, did a somersault, then jumped up and ran around the stage waving to the crowd.

The crowd gave the band an enthusiastic welcome and the band picked up where they had left off on March 9. I would have to rate the April 1 concert one of the best I have ever seen.

30. Moon reportedly pays nine New York cabbies $100 each to blockade each end of a side street so that he can throw furniture out of his hotel room window.

May 1976

22. Parc Des Expositions, Colmar, France.

25. Palais Des Sports, Lyons, France.

31. The Who Put The Boot In concert at Charlton Football Ground, Charlton, London, enters *The Guinness Book Of Records* as the loudest performance ever (120 decibels) by a rock group.

Pete Townshend: It rained a lot and Keith brought Elizabeth Taylor. He came in and said, "Elizabeth's in the other room. She wants to meet you." And I said, "Tell her to fuck off." The whole day was a nightmare. I got home and my wife and kids were asleep, and I thought, "What is this about?" But people who were in the audience tell me the show was magic.

Barbara Charone (reviewer, *Sounds*):

> Charlton was magic because it pulled the very best out of The Who . . . the lasers were just decoration. The Who were the real magicians . . . absolutely brilliant.

June 1976

The Who become the first recipients of the Nordoff-Robbins Music Therapy Centre Silver Clef Award.

5. Celtic Football Ground, Glasgow, Scotland.

12. Vetch Field, Swansea, Wales.

Steve Davies (audience): I came to The Who quite late in their career, around the time of the *Who's Next* album and the *Tommy* film. I was 16 in 1976, and they weren't doing a lot of British dates that year. Vetch Field came in the middle of three football ground shows, and I convinced my dad to drive me and three friends (including David Hughes who later played with Orchestral Manoeuvres In The Dark) down to Swansea.

Gates opened about noon, and the first band came on about 2 p.m. I admit I was profoundly disinterested in the opening acts, AC/DC, Alex Harvey Band and Little Feat, and by the time The Who came on in the early evening, I was cold, bored and hungry, but their performance raised me above all of that.

We had started in the middle of the crowd but managed to push to the front by the time they started. What really struck me was the power of Daltrey's voice, which seemed huge for a bloke who by my standards was already quite old. I also remember Moonie standing astride the drums, and the green lasers piercing through the smoke. They were among the first bands to use lasers in their stage show, and it was still very unusual in those days.

July 1976

7. Pete Townshend opens the Meher Baba Oceanic in Ranleigh Drive, Richmond, London.

Pete Townshend: For a few years I had toyed with the idea of opening a London House dedicated to Meher Baba. In the eight years I had followed him, I'd donated only coppers to foundations set up around the world to carry out the Master's wishes and decided it was about time I put myself on the line. The Who set up a strong charitable trust of its own which appeased, to an extent, the feeling I had that Baba would rather have seen me give to the poor than to the establishment of "yet another" spiritual centre.

Richard Barnes: Pete's intentions were highly laudable. He had hopes for the project and was very ambitious. He even had the cash to back all his grand schemes and was doing so. However, he never really saw things through to the end. He was constantly initiating new ideas and projects, but in a few days or weeks his mind would have raced ahead to something new and he'd be changing everything again. He'd have builders in to alter the place, pull down a wall and then erect another somewhere else. A few weeks after the paint was dry, he'd have the new wall taken down and the place altered again. At first there were facilities for filming and editing, then it was video, then it was recording. Pete was like a rich kid with too many toys.

The place was supposed to be an English Baba centre but, apart from Pete's secretary, it was, for the first year or so, full of Americans. Many were very sycophantic, and I fully expected one day to see the photographs of Baba on the walls replaced by those of Pete. Pete was only trying to give people the opportunity and the facilities to carry out their own creative Baba projects.

He also set up a number of companies under the banner of Eel Pie Ltd. I was staggered at the stupidity of some of the people Pete had given key jobs. By mistake, the tape would be wiped off after a day's recording session, or a video would be ruined because somebody forgot some vital function. The whole place was deadly amateurish but with the budgets of professionals.

Many people took advantage of his idealistic good nature; not that they were calculating but, in the main, just inept and hopelessly disorganized – someone would quite gladly spend all day in a company car looking for a box of staples. The Baba Centre evolved just like one of Baba's parables. It became far removed from having any real feeling of love surrounding it, as mountains of expensive technology seemed to amass itself. The incongruous combination of recording studio and Baba workshop under one roof was a typical, badly thought-out move by Pete. The whole place seemed to be a reflection of his own confused state of mind at that time.

August 1976

3-4. An American mini-tour begins with two nights at the Capital Center, Largo, Maryland.

7. A new single, "Slip Kid", is released in the US. The same day, The Who play at the Gator Bowl, Jacksonville, Florida.

Chris Charlesworth (journalist): This was the last Who gig I saw with Keith on drums. They were closing an open-air all-dayer in a big stadium, in muggy, unpleasant weather after an ill-judged, weak supporting cast had limped on and off stage to little purpose. A greedy promoter had overcharged and Florida was never Who territory, so the crowd numbered 35,000 instead of a potential 60,000. This hurt their pride and they were angry at what had happened, furious in fact, and having watched The Who at close quarters scores of times by then, I knew all too well that anger could bring out the best or the worst in them. Sharp words were exchanged backstage and I kept my distance. Only Keith, fuelled as ever by Remy Martin brandy, seemed sociable. But, come showtime, there was an extraordinary transformation and all their fury, all the frustration and pent-up rage that spilled out of Pete and Roger, was channelled into the music, and they played an absolute blinder, as powerful as any show in the classic 69–71 era. The Who at their almighty best came flooding over everyone in that stadium that night. At the end they smashed their equipment in an orgy of gleeful destruction and the crowd exploded with endless ovations because they'd never seen or heard anything like it before, nor would they ever again.

Afterwards, backstage, in the calm of the caravan that served as a dressing room, I clearly remember sitting down next to Pete and remarking to him on how good this show had been. Exhausted, slumped in a corner, his fingers shredded and covered in blood, his skinny, loose-limbed body wrapped in a towel, he knocked back a huge beaker of brandy in one gulp. There was a strange faraway look in those deep blue eyes of his as he looked up at me. He thought for a minute, fingered the Meher Baba badge that hung from his neck, then managed a wry smile. "We were playing for the people who weren't there," he said.

9. The US mini-tour ends at Miami Baseball Stadium, Miami, Florida.

Pam Brown (reviewer, *Creem*):

They played 20 songs over a period of two hours, spanning their history from "Summertime Blues" and "Can't Explain" through *Tommy* and their current hits from *The Who By Numbers*. Everything was superb; Pete Townshend is still the greatest guitar showman of all time – age has not lowered his jumps, weakened his splits, or altered the quality of his unique playing style. Roger Daltrey sings more beautifully than ever; years of practice and solo endeavours have increased his range and melodic abilities to the hilt. It's thrilling to watch him circle the stage like a caged animal. Keith Moon is still the wonderfully mad drummer – so what if he drinks too much and has fun at parties; he's still great. And John Entwistle goes on writing, playing, singing . . . just being his steadfast sturdy self. The Who are an establishment; they will last as long as they keep touring and recording.

September 1976

18. Keith Moon attends The 2nd Annual Rock Music Awards at the Hollywood Palladium, and goes on to the post-show party at the Beverly Hills Hilton in the company of Aerosmith's Joe Perry and Steven Tyler, Stevie Wonder, Peter Frampton, Mick Jagger, George Benson, Elton John, Ron Wood, Rod Stewart, Donna Summer and Fleetwood Mac.

October 1976

6. The last leg of the Who By Numbers tour kicks off at Veterans Memorial Coliseum, Phoenix, Arizona.

Pete Townshend: In late '76, I was actually feeling pain on the stage. I've got one ear which is damaged. It can't resist certain frequencies. It's got no muscle or hairs in the ear to do anything with those frequencies; so the sound goes right to the eardrum, and it's quite painful.

One doctor advised me to learn how to lip-read. I said, "You can't be serious!" He said, "Learn to lip-read." As it happens, I can already lip-read, 'cause on the stage we do it to communicate with the sound man. This doctor said, "There's a possibility, if you go on the way you're going, that you could be deaf by the time you're forty." I said, "Listen, I'm only thirty-three. You're tellin' me that I could be completely deaf in SEVEN years?" "Yes," he said, "it's a possibility. The only other thing you can try to do is conserve your hearing." He said I'll definitely be deaf by the time I'm 50. Totally deaf. And I just started to think, I'm a musician, but most of all, I love music. I love listening to it. I like hearin' what people are sayin'. And I started to think quite seriously that I'd prefer to be blind than deaf. People chuck platitudes about Beethoven, but at least he could write music.

7. Sports Arena, San Diego, California.

9. Compilation album *The Story Of The Who* enters the UK album chart, where it will peak at No. 2.

9-10. The Who share the bill with The Grateful Dead at the Oakland-Alameda County Stadium, Oakland, California.

Pete Townshend: With the Dead, it was all on stage. They were having a good time. They enjoyed one another's company. One of them might walk off halfway through and go chat with somebody. It was slow, it was easy. They were taking their time. They were being almost mystical about the process.

Jerilyn Lee Brandelius (Grateful Dead staff): On the second day, they opened the show. We were sitting in the dressing room during the break. Pete Townshend came in and he said to Garcia, "I've seen you play three sets and I'm wondering how you figure out what you're going to play. Because it doesn't seem to me like you have a list or anything like that. We've been playing the same set on the entire tour. The same songs." Jerry said, "Gee, man, I don't know. I never really thought about it. We just kinda get up there and do it." Pete said, "Wow, that's incredible. That's just amazing."

A couple of weeks after this conversation, we were on the road somewhere and [Grateful Dead rhythm guitarist, Bob] Weir said, "I've been thinking about what Pete Townshend said. I think we should make up a set list." The guys went, "Ahh, Weir. Stuff it." He was going, "No, no, no. I think we should have one." So they said, "Okay, Bob. Make up a set list, we'll play it." They made up this list of songs and they went out there and started playing. They were playing along and they came to a point where Weir was supposed to know the list. They turned to look at him. Weir looked back at them and they all stopped playing. They just stopped. Because they didn't know what they were supposed to play next.

Pete Townshend: They were not striving for success. There was no stress. There was no success ethic. They were moving like gypsies across the planet and they just happened in that place. I always knew they would carry on until Jerry Garcia was old and grey.

13. Alameda County Stadium, Oakland, California.

14. Seattle Center Coliseum, Seattle, Washington.

16. Northlands Coliseum, Edmonton, Canada.

18. Winnipeg Arena, Winnipeg, Canada.

21. North American tour ends at Maple Leaf Gardens, Toronto, Canada, followed by a lavish end-of-tour party.

Pete Townshend: It was the first party I had been to for at least five years that meant anything to me. I don't go to a lot of parties, but I'm glad I made this one. I suddenly realized that behind every Who show are people who care as much as, or even more than, we do. Talking to the individuals who help get the show together enabled me to remember that audiences care too.

Then we rushed back to England and had no new album, nothing happening, no feeling of existing and, every time we picked up a paper, there were snivelling little brats knocking us.

30. A reissued single of "Substitute" enters the UK singles chart.

November 1976

19. The Sex Pistols release "Anarchy In The UK".

Pete Townshend: When the New Wave came along, it was a great affirmation. Aye, we're not dead yet. It freed me and allowed me to be myself. It dignified and allowed me to be cast to one side. I felt very uneasy with the way The Who were inevitably on the road to mega-stardom. I believed that the punk movement would free me from that. It did.

It was the closing of a circle. It was part of what had been nagging at me. It didn't seem the music business was ever gonna get back to rock again . . . We were getting older, more mature and settling down.

20. The re-release of "Substitute" peaks at No. 7 in the UK singles chart.

1977

The years 1977 and 1978 were, in terms of activity under the umbrella of The Who, exceptionally low-key. The band pursued solo projects and collaborations, the most significant of which are detailed below.

January 1977

Roger Daltrey is in Ramport Studios, Battersea, London, working on tracks for his album *One Of The Boys.*

At The Speakeasy, London, Townshend gets into an argument with the Sex Pistols.

Pete Townshend: The song "Who Are You" was the product of one particular day on which two things happened: I met the Sex Pistols and I was stitched against the wall by a guy called Allen Klein, who had a piece of The Beatles and has a piece of the Stones and who had always wanted a piece of The Who. I went to this meeting and discovered that somehow he'd managed to buy into my publishing company. And I hated him. I hate him still. I can't bear him. I can't bear the fact that he's a part of my life.

It was an 11, 13, 14, 15-hour meeting in this Poland Street office and we only got out about 10 o'clock at night. I was with Chris Stamp, and he said, "C'mon, Pete, fucking relax. Let's go see some punk bands. Draw a line. Let's go forward, forward. Modernism!" So I said OK, and we went to look for some punk bands and we couldn't find any. So we went to The Speakeasy, and lo and behold, two of the Sex Pistols were there, and I fell on them like a hungry wolf and what they got was my anger and frustration at having been fucked up the arse by this guy that I hated, and he'd managed to get hold of one of my testicles, and I was just saying to them, "It isn't fucking worth it. If you want it, you can fucking take it. I don't want it. Rock'n'roll is something good. If you can make something good of it, take it, but I have been degraded, humiliated, and ultimately tortured and tossed aside like a rag by this industry." And their response was, "Oh. What a shame. We really like The 'Oo." And it just made me so angry! I ran out in the street and at 2.30 or 3.30 in the morning I was in Oxford Street, asleep in a doorway with a piece of paper in my hand, and a policeman woke me up.

I can't remember exactly what was said, but it was like this. He said, "Sir, if you can prove to me that you can get up and walk away, you can sleep in your own bed tonight." So I went, "'Oothefuckareyou?" Hahaha! So he said, "I, sir, am Police Constable So-and-so, and I know who you are – otherwise I wouldn't be making you this offer in the first place."

So I stumbled away, but with this lyric in front of me, a few verses about this, that and the other that were starting to kind of emerge, about being in this meeting – "Eleven hours in the tin can, there's gotta be another way" – and I just quickly scribbled out "Who the fuck are you?", wrote the verse about the policeman: "Woke up in a Soho doorway, policeman knew my name . . . said you can get up and walk away."

So there was the song, a song about the humiliation of that whole day, the degradation, the absolute end that it represented. And the end, in an interesting way, was again distorted by the fact that when The Who went into the studio and played it, it sounded like an anthem. So resentment, and pathos, and apathy turned again to empowerment and anger and defiance.

February 1977

Pete Townshend, Ronnie Lane and Eric Clapton work on the *Rough Mix* album at Olympic Studios, Barnes, Richmond, and Eel Pie Studios, London.

Ronnie Lane: I was having a brain trauma.

Pete Townshend: He nagged me to do it.

Glyn Johns (producer): A couple of years after I'd worked with Ronnie Lane on "How Come", I made the *Rough Mix* with him and Pete Townshend, and that was also where I met Eric [Clapton] again. Before that, I didn't know him very well, and I didn't get on with him, but he and I became close friends during the making of that album, which I think is one of the best records I've ever made.

Pete Townshend: I got angry with Ronnie about halfway through the sessions because I thought he was a drunk, just a drunken pig. I don't know why I was being such a hypocrite, as I used to drink far more than he. But he was falling all over the place, and I got angry with him in the hallway and pushed him. I punched his right shoulder to emphasize a point, and he went flying down the hall. It was then I realized he was sick. [Lane was in the early stages of multiple sclerosis.]

Glyn Johns: Townshend had written an instrumental specifically for Eric to play on – which I still think is rather odd, since I never thought it was that great, nor could I really see what it had to do with Eric. I had to tell him (Pete) that at that point, Eric and I didn't get on, and I wasn't sure if it was a very good idea, and I wondered if we really had to do it. He said he really wanted it, so I felt it would probably be all right just for one session. We cut the track, and Eric came and played on it, and we got on fine. It was harmless enough, but Eric didn't play that well – I don't think it was that easy for him to play actually, and it wasn't that great, a fast up-tempo thing. After we'd finished the track, Eric hung around while we carried on recording, and he came back the next day and ended up hanging out for the rest of the week, because he enjoyed the experience, I suppose. He and Ronnie became good friends and he and Pete were already very good friends.

Pete Townshend: Ronnie's contribution to my stuff was much, much deeper. He has always encouraged me to do stuff away from the mainstream Who clichés. You can get in a rut, and it must affect the way you work. On a song like "Street In The City", it's something I wouldn't have done before. Ron was knocked out when we heard the playbacks. It gave me a kick to see that.

March 1977

Pete Townshend instigates legal proceedings to dissolve managerial ties with Kit Lambert and Chris Stamp.

Pete Townshend: I felt myself being pulled in two directions and in the end I had to let go of my friendship with Kit and Chris and run with the band. If two of your kids are drowning, which one do you save? You don't necessarily save the nearest. Somewhere along the line you make a choice which may be deemed selfish. In retrospect, I made the right choice.

30. At his studio in Goring-on-Thames, Berkshire, Townshend records several demos that will end up on the album *Who Are You.*

Keith Richards (guitarist, Rolling Stones): In actual fact, Pete made better Who records than The Who. He used to go there with the album already finished and the rest would simply come up with some dubs, but his was 10 times better than the finished product. It was a matter of them imitating what Peter had already laid out, kinda Hitchcockish.

April 1977

21. Keith Moon drums with Led Zeppelin at the Forum, Los Angeles.

29. Pete Townshend guests with Eric Clapton at The Rainbow, London.

May 1977

14. Roger Daltrey single "Written On The Wind" peaks at No. 46 in the UK chart in its week of entry.
7. Paul Weller spends his 19th birthday trying to track down his hero, Pete Townshend.

June 1977

4. Roger Daltrey solo album *One Of The Boys* enters the UK chart at its peak, No. 45.

Roger Daltrey: I was ruthless with the material. I listened to about 500 songs, and it's very difficult to find good songs. I'm not a natural songwriter. I can't sit down and come up with 10 great songs like Pete or some of the other songwriters can do but also I don't really like doing old material that's been popular.

September 1977

17. Roger Daltrey solo album *One Of The Boys* peaks at No. 46 in the US.
30. At Ramport Studios, Battersea, London, producer Glyn Johns records strings to add to the song "Had Enough".

Roger Daltrey: I had a punch-up with Glyn Johns, mainly because he put strings on John's track "Had Enough". I went into the studio in the afternoon the day before they put on the strings. I thought, "Fucking hell, strings on a Who track?" When I heard it, it was just slushy strings and I don't like slushy strings.

I don't mind orchestras. I like them triumphant. There's things you can do with strings that can be really good and exciting but what he'd done on this I didn't like. He said, "What do you think?" And I said, "Don't like it much." And he went up the fucking wall. So I think he smacked me and I smacked him and that's how we were in those days. No big deal. I've read his recollections of those events about him always trying to get me to sing different. That's bollocks!

There's not one rock'n'roll singer who's ever sung in more different styles than I have. Don't give me that bullshit! From "Tattoo" to "Behind Blue Eyes", with that softness and vulnerability, to "Who Are You". Don't give me that shit that he was trying to do that, he wasn't.

It's just that I disagreed with him about the direction of the album. I still don't think Glyn was the right producer for that album. He was the right one for *Who's Next*, because we had already done all that kind of pre-production work and all he had to do was mike it up and get it down on record and mix it. I do like the record but basically the mixes are down to Jon Ashley, they weren't down to Glyn Johns at all. I love "Music Must Change" and I love "Who Are You".

Roger Daltrey: That was just when he [Keith] was really bad on the alcohol. He'd just started to go for a cure . . . We had to make a record and we had to get it finished. John and I were quite prepared to get in another drummer to finish the record, which is not the same as getting Keith out of the band. It was a totally different thing. It was totally, totally untrue.

October 1977

4. The Who are working in Ramport Studios, London, on "Who Are You", title track of their next album, but the now seriously alcoholic Keith Moon is in very poor shape.

Keith Moon: In the two years off I was drifting away with no direction, no nothing.

Pete Townshend: I got him behind the drums and he couldn't keep the song together. He couldn't play . . . But before I said anything, he went, "See, I'm the best Keith Moon-type drummer in the world!" There was nobody to top him. But, unless you wanted that, you were fucked, and it so happened, on that song, we didn't.

A couple of days after, he started to call me up just to say goodnight and I love you. He did that about ten times and you could tell he was crying a little. He'd say, "You do believe me, don't you?" I'd say, "Yes, but you're still an asshole."

Roger Daltrey: He had this desperation to be loved, really loved by the people he cared about. Keith had the comedian's disease of trying to make people laugh all the time, but inside he was incredibly unhappy.

Pete Townshend: It was terrible when we realized that Keith, though not actually dying, was somehow gone. He'd changed and he was so much the epicentre of our life.

15. *Rough Mix*, the collaborative album by Pete Townshend and Ronnie Lane, enters the UK album chart, where it will peak at No. 44.

Pete Townshend: I think they [MCA Records] kind of flushed the album. They printed seventy-five thousand copies and held back about fifty thousand. People were going out to buy it and couldn't find it. I suspected conspiracy. I think MCA were worried the money they'd invested in The Who would be lost if

I went out and pursued a supergroup career.
18. "Sister Disco" and "Love Is Coming Down" are recorded at Ramport Studios, Battersea, London.
24. Work starts on recording "New Song" at Ramport Studios.
27. Work on "New Song" continues at Ramport Studios.

November 1977

Rolling Stone magazine carries a lengthy article written by Pete Townshend.

December 1977

15. In the middle of a disastrous Who concert at the Gaumont State Theatre in Kilburn, London, a drunken Pete Townshend shouts at the crowd, "There's a guitar up here if any big-mouth f***ing little git wants to take it from me."

1978

March 1978

13. "Trick Of The Light" and "905" are recorded at Ramport Studios, Battersea, London.
14. "Guitar And Pen" is recorded at Ramport Studios.

May 1978

25. Drummer Keith Moon plays his last gig with The Who – their second secret UK gig for the movie *The Kids Are Alright*, at Shepperton Studios Sound Stage, London.

Dave Lewis (journalist): We were all taken into Shepperton Studio canteen and fed and given large amounts of wine. This obviously got us into the mood.

Richard Evans: We all assembled in the sound stage where Jeff Stein was to film The Who playing "Won't Get Fooled Again" on account of how they had cocked it up when he'd filmed them in Kilburn.

Me and my friend Sonnie were right in the front between John and Roger. Behind us was the camera, on a dolly, tracking back and forth. After various takes of "Won't Get Fooled Again", the band decided they'd just carry on and do a regular gig for the hundred or so people who had turned up.

Dave Lewis: Even though it was a bit ragged, Pete in particular seemed to enjoy himself.

Richard Evans: We got talking to a couple standing next to us. The bloke was a bit of a ted and the girl was an American called Chrissie who kept screaming, "Keith! . . . Keith! . . . Keith for president!" They told us they'd got a band together and they'd just got a record deal with Warner Bros. "Oh, yeah? What's your band called?" I asked. "The Pretenders," she said.

Dave Lewis: Afterwards we all went into the garden to be photographed for what was originally intended as the sleeve of the new Who album. We stood in four lines, and at the front of each was a member of The Who.

26. Further filming at Shepperton.

Dave Lewis: We went back the next day, when they filmed the laser show used in the middle of "Won't Get Fooled Again". This took about three hours and Keith played his drums all the time . . . he never flagged. He was just like a big boy with a huge grin.

Dougal Butler (personal assistant to Keith Moon): I feel genuinely sorry for Keith. He is not capable of coping on his own . . .

June 1978

4. Keith Moon and his girlfriend Annette fly to Mauritius for a holiday.

July 1978

3. Keith Moon behaves so badly on the return flight from Mauritius that he is thrown off the plane in the Seychelles.

14. "Who Are You" is released as a single in the UK.

Pete Townshend: The abyss that I fell into after *Quadrophenia* wasn't a suicidal, apathetic abyss, it was actually quite a venomous one. It was a very violent, cynical mood. *Who Are You* is one of my favourite Who albums, probably because it's the most honest Who album. It shows how out of step we were with the music of the time and also kind of anticipates, or welcomes, punk, which proved to be a further distraction for Keith, who was killing himself in front of everybody's eyes. I was also drinking a lot, huge amounts by this time, and my drinking was affecting my personal behaviour. I was doing things that either I didn't remember or greatly regretted after I'd done them. And yet my writing was getting better and better.

22. "Who Are You" enters the UK singles chart.

August 1978

Franc Roddam (director, *Quadrophenia*): I was working on *Quadrophenia* in offices on Wardour Street. It was in the early stages of casting the film and one of the people I was thinking about to play Jimmy was Johnny Rotten.

One night, after work, Townshend turned up at the office. Johnny Rotten wanted to go out for a drink, and they went into The Ship. Rotten has a legendary capacity to drink . . . Townshend was determined to prove he was as cool as Rotten, so he started drinking vodka, and in the end he was drinking it from the bottle.

So I was in the middle of this competition – Johnny downing the lagers, being very cool and surly, Townshend trying to be magnanimous but, at the same time, some of his old anger was coming out.

After we were well pissed, we went off to a club in Camden to see some punk band. Townshend was driving. He had a family car, a Volvo estate, which Rotten thought was absolutely fucking crass. Townshend by this time was massively drunk and still intent on showing off to Rotten, which was the funniest thing. We were driving down past Regent's Park and came to some traffic lights, when Townshend stops abruptly and the car behind bumps into us very gently. It was a little Ford Escort with a family in it. Townshend was so enraged that he goes forward about 10 feet, then backs into the car. He does this about ten times.

Then Pete accelerates suddenly and shoots off to get away from this car. As he takes off, there's a nurse on a bicycle, and he hasn't seen her. I'm in the back and I lean over and take the wheel, steer away from the nurse and point us back on course again.

Pete immediately throws his hands in the air and says, "You fucking drive!" So he's got his foot on the accelerator while I'm steering from the back.

Rotten just sits there, completely impassive, all pale skin and spotty, saying, "Daft bastard!"

7. The Who's first manager, Pete Meaden, commits suicide.

18. The album *Who Are You* is released in the UK.

25. The album *Who Are You* is released in the US.

26. "Who Are You" peaks at No. 18 in the UK singles chart.

Late August: Keith Moon is called to CTS Studios, Wembley, to overdub drum tracks for the soundtrack of *The Kids Are Alright.*

Pete Wandless (engineer, CTS Studios): I could barely recognize him. I knew it was him, but he was very puffy, very slow. He just looked like he was past it. His skin had taken on that pallor people have when they really are not looking after themselves, quite a greyish colour. I was quite shocked when I saw him, because he wasn't the guy I'd been watching on the screen for the last three weeks. Keith was the youngest member of the band and yet he looked 10 years older than the rest of them.

He got halfway through, and we had to stop the tape. He leaned forward, resting on his two drumsticks on the toms, and he looked through the glass, like, "God, do I have to do this? It's hard work."

September 1978

7. Keith Moon attends a Buddy Holly Week party at Peppermint Park, London, along with Paul McCartney, Carl Perkins, Mickey Dolenz of The Monkees and others. At midnight, they all watch the film *The Buddy Holly Story* at the Odeon Cinema, Leicester Square.

Kenney Jones (drummer, Faces): We were talking with Paul and he said, "I've got this idea I want to call Rockestra, where I'll get a load of musicians together. I want you, Keith, and John Bonham, with all these other guitarists, Pete Townshend and Eric Clapton." Keith and I were enjoying each other's company and, as we left, we decided the idea was fantastic.

Roy Carr (journalist, friend): He looked like a caricature of himself. He was crying – you don't know if he'd put it on or if he was just over-emotional.

Roger Daltrey: Keith had started to have a really bad time, I was the only constant because I was at a period then where I didn't do any drugs. We got closer and closer and closer, till right towards the end when he was cleaning himself up and he finally got off the drink and the drugs. I had a pact with him, because he said, "I've got to tour, we haven't toured for three years – drummers have to work."

But he'd put on all this weight, and he was broken-hearted. And I said, "Look, Keith, if you get yourself set, we'll get you a training programme, and I'll make sure we tour." That was the deal, though God knows how I was going to make sure we toured. But anything to get him to get himself in shape. And we were working on it, and then, boom – he died of the bloody drug that he was taking to cure him.

8. At 3.40 a.m. Annette Walter-Lax finds Keith Moon dead in his apartment in

Curzon Place, London, from an overdose of Heminevrin, a drug prescribed to him to help him combat his other addictions.

Annette Walter-Lax: When he took Heminevrin, he acted drunk and when he was drunk, he wasn't always very pleasant.

I went in to look at him and he was lying on his tummy. His left arm was hanging off the side. And I was getting agitated, worried, because I thought he was going to wake up hungry. I had this menu from a Chinese restaurant and I sat there with this menu by the phone, thinking, "Should I order something now, because he's going to be hungry when he wakes up."

I went in the bedroom again, and there was this awful quietness. You can normally hear when someone is asleep, but it was stone quiet. It was a silence I can't describe. And then, when I went up to him and turned the light on, turned him around, that was when I saw he was dead.

John Entwistle: The worst thing is that none of us were there when he died. We must have saved his life thirty times, picking him up when he was unconscious and walking him around, getting him to a doctor.

Roger Daltrey: The Who as it was, is finished . . . dead and gone with Keith. There is no question of us simply finding another drummer because it can't be done. It wouldn't be the same. Keith was the best drummer in the world. A hundred others couldn't replace him.

Pete Townshend: I don't feel guilty. I feel a sense of inadequacy at being unable to recognize how ill he was. I'm angry with Keith for dying, and I'm angry with the world. It's like if you lose a child, you're angry with the system for not saving that child.

I'm angry with us for not understanding that Keith's whole thing – "I am a crazy, wacky, wild rock star and I can do anything" – was, as they say, a cry for help, and he never got it. What he actually got was his disease fed and fed and fed until finally he died.

Roger Daltrey: The truth is, with Keith it was a phone call that we knew was going to happen one day. He lived nine lives and I'd seen him nearly die several times. When people talk about living on the edge, they don't know what living on the edge is like until they had seen how Keith Moon used to live. I've never met anyone who lived like Keith Moon. He really lived on the fucking edge, oh, yeah.

I love him and I miss him, God I miss him. The world misses him. He was a wonderful human being. Although he had this narcissistic streak in him, his main aim was to entertain people. Mostly at his own expense and in the end at the expense of his own life.

9. *Who Are You* enters the UK album chart at No. 6, its peak position.

Pete Townshend: I wish the band had stopped when Keith died. We were about to stop, but I felt we had to go on and finish off somehow.

Roger Daltrey: We were on a treadmill and when Keith died, we stayed on that treadmill. We should have taken time and thought about what we were. But we just buried our heads in the sand and pretended we were the same band. But we weren't.

13. Keith Moon is cremated at Golders Green Crematorium, London.

John Entwistle: I told a few jokes. We were standing there, it was Eric Clapton and myself, looking at these fifty yards of flowers, and I said to him, "It's just as well Keith isn't here. It would have really aggravated his hay fever." Keith had awful hay fever. He used to turn up with a towel over his head in the limousine when people sent flowers.

16. "Who Are You" enters the US Top 40 singles chart.

20. *Who Are You* is certified as a gold album in the US.

October 1978

21. *Who Are You* peaks at No. 2 in the US album chart, held off the top slot by the *Grease* soundtrack.

November 1978

4. The single "Who Are You" peaks at No. 14 in the US.

December 1978

2. A new single, "Trick Of The Light", is released in the US.

22. Kenney Jones, formerly of The Faces, takes over as drummer in The Who.

Kenney Jones: I feel a bit weird about joining The Who, because Keith is dead. If Keith had left the band, and then they asked me, I'd be fine. But Keith is gone and I miss him.

Pete Townshend: Keith's death made us think very carefully . . . It prompted us to realize that it could just as easily have been any one of us. The Who were sleepwalking along the edge of a cliff, the band had become a celebration of itself and was slowly grinding to a halt. But no one would take a decision to call it a day . . . I decided to become more involved again. To get out and work.

Roger Daltrey: I just felt that Keith was such an extraordinary drummer, to try and replace him was just ridiculous. We had the chance then to be completely free to do literally anything. We could have done so many experiments. We could have added a string fucking quartet if we wanted to.

People were expecting nothing because the Who that people had known at that point had stopped. We just filled the gap and pushed it back into the same slot with a drummer who was quite obviously the completely wrong drummer. No one supported me at the time, including most of the fans. I used to get real vehement letters from fans saying how could I be so nasty to Kenney. I was never nasty to him. I was just stating my feelings about this because I don't feel he's the right drummer.

I'm not saying he's a bad drummer. I'm not saying he's a bad guy. I didn't dislike the guy, but I just felt he wasn't the right drummer for The Who. It's like having a wheel off a Cadillac stuck on to a Rolls Royce. It's a great wheel but it's the wrong one. I took a lot of shit over that from fans and from everyone.

1979

Early 1979

In the wake of Keith Moon's death, Pete Townshend embarks on an extended period of serious drinking and extra-marital encounters.

Pete Townshend: I felt, "Well, he's gone, that means I've got a bit more licence." I was freer, somehow.

I suddenly realized that this gawky kid, who had a hard time even looking in the mirror, was discovering a middle-aged charisma which was hypnotizing women. I looked back at this terrible, troubled, self-obsessed life I'd had and it wasn't the ugly duckling turning into a swan, but rather the ugly duckling turning into Rambo.

It confused me, wondering whether it had happened because of a genuine personal emergence, because women love a drunk, because I'm a superstar, or there's a chance they might get their hands on my money. It took me a long time to come to grips with it.

Kenney Jones makes his live debut as drummer with The Who in France.

Kenney Jones: It was difficult to get used to when I first joined the band. And learning all their songs was really a nightmare. I only had five days to learn 10 years of material. And my memory was really terrible. All I could remember were Faces songs. And everyone thought I knew all the songs. I said, "I don't know your songs. I'm not that much of a fan. I don't go home and play your records all day."

My first gig with The Who was promoting the film *Quadrophenia*. We did a live show in the south of France. So I was doubly paranoid, you know, with all the glory attached to Keith. I tried to keep it simple. But I thought there was no way I could do it, because all the Who songs are quite complex, with weird accents and counts. Yet with the nods and the winks from Peter and John, it was great. I don't actually read music, so I thought I'd make some notes. I had these great big circles and Xs and accents. It became a joke at the end, because everyone would sneak up and have a look at my notes and fall about laughing.

April 1979

1. A new single, "Long Live Rock", is released in the UK.
28. "Long Live Rock" enters the UK singles chart.

May 1979

2. On the day that the film version of *Quadrophenia* is premiered, Kenney Jones makes his live UK debut as drummer with The Who at The Rainbow Theatre, London.

John Entwistle: I don't have to worry so much about the drums now. Keith was so unpredictable . . . I used to worry if he would go out of time. Kenney is a lot more consistent, and he's a lot easier to play with. Keith was the hardest drummer in the world to play with.

Roger Daltrey: Moon's function wasn't to go "boom-chick, boom-chick, boom-chick." He used to play that way because it used to tie the whole thing up. As soon as you put Kenney Jones . . . all he used to do was – "boom-chick, boom-chick, boom-chick" – it was fucking horrible! It used to drive me crazy! I used to want to die on the stage. I was gonna buy him a pair of brushes.

Pete Townshend: I cared about doing it for all the wrong reasons. I carried on doing it for Roger, for John, for the fans. I carried on doing it because I had a contract. I carried on doing it because I had 30 employees. I carried on doing it and I shouldn't have.

11. A film profile of The Who appears on the BBC TV show "Nationwide".
12. As The Who begin a brief French tour at the Arenes de Frejus, Frejus, the movie *The Kids Are Alright* is released.

Pete Townshend: The movie is good. It's not exactly a documentary of The Who or its history or anything like that: it's just a collection of whatever was available. Some of it's TV trash and some of it is very good live footage and some of it is very bad live footage. Kind of a bit of everything. It's fun though, I think. It's a film about the group, not me. And *Quadrophenia* is a powerful film. We don't appear in it and there's not a hell of a lot of music, but we're proud of it.

Roger Daltrey: I can't be objective about it. To me it was wonderful to see. It was Moon's film. I love it for that. I don't think it was well directed or even well put together as a piece of footage on Keith Moon and the band. It's all right. What I like about it is it's completely unpretentious. I don't think anyone can deny that.

17. Second of two gigs at the Pavilion De Paris, Paris, France.

Richard Evans (audience): The two nights at this former slaughterhouse were sell-outs for The Who. I was at the Thursday night show and it was a great gig, very tight. The French audience really went nuts for The Who. Kit Lambert turned up for this show.

June 1979

8. Apollo Centre, Glasgow, Scotland.
9. Playhouse, Edinburgh, Scotland.
27. Townshend performs at the Amnesty International Comedy Gala, popularly known as The Secret Policeman's Ball, in Her Majesty's Theatre, London, duetting with classical guitarist John Williams. During the encore, sozzled on brandy, Townshend falls asleep on stage.

Martin Lewis (producer): Only three people noticed. I thought, "Christ, how will they get out of this?"

30. Soundtrack album to *The Kids Are Alrigh*t enters the UK album chart at its peak position, No. 26. It will fare better in the US, reaching No. 8.

July 1979

7. *The Kids Are Alright* soundtrack album enters the US album chart.
13. Pete Townshend appears for the first time with a group other than The Who,

at a two-day series of concerts organized by the Anti Nazi League under the banner of Rock Against Racism.

21. "Long Live Rock" peaks at No. 48 on the UK singles chart and No. 54 in the US.

August 1979

16. The film of *Quadrophenia* is premiered in London.

18. The Who play at Wembley Stadium, London, with AC/DC, Nils Lofgren and The Stranglers.

September 1979

10. Kenney Jones makes his US live debut with The Who at the Capitol Theater, Passaic, New Jersey.

Pete Townshend: Kenney Jones has been a tremendous blood transfusion. Not just as a player – 'cause he's different from Keith, very much a fundamental backbone drummer – but he's a much more positive individual. Keith was a very positive musician, a very positive performer, but a very negative animal. He needed you for his act, on and off stage. Kenney fits in very well as a person with the other guys in the band.

Roger Daltrey: I have an incredible wife. I fuck around, sure. And she knows about it. If she fucks around I'll say, "If you do, don't let me know about it." That's my male thing. Sure, I'm a chauvinist pig. I don't care if she fools around as long as I don't know about it. She doesn't mind, either. I probably have the best wife in the pop business.

She's just everything I want in a woman. Probably she's more intelligent than me on every level. That's probably what it is and it's great. She can be servile, dominant. Totally satisfying woman. She never comes on tour because she never wants to.

13-18. Five gigs at Madison Square Garden, New York.

October 1979

Roger Daltrey appears in horror film *The Legacy.*

5. Compilation *The Kids Are Alright* is certified a platinum album in the US.

18. Bremen, Germany.

November 1979

2. The Who's movie *Quadrophenia* opens in the US.

Pete Townshend: We produced it, and it is English director Franc Roddam's first feature. It's not based on the music of *Quadrophenia*, but on the story of a kid from Shepherd's Bush named Jimmy, and the trouble he has with the other kids on the street and his family and all that stuff. What's great for me about *Quadrophenia* is there's nothing to explain. It's just a straight story that everybody understands. So much of the talking that went on about Tommy was trying to fill in holes.

3. "5:15" peaks at No. 45 in the US singles chart.

10-11. Conference Centre, Brighton.

16-17. New Bingley Hall, Stafford.

17. Soundtrack album of the film of *Quadrophenia* peaks at No. 21 in the UK.

30. Another US trek begins at the Masonic Auditorium, Detroit, Michigan.

December 1979

3. Eleven fans are trampled to death in a rush for seats at a gig in Riverfront Coliseum, Cincinnati, Ohio.

Pete Townshend: The stampede could have happened at any rock concert. It was much more a symptom of the kids who go to rock'n'roll concerts – being young, getting drunk, doing whatever shitty drugs are available. It can happen at a football game or high school reunion – and it does. But that doesn't mean you don't feel guilty, not that it happened but that it was a symbolic moment and we could have handled it right, but we didn't.

I was drinking so hard at the time I wasn't conscious of what I was saying. And I said some dumb things. I said some things that hurt the victims' families. I remember saying, "It seems that everybody wants us to shed the theatrical tear and to say 'sorry'. Whereas what we have to do is go on." The fact is that we didn't have to go on. We could have stopped, and I think we should have stopped. We should have stopped the tour.

I don't quite know why we didn't. I suppose we didn't, to put it bluntly, because there was too much money at stake. It would have been a big legal mess to cancel tour dates, but we should have. It's obvious that we should have stopped. The idea that "we're going to Buffalo and we're doing this for those kids" was rubbish. The kids were gone. We then should have attended to the families. We should have stayed in Cincinnati. It looked as if we had gone in like commandos, created this havoc, then fucked off to do the same things somewhere else. Our advisors, our lawyers and everybody else were just completely wrong, inhuman and stupid. Everybody was stupid – the record company, the manager, my lawyer, the fans – they were all stupid, completely stupid. Never, ever have I come across a chunk of humanity as stupid as the people with whom I interrelated. As I sat on top of all those stupid people as Mr King. Stupid. I mean, we had to go on for rock'n'roll? What shit! It's like *Wayne's World*, "Rock'n'roll!" That's what we did after Cincinnati. "Rock'n'roll!" Eleven kids dead, but what the fuck?

Roger Daltrey: It's like somebody getting killed in a car crash on the way to a Frank Sinatra concert. I mean, what can you do? In the end we're all responsible for somebody farting in Tokyo, if you believe the theory of chaos. What would have been the point? If it happened when we were in the hall and we could have controlled a situation then I would have felt totally different. Totally different and totally responsible and held my head and said, "This is the end."

But the fact is, it happened before, I wasn't even at the hall. You have to remember it would have been an even worse catastrophe if we hadn't played that night. That's why they didn't tell us. There would have been a total riot. There had already been those people killed on the way in. There could have been more people killed on the way out.

I think that there were some people who should answer to it. I don't know whether they did. It's all in the past now. I can live with my conscience on it.

Pete Townshend: The amazing thing, for us, is the fact that – when we were told, told about what happened at that gig, that 11 kids had died – for a second, our guard dropped. Just for a second. Then it was back up again.

It was, fuck it! We're not gonna let a little thing like this stop us. That was the way we had to think. We had to reduce it. We had to reduce it, because if we'd actually admitted to ourselves the true significance of the event, the true tragedy of the event – not just in terms of "rock", but the fact that it happened at one of our concerts – the tragedy to us, in particular, if we'd admitted to that, we could not have gone on and worked. And we had a tour to do. We're a rock'n'roll band. You know, we don't fuck around, worrying about 11 people dying. We care about it, but there is a particular attitude I call the "tour armour" – when you go on the road you throw up an armour around yourself, you almost go into a trance.

I think the way festival seating was blamed, wholesale, for practically all the problems, was quite a nasty, negative over-reaction – because I like festival seating. When I go to a concert I don't want to have to fucking sit in a numbered seat, and get clobbered over the head every time I stand up. I like to be able to move about, I like to be able to dance if I want to, or go and buy a Coke if I want to, or push my way to the front if I want to or hide in the back if I want to! I also know, from the stage, that you get the best atmosphere with festival seating.

Immediately after the Cincinnati gig, to protect ourselves partly from legal recriminations, we doubled, trebled and quadrupled external security at halls. The problem with Cincinnati was external security, external control: external people control. People in large numbers need controlling. They're – they're like cattle. But a lot of kids complained; everywhere they'd look there was a cop. It spoiled their evening for them. They felt, okay, it happened in Cincinnati, but we don't need that. There was an article in the paper in Seattle, complaining about the fact that there was too much security. It said, "This isn't Germany. The kids in Seattle don't rampage. There's never been even a slight injury at a concert . . ." et cetera, et cetera, et cetera.

The other side of it is worth mentioning: the fact that The Who don't just get their strength from wearing armour. We did go home, and we did think about it, and we talked about it with our families and our friends. I went home to about 10 letters, from the families of the kids who'd died: letters full of deep, deep affection and support and encouragement. It wasn't like these people were being recriminatory. The father of the girl who died who had two children was writing to say that it would hurt him, the family, the friends of the family and friends of the girl, if they knew that because of what happened, because of her death, we changed our feelings about rock. They understood her feelings about the band, and about the music – you know what I'm saying?

We actually left the States – I know Roger and I had a long conversation about it – with an incredible feeling of, without being mordant about it, of love for the American people. Everybody had been so positive, and so supportive and understanding – even to the point where people would come up to me and say, "We know it wasn't your fault." And to some extent it was our fault. It's not exactly the way the Cronkite report made it look, but there was a great share of responsibility there, and people were so willing to – not so much forgive, but firstly to get us back into shape, so that perhaps it was possible for us to behave in a truly realistic, responsive way about the whole thing.

I watched Roger Daltrey cry his eyes out after that show. I didn't, but he did. But now, whenever a fucking journalist – sorry – asks you about Cincinnati, they expect you to come up with a fucking theatrical tear in your eye! You know: "Have you got anything to say about Cincinnati?" "Oh, we were deeply moved, terrible tragedy, the horror, loss of life, arrrrghh" – What do you do? We did all the things we thought were right to do at the time: sent flowers to the fucking funerals. All . . . wasted. I think when people are dead they're dead.

Roger Daltrey: I think it might have made him reassess because he was quite heavily into drugs at the time. We didn't find out until after the show [about the tragedy].

Pete Townshend: What made me stop thinking the show had to go on was obviously Cincinnati. It was a terrible lesson to have to learn. For a long time, I couldn't live with that. It was directly responsible for me literally, emotionally falling apart.

28. The Who play on the second of three consecutive nights of fundraising Concerts For Kampuchea at the Hammersmith Odeon, London.

29. The final night of the Concerts For Kampuchea sees Townshend join 19 other musicians, including John Bonham, Robert Plant, John Paul Jones, Ronnie Lane and Linda McCartney, in Paul McCartney's Rockestra.

Steve Holly (drummer, Paul McCartney): It was during Pete's over-the-top cognac days. Just before we all went on, this poor wardrobe girl had popped into Townshend's dressing room to make sure everything was OK. To her horror, she discovered he wasn't wearing the gold lamé top hat and tux jacket Paul had made up for everybody and, what's more, had no intention of doing so. "I'm not wearing that fucking shit," the surly guitarist roared. Townshend was certain Paul was having him on and never actually expected that anyone else intended to appear on stage in the admittedly tacky outfit. Of course, everyone else was wearing the getup, which left Pete paranoid about being out of step with his colleagues.

1980

January 1980

Surprise appearance with The Clash at the Brighton Centre, Brighton, during their encore.

February 1980

Pete Townshend: Three years off the road has helped it to recover a little bit. We're playin' a lot more quietly on the stage, and that helps a lot, 'cause I don't come off with such a high ringing and don't feel any pain.

16. Townshend records some demos of solo material, including "Athena", at Warner Bros Studios, North Hollywood, California.

Pete Townshend: In 1980, when I was never sober, I was writing songs that were not right for The Who. Some people said that my solo albums should have been Who albums, though Roger never said those words out loud. The songs were personal, and they reflected what I was going through.

March 1980

27. The Who begin a period of sustained touring with a show at Grugahalle, Essen, Germany.

Pete Townshend: What made things even worse was the long period of sustained touring that the band did immediately after my first solo album, *Empty Glass*, came out in 1980. We did about four months' work spread out through a year. I wasn't home very much, and when I was, I hit the bottle heavily. My wife and I grew more and more estranged until eventually there was nothing really there, apart from my relationship with my children, which I maintained as much as I could. We decided it would be best if I went to live in a hotel or in my club in London. I did that and soon I became involved in a much higher level of promiscuity than ever before. It was not through any increase in appetite. I was just so socially demented all the time that I didn't realize what I was doing. I was very gullible. When I was on the road, I would often wake up in the morning with a roomful of girls whom I'd never seen before, simply because I had been so drunk the night before that I didn't throw them out or politely ask them to leave or whatever it is that you do.

April 1980

5. Pete Townshend's solo single "Rough Boys" enters the UK singles chart.

14. Another North American tour begins at the PNE Coliseum, Vancouver, Canada.

Mike Kellie (drummer, Only Ones): I pulled a couple of strings to get us on the tour. Pete wanted us on because of our friendship and because he believed in the band and liked where we were coming from.

John Perry (guitarist, Only Ones): We'd play 12,000 seaters, go down really well, and there'd be people shouting up from the front rows, "What's the group called?" Somebody had omitted to see that our name went on the posters.

26. "Rough Boys" peaks at No. 39 in the UK singles chart.

Pete Townshend: The song is actually taunting both the homosexuals in America – who were, at the time, dressing themselves up as Nazi generals – and the punks in Britain dressing the same way. I thought it was great that these tough punks were dressing as homosexuals without realizing it.

30. The film *McVicar*, featuring Roger Daltrey in the title role, opens in London.

Roger Daltrey: I'm a good actor, and like all actors, I'm always learning. What can I say? I'm always willing to take a gamble and go to something that is against my type. And I've done some good roles and got some really good notices. I'm very happy with the way it has gone. It is not easy to break the mould of a rock star, because the image has to be so strong to be a rock star.

May 1980

3. Townshend's solo album *Empty Glass* enters the UK album chart, where it will peak at No. 11.

Pete Townshend: I always had quite a nice voice, but I never owned it until 1980, when I did my first solo album, *Empty Glass*, with [producer] Chris Thomas. He said, "Why don't you just sing?" And I said, "Because I sound like Andy Williams." And he said, "So?" And I sound like Andy Williams – I've got a beautiful voice.

24. *Empty Glass* enters the US album chart, where it will peak at No. 5.

Mid-1980

At a party in New York, Townshend has his first encounter with cocaine.

Pete Townshend: About midway through 1980 I made the mistake of starting to use cocaine. I became immediately dependent upon it because I loved the feeling of it so much. I'm very much a stimulants kind of character. It also helped me cut through the drunken haze. You sober up when you have a toot, drink more, have another toot, sober up, and of course you repeat the cycle until you're too wrecked at the end of the day to go on.

June 1980

21. Townshend's solo single, "Let My Love Open The Door", enters the UK singles chart, where it will peak at No. 46.

Pete Townshend: Most of my songs are about Jesus. Most of my songs are about the idea that there is salvation and that there is a saviour. But I won't directly mention his name in a song just to get some cheap play.

23. Sports Arena, Los Angeles.

Sylvie Simmons (reviewer):

> They don't get any worse. More to the point, they don't get any different. John Entwistle still moves the usual two inches from the spot and grunts; the nose-on-a-stick still looks heroic, even bashing a bloody tambourine; and, talk about fit, suntanned Roger Daltrey in his little leather jacket and leaping around for two hours straight like some advert for a health farm must have a hell of a leprous pic locked away in his attic back home.
>
> They played all the oldies . . . chucked together in no particular order, yet sounding amazing. The same old ritual except that it still sounds like the first time.

30. The Only Ones, who have been supporting The Who since the start of this tour, are now no longer on the bill.

John Perry: Evidently Roger Daltrey didn't take to us and effectively, we were thrown off the tour, mainly, I believe, because Daltrey was making such a fuss. I think we were expected to socialize more with them – do a bit of good-natured drinking and back-slapping, but we were quite reticent. In my case, the reticence was based on respect. It seems that Daltrey interpreted it as us being some stuck-up punk band who thought we were better than them.

Townshend and Entwistle were the ones I really respected, but Pete wasn't easy to communicate with . . . he was drunk or coked-out or whatever. I thought we were getting on great but we were asked to leave after the LA dates.

July 1980

5. Townshend solo single "Let My Love Open The Door" enters the US Top 40.

August 1980

11. Empty Glass is certified as a gold album in the US.

Pete Townshend: Alcoholism produced my most morally bereft period – 1978 through 1980 – and *Empty Glass*, which most people think is my best solo work. That album is, in a sense, a cry for stability, a cry for an empty glass, for sobriety and for a return to values that I held above everything else. But the reason the cry was authentic was that I was in real trouble. The album is like a war medal. I went through hell and I don't undervalue it, but I don't aspire to do it again. The 14 years since then, being sober, are far preferable, though a few months ago I decided to go on a bender.

20. Townshend's solo single "Let My Love Open The Door" peaks at No. 9 in the US.

Pete Townshend: I released *Empty Glass* and then went on to do the Who tour, and I could see the difference immediately. There were all these girls coming backstage asking, "Which one of you wrote 'Let My Love Open Your Door'?" So there were all these girls, very different from the Who audience, the Who Rottweilers, I called them. Even the women were quite macho – they had to be to survive the front-row nonsense. Maybe five per cent of the audience was female at Who concerts, whereas I seem to have a mixed audience. Then I started to get letters from young gay men who were delighted with "Rough Boys", because they thought that I had come out, so they were in the audience, too.

23. Roger Daltrey album *McVicar*, the soundtrack to the film of the same name, enters the UK chart, where it will peak at No. 39.

30. Daltrey's *McVicar* soundtrack enters the US album chart, where it will peak at No. 22.

October 1980

25. Roger Daltrey enjoys his only solo hit in the US, when "Without Your Love" enters the Top 40 singles chart, where it will peak at No. 20. Simultaneously, a reissue of "My Generation" enters the UK singles chart, where it will peak at No. 20.

November 1980

4. Recording "You Better You Bet" at Odyssey Studio.

John Entwistle: "You Better You Bet" is a good stage number. But to tell the truth, the last two Who albums are a kind of blank. By the time we were recording them, personalities were clashing. There were different ideas of music policy. General backbiting. People not agreeing with each other. Roger and Pete always had differing opinions about everything, but myself and Keith would make our minds up and usually, things went in the way that myself and Keith wanted, so we never got into four-piece arguments, luckily. After Keith died, those were the hardest times . . .

1981

January 1981

25. UK tour begins at Granby Halls, Leicester.
31. The Coliseum, St Austell, Cornwall.

February 1981

3. The Rainbow, Finsbury Park, London.

Richard Evans: This was a great Who gig. They announced it at the last minute on Capital Radio the afternoon before. Mod kids were camped out all night on the pavement outside The Rainbow in the pissing rain, waiting for the tickets to go on sale at 10 o'clock the following morning.
4. On the second night at The Rainbow, Finsbury Park, London, Townshend drinks four bottles of brandy on stage and plays badly, inciting a backstage row with the other band members.

Pete Townshend: I got used to behaving very badly. Once I was so completely out of my brain that I actually humiliated the band in public. We were playing at The Rainbow in London – this was early '81 – and I kept stopping songs and making speeches to the audience. I kept playing long, drawn-out guitar solos of distorted, bad notes. I'd alter the act, making up songs as I went along. And I knew it was London, and I knew that everybody's friends and family were there, and I deliberately picked that day to fuck up the show. I just ceased to care. I threw my dignity away.

Roger Daltrey: It ended it all for me. I was hurt. I thought we were the best rock band in the world till then. I thought we could change the world. What Pete did proved we couldn't.

Pete Townshend: Far from kicking my head in, Roger was worried I was killing myself. Roger's always said over the last year or so when I was going through a lot of shit, "Listen, stop the band if it'll keep you alive. You're the important one to me." I think what I was doing at The Rainbow was testing that.

27. "You Better You Bet" is released as a single in the UK.
28. Deeside Leisure Centre, North Wales.

Steve Davies: Five years after I first saw them, I went back a second time and came away very disappointed.

This was quite a small venue, maybe 8,000 people, and they were playing much too loud for a place that size, and I got the feeling Townshend only grudgingly played the old hits.

There were a lot of punks in the crowd, and lot of heckling from punters who wanted to hear the early songs like "My Generation" and "Substitute", but Townshend was intent on playing stuff from the new album, *Face Dances*.

He didn't even deal with the hecklers very well. He addressed them in this reedy, whining voice and I found myself quite embarrassed by him, as did my girlfriend of the time.

March 1981

7. "You Better You Bet" enters the UK singles chart, where it will peak at No. 9, giving The Who their last Top 10 single.
9. Wembley Stadium, London.
16. When the UK tour ends at the Arts Centre, Poole, Dorset, the band is so dispirited that upcoming US dates are cancelled.

Roger Daltrey: Ever since Keith died we were always trying to recreate what we'd been with him. So in that area it was a total failure. We didn't do anything new.

Pete Townshend: The Who were sleepwalking along the edge of a cliff. The band had become a celebration of itself and was slowly grinding to a halt. But no one would make a decision to call it a day.

28. *Face Dances*, the first Who album to feature Kenney Jones on drums, enters the UK chart, where it will peak at No. 2.

Bill Szymczyk (producer): Apart from the fact that I had never worked with them before, *Face Dances* was the first album that I had made outside the United States. I went to England to do it, and the first few weeks were petrifying, because it was like history repeating itself. Here I am again with another legend, and it has to be handled in a totally different way from somebody like [Joe] Walsh. The act has to trust you – you have to have mutual confidence in each other, and gaining that confidence can be done in an innumerable number of ways.

With The Who, Pete Townshend and I have known each other socially for about 10 years, and when it came time for them to do a new album, the first with Kenney Jones, and on a new label, it was like a new beginning. Everything was new, so they wanted a new producer, and Pete and I had hinted to each other over the years that we would like to make a record together.

One of his favourite albums is *Hotel California*, and really, that's what got me the job with them, that album. Your reputation goes before you, and it's like, "You hear the way that sounds? Do that to me." But with The Who, it was very difficult sometimes to maintain my objectivity – I found that I had crawled into the forest and couldn't see the trees, which was difficult, because it was such a big shot for me. It took almost a year to make *Face Dances*, but it wasn't constant work – they toured three or four times, and in actual studio time, it took about five months.

John Entwistle: We'd do the backing tracks in groups of three. We'd do three and then take a break and then do three more of the same thing. I think that the backing tracks took us ages for that album. Then he'd take a group of three of the best ones and cut them to little pieces and stick them back together again.

I mean, the tape would go round and it would be stripped, editing bits out. It was kind of a strange way of doing it for The Who. It was Kenney's first album with us as well. And we were doing stuff like, "I prefer that bit because of the bass and there's a good drum break there. I want that bit." It just seemed an incomplete way of recording. Those are the only ones that took any length of time. We were usually real fast. Most of the time, with the exception of when we were doing stuff like "Won't Get Fooled Again" or "Baba O'Riley", we were playing to tapes then. Usually when we went in we'd hear the song for the first time the day we recorded it.

Roger Daltrey: I love *Face Dances*. I love all the songs on *Face Dances.* Imagine if they had been played with a great drummer, as they are when we play live now with a drummer like Simon Phillips or whoever I take on the road with me on my tour, you can hear what the potential of that album could have been. Listen to the drums on that album and you tell me if they're any fucking good. As a fan yourself and someone who is writing this article, do you think they're any fucking good?

Kenney Jones: On that record, I liked the songs, but I just thought the chemistry of the band and producer wasn't right. The sound was too laid-back, like rubber. It simply wasn't right.

Bill Szymczyk: I have to tell you one thing – the songs that Pete Townshend wrote are just amazing, and when I can stand back from it and listen to it as a whole, the album is brilliant, and as a writer, Pete has grown by leaps and bounds. I think that Kenney Jones has been a great addition to the band, and I really love the record, but it was such a big deal to me that I can't be certain that I'm being completely objective about it.

April 1981

4. "You Better You Bet" enters the US Top 40 singles chart. On the same day, the album *Face Dances* enters the US album chart, where it will peak at No. 4.
7. Kit Lambert dies from a brain haemorrhage caused by falling down a flight of stairs at his mother's home.

Simon Napier-Bell: I saw him just a few days before he died. We were at this club, Yours And Mine, which was the great showbusiness seedy gay club in London. For three or four years he'd been in a bad way. He no longer told the great monologues he once did, and he'd fall into a coma in the middle of his soup – his drug-taking was just in excess.

He'd also been declared bankrupt and he was living on £200 a week as a ward of the court, although he had millions in his bank account. I imagine that he'd get the money every week and immediately use it to pay for the previous week's heroin. He would also borrow money from The Who, or fiddle his expenses . . .

But that night at Yours And Mine, he was on top form, shouting over the music about some experiences he'd just had in a railway station in Rome, and how he was going to go and live there in a hotel, it was all to do with his Rome rent boys. He was great. I thought he'd maybe got control of himself again, but then a week later he was beaten up, went home to his mother's and fell down the stairs.

Pete Townshend: I had even more licence . . . I felt I could get away with even more . . . I just took anything I could lay my hands on as a way of passing the time, because I hated the sensation of not being drunk.

28. Grugahalle, Essen, Germany.

Pete Townshend joins The Grateful Dead on stage after The Who had performed a full set for the German TV show "Rockpalast".

Rock Scully (manager, Grateful Dead): Pete Townshend called me and asked for the Grateful Dead to come bail them out of their European tour when The

Who were breaking up. Pete wanted us to be the co-band with them and do London and Germany. It was such a great opportunity. We were going to go to one TV station in West Germany and play this rock TV show that went to 32 countries. It was like doing a whole tour of Europe in one city and with The Who. Garcia was very reluctant to go because there were no drugs and he was strung out and he didn't know what to do about that. I had to go to the rest of the band and tell them how Jerry was going to be covered. I had to have Pete call back and say he would have somebody there at the airport to meet Jerry and we didn't have to worry about it. There would be something there for him the moment he arrived. Pete was already clean but he knew where Jerry was coming from. Then we had to convince Jerry. First, I had to convince all the rest of the band that this would be a really good trip to do and then in a band meeting, everybody went, "Jerry, we've got to do this," and then Jerry went for it.

Pete Townshend: I think it was in Germany that Jerry said to me, "I know none of this stuff is academic enough for you. Do you want to play some Wagner?" I said, "Come on, let's try. Götterdämmerrung? What key is it in? Let's go for it."

May 1981

9. As "You Better You Bet" peaks at No. 18 in the US, a new UK single, "Don't Let Go The Coat", enters the UK chart, where it will peak at No. 47.
30. At Brockwell Park, London, Pete Townshend is second on the bill to Aswad, in an all-day concert arranged by the Trades Union Congress (TUC) as the culmination to the People's March For Jobs campaign.

Mid-1981

Townshend discovers that his reckless lifestyle has left him £1m in debt, and that his creditors are attempting to seize his house and other possessions.

Pete Townshend: I had to go to Karen and say, "Can we raise money on the house? Can you sign this piece of paper, which allows the bank to do this and that? Can we sell our country home?"

June 1981

Townshend ceases work on his second solo album.

Pete Townshend: Everything got increasingly worse until about June or July of

1981, when I was making my second solo album. I had to stop making it, because I literally couldn't work. I was becoming exhausted through being in a recording studio.

This really got to me, because rock'n'roll should be all fun, all pleasure. There's quite a lot of guff talked about the pressures and the rigours of the road, but if people don't like it they shouldn't do it. It's not happiness that you're seeking. It's pleasure. Pleasure through music, highs, euphoric feelings – all these extremes. I couldn't stand this fucking feeling of being wrecked all the time, and feeling that I was going to be sick.

I went to this doctor and he prescribed some sleeping tablets, some high-power vitamins, and an anti-depressant, or tranquillizer of sorts, called Ativan [chemically similar to Valium or Librium]. Now these Ativans were really the business. They made me feel incredibly good. I felt as if I could cope with everything.

September 1981

After his first experience of heroin, while drinking with Paul Weller and Steve Strange, at Club For Heroes in London, Townshend collapses and is rushed to hospital.

Pete Townshend: In the nightclub that evening, a so-called friend of mine in the music business said to me, "You look really smashed." I said, "Yeah, I am." He said, "I've got something for you." And he took me in a toilet and gave me an injection of heroin. Apparently, I had used heroin in front of a few gossips one night, and word had gotten around that I was a heroin addict. So this guy thought I was suffering from withdrawal and that he was doing me a favour, when in fact I'd simply had too much to drink. Anyway, the shot of heroin temporarily killed me – my heart stopped. When they carried me into the hospital, I was dark blue. The nurse actually had to rip off my shirt outside the hospital and beat me back to life.

18. *Face Dances* is certified as a platinum album in the US.

November 1981

Townshend starts work again on his second solo album.

Pete Townshend: About a month before Christmas, I decided to go back into the studio again. And there was this French woman hanging around all the time, and she asked me, "Have you got any junk?" And I said, "No." And she said, "Well, how the hell are you managing?" So I said, "Managing what?" I suddenly cast my mind back and I remembered a series of events that had happened to me throughout the year. The most notable incident was being carried out of a nightclub and taken to a hospital with a drug overdose. I had not been able to remember the circumstances except that, when I got to the hospital, a nurse found needle holes in my arm.

After this happened, I rang up a friend of mine who was a dealer in cocaine. Incidentally, he is now dead at 26 years of age. He died of an OD last week, just before I came away. Anyway, I rang him up and asked him, "Have we been doing any, you know, smack?" And he said, "Yeah. Sometimes I put a bit in with the coke, but not enough to cause any problems." But you see we'd been doing a lot of freebasing . . . So when the Ativan stopped working, and I turned to heroin, it did not take long for me to become well and truly hooked. I just sort of topped off a habit, I guess.

I'd been freebasing two or three grams of coke, which required about half an ounce of coke to produce; I was smoking about one gram, sometimes more, of heroin; and on top of that I was usually taking about eight to ten Ativan tablets plus two or three sleeping tablets to get to sleep at night – I was a walking pillbox.

December 1981

Following another horrific drug binge, Townshend is invited to return home for Christmas by his wife, Karen.

Pete Townshend: I reduced myself to a gibbering heap of rubble and then woke up in some venue having injected myself with whatever was available. I was literally just barely breathing, covered in blood, warts, slime, phlegm and vomit.

I was still surrounded by people who wanted to get close to me though. People did care about me, people did come to my rescue.

31. While trying to come to terms with the fact that overspending has left him £1m in debt, Pete Townshend visits the office of his publishing firm, Eel Pie.

Pete Townshend: It was frightening and I dealt with it by drinking too much. I was very drunk one New Year's Eve and went into my Soho office to find 40 employees, none of whom I'd ever met. They were accountants who'd been brought in to "save" me. I thought, "When this happens, I'm supposed to throw myself off one of the duller Thames bridges." Instead, I called my manager, asked for £1 million, and he said, "No problem." I soon paid it back. A lot of the time I was running around in a melodrama of my own making.

1982

Early 1982

In California, Townshend undertakes the NET or "Black Box" cure pioneered by Dr Meg Patterson.

Pete Townshend: From the moment I touched heroin, though, I felt as if I'd joined forces with the devil. I went from being unbearably lucky to becoming a powerful foe – my own worst enemy. It was as if I had opted for my self-destruction. It finally dawned on me that heroin was a very bloody adversary, and that I had to be prepared to lose my life in order to gain it again. It was at this point that I got the idea to ring up Meg [Patterson] in California and ask her what I should do. She insisted that I fly out the next day, which I did, and three days later I was straight.

I took a massive dose of heroin to get to California, and the Pattersons met me at the airport in a van and they hooked me up to the machine as soon as I got in.

Dr Meg Patterson: He was so badly into drugs. He looked as if he had been in a concentration camp, but within a week, he was totally changed.

Pete Townshend: NET is a fairly simple thing. It restimulates the brain to produce endorphins. The theory is that the brain stops making its own opiates if you take heroin. You see, drugs literally barge their way in and grab hold of the receptors. Drugs wreak havoc where there was once peace and harmony. So with NET, you use an electrical frequency that will restimulate the problem area.

The first frequencies they gave me were low ones for heroin. I think it was kept on that setting for about eight hours.

I just got this sense of a natural energy flowing into my body. It was as if all sorts of dormant feelings were being rekindled. The inner joy of recovery, and becoming independent from drugs, it produced this tremendous feeling of rejuvenation.

Meg took my Ativan addiction even more seriously than the heroin, which really surprised me at the time, because the Ativan was, after all, prescribed by a doctor.

On the second day, the battery of the bloody machine ran out, or something went wrong. We were totally unaware of this until it became clear that I was going into steep withdrawals. I got the full belt of the symptoms back – the panic, the nose-running, and fantastic cramps, particularly in my arms and legs. When they got the machine working again, I got only some of the symptoms – and they were far less severe. I got a runny nose and I did have muscle cramps. I had a certain amount of difficulty sleeping, but it wasn't too bad, really. I felt fairly warm. But most important of all, I got back the ability to act.

By the second day, in fact, I knew I was on the home stretch. And on the third day, I started to look and feel human again. I started to read newspapers and to write about the way I felt. I remember writing things like, "I want to go out for a walk. I don't believe it." I could really feel my passion for life returning.

Another thing was that I'd had traces of returning sexuality. Initially, that was quite troubling for me, because I'd put down a lot of my problems in relationships to an abnormally dynamic sexual appetite – and a confused sexual appetite. I'd talked to close friends about it and they'd said, "Oh yeah, well, you know, that's pretty much normal if you're an aggressive, high-strung individual. After all, half the people who are successful in business or acting are sex crazy." But I suppose that for about a month, maybe two months, before being treated I'd felt no sexual feelings whatsoever, so the treatment definitely had a rekindling effect.

I think I also wrote that I was still feeling somewhat bitter, or betrayed. But then on the fourth day, I woke up with this aggressive, angry attitude toward life. No, arrogant is perhaps a better word. I believed that I could take on the world. Later on, though – on the fifth day, I believe – I started to get depressed. Meg would then turn the machine up to a high frequency for an hour or so to stimulate the cocaine-type receptors in the brain. And if it was left on too long at this setting, I would start babbling away and everything in the room would start to go *woooooooo.*

The intensification of colour and sound, often in a very pretty way, was just like acid. But there was no confusion of sense channels – that didn't happen. I really felt up until the next day, when I woke up nauseous and achy. A lot of the withdrawal symptoms had actually returned in their own shape.

Before, when I tried to stop using heroin unaided, I not only suffered severe withdrawal but was completely unable to get out of bed, even to carry out the most minute task. If the phone rang next to my bed, it might take me 10 hours to pick up the receiver. I'd be so far gone I hardly knew what I was doing. The major difference with Meg's treatment is that you immediately get back the ability to act. I didn't suffer from that horrible kind of paralysis.

Somehow I managed to come through all of this with my brain still intact, with enough common sense and dignity to re-establish my family. And by re-establish my family, I mean I was allowed back, as it were. I had to acknowledge everything that was wrong with my life. What had gotten me into so much trouble to begin with was my refusal to face up to various problems. So one of the first things I did after getting back was deal with the bank.

I gave them my record contract and said, "Listen, hold on to that. Don't charge me any interest. I'll get on with delivering the record and you just take the lot. I'll pay you over three or four years." I also sold a lot of assets. I closed my bookshop and sound equipment company. I sacked a few people. I raised the rates at my recording studios. I cut down on personal spending. I sold my Ferrari and my boat.I also managed to convince the guys in the band that I would stay alive if they allowed me to work with them again.

April 1982

29. At the 27th Ivor Novello Awards in the Grosvenor House Hotel, London, The Who are given the Outstanding Contribution To British Music Award.

Roger Daltrey: We were getting along well. We were trying to support a man we thought we were going to lose. He was very badly into drugs. This wasn't just an alcoholic binge. This was someone who was kind of nodding out on the big one [heroin]. You try and pull together. You avoid all of those situations which can make people go back on that. So maybe we were too soft. Maybe the lack of the in-fighting did help destroy the band. I don't think it did. I think Pete had already made up his mind.

June 1982

At Turn Up-Down Studios, Townshend works on demos, including a song called "I've Known No War".

Pete Townshend: On "I've Known No War", we used a series of rhythmically modulated frequencies. For instance, we'd start with two notes that had a certain amount of inter-harmonic distortion, which was basically fairly pure frequency-wise. Then we'd break the sound up rhythmically. You have to listen to it with very, very, very open ears – that's the only way I can describe it. You listen to the music it creates in your head. It's strange, but people are quite content to listen to a series of chords without needing melody, because the catalytic event occurs in their mind – that's where the melody is created.

July 1982

3. Townshend's solo album *All The Best Cowboys Have Chinese Eyes* enters the UK album chart, where it will peak at No. 32.

21. Dominion Theatre, London.

The inaugural Prince's Trust Rock Gala sees Townshend join in the "house band" alongside Phil Collins, Mick Karn, Gary Brooker, Robert Plant and Midge Ure. Also on the bill are Madness and Jethro Tull.

24. *All The Best Cowboys Have Chinese Eyes* enters the US albums chart, where it will peak at No. 26.

August 1982

21. Townshend's solo single, "Uniforms (Corps D'Esprit)", enters the UK singles chart, where it will peak at No. 48.

September 1982

4. The Who's new single, "Athena", is released in the US.

9-10. The Who perform their only UK dates of the year at the National Exhibition Centre, Birmingham.

Pete Townshend: After the Rainbow fiasco (in February '81), I had difficulty proving to Roger in particular that I was going to enjoy working with The Who, and that it was important to me that the band end properly, rather than end because of my fucking mental demise. I love the group. What I couldn't stand was the tension of not knowing when it was going to end. I just had to know when it would finish – I couldn't stand the indecision. So we agreed to wind everything down between 18 months and two years from that time.

John Atkins (reviewer, *Generations* magazine):

> The atmosphere of the show was terrific and I think many people sensed that this would be the last time they might see the band. Pete told the audience that The Who would be doing a "proper British tour next year",

but of course they never did. They sounded immaculate and powerful, and gave great hope for the future, displaying none of the apathy that seemed to set in midway through the subsequent US tour. It was really a last gasp for the band, of course. It just happened to be a good night from an era when they had stopped having good or bad nights and performances now merged into a highly regulated uninspired stability. Once again, Pete was on top form, playing stupendous solos. This was the first show where Roger played guitar – unfortunately it was hardly noticeable! I thought the flashbombs that exploded at the start of "Won't Get Fooled Again" were wholly unnecessary; this band never needed such things in the past. Some fans, I know, just couldn't believe they'd witnessed a Who show without hearing "My Generation". Post-concert entertainment was provided immediately afterwards in the grounds of the National Exhibition Centre. Several exuberant (male) fans stripped naked and swam towards the centre of a huge ornamental lake and succeeded in stopping a giant water fountain.

11. *It's Hard* enters the UK albums chart, where it will peak at No. 11.

Roger Daltrey: *It's Hard* should never have been released. I had huge rows with Pete. Pete had just come off detox and he was really looking for help. We did *It's Hard* in the studio and the band was rehearsing before Pete got out of the clinic just to try and keep a vibe up, to try and support Pete. But when the album was finished and I heard it I said, "Pete, this is just a complete piece of shit and it should never come out!"

Kenney Jones: It was amazing what we came out with, because we only had two songs. The rest were a bunch of riffs. And, because we approached it more like a workshop thing, it brought us all back together.

Roger Daltrey: It came out because as usual we were being manipulated at that time by other things. The record company wanted a record out and they wanted us to do a tour. What I said to Pete was, "Pete, if we'd tried to get any of these songs on to *Face Dances*, or any of the albums that we've done since our first fucking album, we would not allow these songs to be on an album! Why are we releasing them? Why? Let's just say that was an experience to pull the band back together, now let's go and make an album."

22. The Who's farewell tour of the US begins at Capital Center, Largo, Maryland, supported by The Clash and David Johansen.

25. As the new single, "Athena", is released in the UK, the album *It's Hard* enters the US albums chart, where it will peak at No. 8.

October 1982

2. "Athena" enters the UK singles chart, where it will peak at No. 40.
9. "Athena" enters the US Top 40 singles chart, where it will peak at No. 28.

November 1982

3. *It's Hard* is certified a gold album in the US.

December 1982

17. In Toronto, at Maple Leaf Gardens, The Who play their final live concert, having grossed $23m on the 39-date tour. Their album *Who's Last* is recorded at this gig.

Roger Daltrey: We finished the farewell tour. And we had one more album to deliver and Pete went away and said he was going to start writing it. If you've ever tried to come in and co-write with Pete and inquire how things are going you'd have the door slammed in your face. He worked himself into an insular situation, as far as we were concerned.

It used to be incredibly difficult to sit down feeling useless because you can't do anything until Pete's done it. That is not easy work, believe me. It's much harder to do nothing than it is to be in there beavering and trying to do something. That's the kind of position he put us in.

Pete Townshend: I didn't handle it properly. I didn't look at what was really going on. I think I didn't know how to. When I would actually talk about the other members of the band having their agenda and me being irritated about the fact they might want to go out and work but I couldn't possibly do so, I wasn't saying they didn't feel it like I felt it, because they did. It's just that I couldn't work out how I could possibly go back. And on top of that, there were obviously other things – Keith Moon's death and the like. I was badly, badly, badly burned when I came out of The Who, and I think that's the only way that I can express it.

Emma Townshend (daughter of Pete Townshend): I'd seen my dad come back after a six-month tour away with something close to paralizing shock. He sat down while his bags were still being brought in and just totally started to shake with sobs – and I'd watched mum keep things together in those long absences while she did a full-time degree. I'd even been banned from ever opening my own front door – the number of weird people I've met is on the high side.

1983

February 1983

8. Townshend receives the Lifetime Achievement award at The Brits, in the Grosvenor House Hotel, London.

Pete Townshend: After finishing the 1982 tour and being confronted with going to the studio yet again with his band, which I thought was really bereft, I had the courage to say, "Fuck it, it's over." From that moment on I've been in complete control of my life. I've had time to sit and look at which part of my life I want to turn into a continuum and which part of it I want to leave behind. It has been done by choice, with a plan, and *Tommy* on Broadway is part of it.

In 1982, in the middle of a Who recording session, I said, "This is it. I've had it. Goodbye. I'm out. It's done." Then the lads all said, "You can't quit," and I said, "The fuck I can't." They said, "But we'll have to pay back Warner chief Mo Austin his $2 million!" and I said, "Listen, if I have to work for the rest of my fucking life to pay him back I'll do it, but I'm out. It's over. I'm going."

April 1983

9. *Scoop*, an album of Townshend's demos and out-takes, enters the US album chart, where it will peak at No. 35.

John Entwistle: When Pete did those albums of rarities and out-takes he went back and changed a lot of his demos, made them even better, so it sounded like we'd copied what he'd done. You have to realize that Keith and me, as individuals, were each at the top of his instrument, so there's no way we'd have just copied the demo.

That's what used to irritate me about Keith Richards. His idea was that Pete just brought stuff in and we copied it exactly. Complete bullshit.

Roger changed bits of melody line and stuff. Songs would end up co-written but the Townshend, he wouldn't split it between us.

Maybe if The Who had taken an equal cut of the publishing, the group might still be together. But, hey, some people don't have to work and some people do.

He was doing all the hard work, obviously, by writing the songs, but the songs were solely attributed to Townshend rather than The Who and that isn't really the truth.

Mid-1983

Roger Daltrey: Halfway through '83 he came to us and said, "No one's phoned me up and asked me how it's going." And that came out of the blue because up until then if we had phoned him up, he would have told us to piss off! He said, "I'm going to finish the band." And that was the end of it.

So I said to him, "If you can't write, let's all sit in a room. If we look at four walls, let's give it two or three weeks and take out instruments. I'm sure we'll come up with something good, Pete." But it didn't work. He was not prepared to share, which is very sad.

November 1983

26. A reissued EP, *Ready Steady Who!*, enters the UK singles chart, where it will peak at No. 58.

December 1983

16. The Who officially split up.

John Entwistle: I wanted to get on with my solo career. I thought there were much greater heights to go on to. And after four years of that, I realized that there weren't any heights to go on to. You'd always get dragged back and have The Who thrown at you. "When are The Who getting back together?" We all realized that The Who would have to get back together again, because they wouldn't let us do anything else. But yeah, I was full of grandiose ideas when The Who broke up for the first time. But it doesn't take long to spend five million dollars.

Roger Daltrey: For me the end of The Who was very sad, because it ended up in almost a very selfish exercise. But I suppose we were all being selfish. I'm being selfish for wanting to keep it going. As much as I think that Pete has written some incredible songs, some incredible songs, the magic that the band gave those songs far outweighs the importance of those songs.

That chemistry was a gift from the heavens. It really was. For us four people to meet up and be able to create that, something that came from Pete on one level and take it to the next level, I've always seen that as the important thing.

1984

March 1984

Daltrey solo album *If Parting Should Be Painless* peaks at No. 102 in the US, and is widely criticized in the press.

Roger Daltrey: If I ever get a good review in the music press over here [in the UK] I shall go and bloody give up rock'n'roll . . . *Parting Should Be Painless* was how I felt then. I'd do it again the same in those circumstances. A lot was going down with me. I was destroyed. The Who was breaking up, that's what that album was about. When you go through a break-up like that you are wounded. If people don't understand that album, it's because they've never been wounded like that. I was just upside-down, inside-out, confused.

June 1984

21. Townshend goes to see Eric Clapton play in Roger Waters' band at Earl's Court, London.

July 1984

28. Paul McCartney is in AIR Studios, London, mixing a disco version of "No More Lonely Nights". In the studio next door, Rolling Stones vocalist Mick Jagger is recording with The Who's Pete Townshend.

November 1984

10. Meatloaf's album *Bad Attitude*, featuring Roger Daltrey on guest vocals, enters the UK chart, where it will peak at No. 8.

Roger Daltrey: It had been a very painful break-up from The Who, and I didn't want to do it any more, simple as that. Then after I did that duet with Meatloaf, I suddenly realized how much I missed that part of it. But doing it on my own was much, much more difficult than I ever imagined.

17. *Who's Last*, a document of the band's final concert, enters the UK chart, where it will peak at No. 48. It will reach No. 81 in the US.

1985

July 1985

13. There are reports of arguments when the band reunites briefly to play at Live Aid in Wembley Stadium, London.

Roger Daltrey: We did not have a row backstage at Live Aid. Where it came from, we were having a photo taken by David Bailey or someone, we'd just come off stage and we were all wringing wet, and he says, "Well, all get in close together." And I made the quip of "What, and pretend we're friends?" Very tongue in cheek, and that was the "row".

None of us wanted to do it as a group. We all offered to do it individually, and there was talk of Pete and I doing it with Phil Collins and David Bowie, but we didn't want to re-form the group. The Who was finished and that was it. But Bob Geldof being the persuasive little sod he is said it would make such a difference to the charity if The Who did it, and you can't refuse that kind of request. I didn't want to do it. I didn't want to be reminded of what I'd lost.

Bob Geldof: At the end, Townshend and McCartney had decided they'd get behind me and grab hold of my legs and hoist me on to their shoulders. I nearly died of embarrassment. It was terrible. These people were pop greats. "Please put me down. I really don't want this." I remember thinking. It may not mean much to someone not interested in pop, but looking back, I am still embarrassed but intensely proud that I was carried on Paul McCartney's and Pete Townshend's shoulders.

Roger Daltrey: What was great was that at the end of it, I could accept that that was the end. I could say, "Great, lads, had a good time." I walked away from it thinking that it didn't hurt. That was what was good about Live Aid – it was like puncturing the boil.

October 1985

12. *The Who Collection*, a compilation, enters the UK singles chart, where it will peak at No. 44.

November 1985

1-2. Two nights for the 'Oo Charity at Brixton Academy, London, with Pink Floyd's Dave Gilmour playing guitar in Townshend's band.

2. *Under A Raging Moon* by Roger Daltrey enters the UK albums chart at its peak, No. 52.

Roger Daltrey: All of my solo albums outside of The Who were always deliberately different, different kind of music, different style of singing, everything, because I was always very conscious that my voice when I sang with The Who belonged to The Who. For me, it would have been treachery to go and make an album where I sang the same as The Who on a solo record. But once The Who was finished my voice came back to me, it was mine again. so on this album I wanted to sing like I sang with The Who – but I didn't realize how difficult that would be without The Who. Something subconsciously used to happen that used to make it very easy for me to sing. Once I got into the studio on my own, I had to start analyzing where that part of me came from. And it was a very painful experience! I thought, for the first few weeks in the studio, I can't sing like that any more! And only when I analyzed it did I realize how far inside me that energy and that part of my voice and my feelings are. It's right in my heart!

30 Pete Townshend's album *White City,* enters the UK albums chart at its peak, No. 70.

Pete Townshend: The central point I'm attempting to make [with *White City*] is that men have been brainwashed into sacrificing themselves for causes which are said to be greater than themselves and which they don't understand. We as a society have all been complicit in encouraging them to sacrifice themselves. Now that the idea of great patriotic causes has been tarnished, we see a tragedy unfolding: the tragedy of young men in the past who willingly threw themselves into futile bloodbaths to amuse chessboard generals and the tragedy of emasculation in the present due to the fact that it's very difficult for Englishmen to find work.

The intent with *White City* was to suggest that it doesn't have to be this way. Originally I was going to call it *The Tragedy Of The Boy.* With the advance of feminism in western society and with women's capacity to have children and bring them up, women can shape the future. I don't object to feminism, but I think men should have a version of it for themselves.

It's unfortunate that sexuality is a component in the nature of freedom. Throughout history, men have satisfied the drive to create and control by leading, writing, and governing. Men gained power through traditionally rewarded acts of heroism, self-sacrifice, and at the most mundane level – and to this day the thing we find hardest to let go of – by doing a hard day's work and bringing home the money. There are so many men who are unable to do that now, and it's backlashing against society in a monumental way.

I work with a refuge for battered women in England, and working there has led me to conclude that domestic violence is often the last resort of men who are lost and emasculated. The popular solution is to separate men from wives and children because society refuses to tolerate violence in the home. Yet for millions of years violence has been the way we've run our countries and protected our causes. We're presently at a fantastic watershed because we're living under a nuclear umbrella. Moreover, the Vietnam War came to a completely unsatisfactory conclusion, so even that old-fashioned kind of warfare doesn't work any more.

An aspect of *White City* that I'm quite proud of is that for once in my life I'm talking about things I know as opposed to expressing opinions as an observer. These aren't opinions. *White City* is a statement of facts – and they're facts I'm already doing something about. When I wrote "Won't Get Fooled Again", which Roger sang with such venom while I accompanied him with great power chords and arm swings, each power chord was another promise. But all it really promised was that there would be another power chord very close behind it. And in the end everyone looks around and says, "Hold on a minute! When are we gonna get the goods?"

December 1985

During a US tour, Roger Daltrey supports Big Country at Madison Square Garden, New York. He sings quite a few old Who songs.

Roger Daltrey: They're just great songs and I'm proud of them. The way I figure it, if I'm going to go out there doing it on my own, sooner or later I'm probably going to get fans who've never heard of The Who, and if I can turn them on to The Who's music, then I'm doing a worthwhile job. It doesn't sound the same as The Who, then again I think it still sounds good.

I love singing. Making records is probably the worst aspect of singing, sitting there in a studio where usually the conditions are bloody awful, and I think I'm a much better live singer than I am a recorded singer. My voice is too big for records. It seems to flatten everything else out. I just want to do it, and it gets a lot out of me that I can't get out any other way.

21. Townshend's solo single "Face The Face" enters the US Top 40, where it will peak at No. 26.

22. Dominion Theatre, London.

The Snow Ball Revue is held in aid of the Chiswick Family Rescue Centre and features a line-up of musicians, comedians and television personalities. The musicians for the show include Simon Phillips, Rabbit, Steve Barnacle, Les Davidson, Billy Nicholls, Coral Brown, Gina Foster and the Kick Horns.

28. Townshend's solo album *White City* enters the US chart, where it will peak at No. 26.

1986

January 1986

11. "Let Me Down Easy" by Roger Daltrey peaks at No. 86 in the US singles chart.

18. "Face The Face" by Pete Townshend peaks at No. 26 in the US singles chart.

22. *White City* is certified as a gold album in the US by the RIAA.

29. Midem, Cannes.

The annual trade show sees Pete roll in with the Deep End line-up which had been seen a few months earlier at the Brixton Academy.

February 1986

9. Townshend plays at the Royal Albert Hall, London in a special concert in aid of the victims of the Colombian volcano disaster. Other artists participating include Chrissie Hynde, Dave Gilmour and band, Annie Lennox, The Communards and Working Week. Pete's eldest daughter, Emma, makes a surprise stage debut alongside dad.

23. Townshend joins The Rolling Stones to play "Barefootin'" and "Harlem Shuffle" during a private party at the 100 Club, London, held to commemorate the death of original Stones member Ian Stewart. Other guests include Eric Clapton, Jeff Beck, Jack Bruce and Simon Kirke.

November 1986

Pete Townshend's album *Deep End Live!* peaks at No. 98 on the US chart.

1987

April 1987

4. Townshend's album *Another Scoop* scrapes into the US album chart for one week, at No. 198.

July 1987

Roger Daltrey releases another solo album, *Can't Wait To See The Movie.*

1988

February 1988

8. At the Brit Awards in the Royal Albert Hall, London, The Who win the Outstanding Contribution to British Music Award.
20. A reissued single of "My Generation" enters the UK chart, where it will peak at No. 68.

March 1988

19. TV-advertised compilation *Who's Better, Who's Best* enters the UK album chart at its peak position, No. 10.

December 1988

6. Pete Townshend declares that he will not tour with The Who.

Robert Greenfield (author, friend of Townshend): I had sat across from Pete Townshend in a cold, draughty room outside his recording studio on the river in Twickenham on the day that Roy Orbison died, listening as he told me how he would not be going over with The Who to tour America one last time even if it was the 25th anniversary of the band. Once the tour began (six months later) reports indicated that the three original band members would each take home between 25 and 30 million dollars. It seemed reason enough for anyone to change their mind.

1989

January 1989

18. Pete Townshend inducts The Rolling Stones into the Rock'n'Roll Hall Of Fame, at a ceremony in the Waldorf Astoria Hotel, New York.

Pete Townshend: In my roasting of the Stones at their induction into the

Rock'n'Roll Hall of Fame, I joked about the fact that I am one of the few people lucky enough to have slept with Mick Jagger. So when it all came out about me, I fought like hell not to comment.

I don't want to deny bisexuality as if I were being accused of child molestation or murder, as if it were some crime or something to be ashamed of, because that would be cruel to people who are gay. But I was bitter and angry at the way the truth had been distorted and decided never to do any interviews again. Not because I had been manipulated but because I didn't trust myself to be precise about what I was saying.

June 1989

21. The Who play a warm-up gig at Glen Falls, New York, prior to a new tour.
24. The 25-date North American tour begins in Toronto, Canada. John Lee Hooker and Nina Simone contribute to sections of the show devoted to Townshend's new work, *The Iron Man*, based on the children's story by Ted Hughes.

John Entwistle: The 1989 reunion tour was good . . . It was the first tour we'd done that made any kind of money. In the past we'd go out for three weeks and come out of it with a couple of hundred thousand each and then take a couple of years off to spend it and go out again for another three weeks. None of us were becoming millionaires. But on the final tour we made so much money we really didn't know what to do with it.

Pete Townshend: The 1989 reunion tour was a piece of cake. I played the acoustic guitar, strummed along while another guitarist over there played all the hard solos and I would just smile at the crowd. I had to do my hair before the show, of course, and jump in the chartered aeroplane afterwards. Hahaha! It was fantastic, such fun and such luxury. It was like, this is the way to live. It was brief, but I loved it. I felt like I was doing my best work every day.

Roger Daltrey: I loved every minute of it. Physically, I was in bad shape for that tour. Very bad shape. I had something wrong with me from birth on the inside that all of a sudden had come to life. It was called a mermangioma, which is a bunch of varicose veins in my guts. I'm okay now, I had it all cut out.

On that tour when I started singing and all the blood would go down because you start pumping your diaphragm, the thing would blow up like a balloon. It stopped me eating. I lost so much weight. God, I was ill on that tour. But the singing was wonderful. And the crowds got me through it. Again, I loved doing *Tommy* when we did it. I didn't like all the guest stars. I'm not that kind of singer. I need to warm up and stay there. Oh, man, is it hard work!

27. The first Who performance of *Tommy* in 19 years is staged at Radio City Music Hall, New York.

Pete Townshend: "I'm A Man" was the song we were playing when I speared myself on my Stratocaster, going, "I'm a maa-aan! Wham wham! Whop!" and the fucking whammy bar went right through my finger and out the other side. I went into deep shock and immediately became a little baby, going, "Ooh mummy mummy!" [see 16 August for full details of this incident]. But it was particularly wonderful playing that song on that tour. It wasn't a Who song but we'd played it from the very beginning. It was probably one of the first R&B songs that Roger allowed us to perform, because of its machismo. He was at that time so insecure about his masculinity that he needed to be macho macho macho. He used to love the songs of Howlin' Wolf 'cause Howlin' Wolf used to sing in this deep, deep voice. Johnny Cash's voice too he used to like. "I'm A Man" was not a song I ever could have written, because I would never have been certain enough sitting on my own, but together we represented this extraordinarily powerful presence, and it was the pinnacle really, especially the version from Radio City, New York, a fucking great version.

I just love the fact that we were able to say it, and somehow it felt right. It really was suddenly just a simple statement of fact. Roger and I would go to the front of the stage and we'd arrived, we were mature now, we could look after ourselves, we were men, and nobody out there would ever argue. It was tremendously dignifying.

July 1989

3. The last of four shows at Giants Stadium, East Rutherford, New Jersey which, between them, have grossed $5,243,672.

John Entwistle: The only tour we ever made money on was the last one [in 1989]. That was three and a half months. We should have charged $140 a ticket.

August 1989

16. While The Who are playing at Tacoma Dome, Washington, Pete Townshend impales his hand on the tremolo arm of his guitar.

Pete Townshend: I picked up the guitar and held it from the tremolo so that everybody could see what had happened. Then I pulled it out and blood started to pump out. And then it fucking hurt. I ran off stage and ended up having oxygen, so I don't remember much after that.

It went through my hand, missing all the nerves and tendons. It just so happened that in Tacoma there's this brilliant microsurgeon who irrigated it with a saline solution for an hour and a half. Next day it was healed.

24. *Tommy* is performed for charity at Universal Amphitheatre, Los Angeles, California. Special guests include Elton John, Steve Winwood, Phil Collins, Patti Labelle and Billy Idol.

September 1989

3. The reunion tour ends at the Cotton Bowl, Dallas, Texas.

October 1989

23-24. Two concerts at Wembley Arena, London.

Sylvie Simmons (reviewer, *Sounds*):

Other than Steve Winwood as The Hawker and Elton John as Mr Pinball, this year's *Tommy* had a new cast. Billy Idol was perfectly cast as the brattish Cousin Kevin. Patti Labelle was every bit as brilliant an Acid Queen as Tina Turner, but the man who stole the show was Phil Collins, who made Keith Moon's dirty Uncle Ernie into a hilarious pantomime figure, in a filthy dressing-gown, socks and underpants, scratching his arse with a beer bottle before offering it to Daltrey.

A sold-out crowd was there to watch. Judging by their age, they could have been the original fans who drooled and swapped intellectual theories about the story when the album first came out. Now, of course, they carried Filofaxes and briefcases to the concert and paid for the £50-£100 charity price tickets on their gold credit cards . . .

26-27. Two concerts at Wembley Arena, London.

1990

Pete Townshend: I bought a 60-foot sailboat in 1990 after the Who tour, because I could not have afforded it before the tour. It was a classic wooden boat, built in Genoa. I entered a couple of races. It was during the time when I wasn't sure if I was going to continue to make records. So there was this kind of early-retirement thing in the air. And I slaughtered everybody. So when you consider retirement, you have to make damned sure it's not just your bank balance that is in shape but also your ability to survive.

January 1990

17. The Who are inducted into the Rock'n'Roll Hall of Fame by Adam Clayton of U2, at the Waldorf Astoria Hotel, New York.

Roger Daltrey: What the fuck is it? I mean, Pete was once quoted as saying, "It's a Hard Rock without the hamburgers."

Every artist, I'm honoured to be on the same planet with them, but some of the industry people that get mentioned at those functions . . . I find it very difficult when I hear people talking about their good old mates from the old days and mentioning names and I know these people have ripped off artists that I've known very well, and unfortunately some aren't with us now. And you think, do I really want to be in the room with some of these fucking people?

February 1990

5. The video *The Who Live Featuring Tommy* is certified platinum in the US.

March 1990

10. The Who appear on UK TV show "Aspel And Co".
20. The video *Who's Better, Who's Best* is certified gold in the US.
29. Compilation album *Join Together* peaks at No. 59 in the UK.

April 1990

14. Compilation album *Join Together* peaks at No. 188 in the US.

July 1990

26. Roger Daltrey wins a settlement totalling £155,000 after winning a case against Home Farm, which he claimed had caused the deaths of up to 500,000 fish in his Dorset trout farm.

Roger Daltrey: I didn't want to grow up to be a trout farmer! It's just something I got interested in and I built a fishery. I built it, I didn't buy it. Then I opened it to the public and people came fishing, so then I had to find some fish, and I thought the only way was to make my own, so that's how I got into trout farming.

Trout farming is very good, because it keeps my head in shape. It's kept me out of all kinds of trouble – your dreams can't go anywhere if you haven't got your feet in the mud, that's the way I look at it. Dreams just float about with no foundation. I couldn't just do trout farming, but it's all necessary, it all has its place.

November 1990

14. *Newsweek* magazine reveals that Pete Townshend is bisexual.

Pete Townshend: I did an interview saying that "Rough Boys" was about being gay, and in the interview I also talked about my "gay life", which – I meant – was actually about the friends I've had who are gay. So the interviewer kind of dotted the t's and crossed the i's and assumed that this was a coming out, which it wasn't at all. But I became an object of ridicule when it was picked up in England. It was a big scandal, which is silly. If I were bisexual, it would be no big deal in the music industry. If I ran down a list of the men who have tried to get me into bed, I could bring down quite a few big names in the music business.

I don't want to deny bisexuality as if I were being accused of child molestation or murder, as if it were some crime or something to be ashamed of, because that would be cruel to people who are gay. But I was bitter and angry at the way the truth had been distorted and decided never to do any interviews again. Not because I had been manipulated but because I didn't trust myself to be precise about what I was saying.

19. Daltrey co-stars in a made-for-TV movie, "Forgotten Prisoners – The Amnesty Files", on the TNT cable network.

1991

June 1991

12. At the International Rock Awards in Docklands Arena, London, Pete Townshend collects a Living Legend Award.

1992

Daltrey releases a solo album, *Rocks In The Head.*

Roger Daltrey: When I did *Rocks In The Head,* I took it down to Pete and said, "Just tell me what you think of the lyrics, Pete, because I think I can write now." And God bless him, he listened to it and said, "Their lyrics are great, Roger." That meant so much to me.

I'm so critical of myself because I lived in paranoia of writing anything for years and years because Pete to me was the ultimate, and it's kind of a hard place to be when you think, "Let me have a go at writing," because what can you do? You have no confidence whatsoever.

1993

Alienated by his drinking problems, Townshend's wife Karen banishes him to a flat in the garden of their Twickenham home.

February 1993

8. The RIAA reports the following US sales figures for Who albums:

Who's Next – 3m
Greatest Hits – 2m
Live At Leeds – 2m
Tommy – 2m
Who Are You – 2m

March 1993

2. Townshend plays at a private party with the Tommy Band, in the West Bank Café, New York.

April 1993

22. The stage show version of *Tommy* opens on Broadway, New York, at the St James Theatre.

Pete Townshend: At first, when I was approached about doing it, I wasn't interested. But I became intrigued with the form. The shows that work on Broadway come down to one magic moment. In *Guys and Dolls*, for me it's singing "If he says the horse can do, can do, can do . . ." There are those moments in *Tommy*, iconic moments. The *Tommy* story and album attained that very quickly. It briefly overshadowed The Who. So it has been good fun to find those moments and re-create them for a new audience. And I am extremely enthused about Broadway. I think that Broadway has many qualities that make it an interesting place in which to work.

June 1993

6. The Broadway stage show of *Tommy* wins three Tony Awards.

Pete Townshend: When *Tommy* was on Broadway, I remember telling Rolling *Stone*, "The main thing I want from my life is dignity." In the end, I don't think I got it from having a Broadway show, but at the time I was hoping that I would. The Who, by definition, is a band which has never, ever, for a moment stood on dignity. Vanity, egotism and grandiosity perhaps, but never dignity. I think dignity has been the one thing that we've always sneered at.

7. Pete Townshend attends the ground-breaking ceremony for the new Rock'n'Roll Hall Of Fame in Cleveland, Ohio.

17. Townshend guests on "Late Night With David Letterman" on NBC-TV in the US.

David Scheff (contributing editor, *Playboy*): Before he arrived, the show's producers were all atwitter. Apparently, one of them had asked Townshend if he would, after performing, destroy his guitar. Townshend had for the most part given up smashing guitars, and he hadn't committed, but the show provided an expensive guitar just in case (Townshend had insisted that the guitar be auctioned for charity if he did it). A cameraman was flustered. "If he's going to smash the guitar, we must rehearse it!" he said.

But one of Townshend's entourage rolled her eyes. "He's not going to break a guitar," she said. "And he's certainly not going to rehearse breaking a guitar."

Townshend arrived in black, his hair cut short, Steve McQueen style, eyes sparkling. First was a rehearsal. It was something to watch up close, as Townshend played the powerful opening riff of "Pinball Wizard". Bandleader Paul Shaffer interrupted. "On the record there's a D in there somewhere," he said, and Pete politely nodded. "Right. Thanks."

Finally, it was showtime. After an opening monologue, Letterman introduced Townshend, who played a fiery "Wizard", D included. When he sang "How do you think he does it?" the Letterman band chimed in, "I don't know." Meanwhile, the producers, in the audience, were concerned about one thing: "Will he do it?" they asked one another. The cameraman waited nervously.

A couple of months later, on the MTV Music Awards show, Kurt Cobain, lead singer and guitarist for Nirvana, appeared to feign fury when he destroyed his guitar. It seemed silly. But when Townshend, on Letterman, as "Wizard" ended, lifted his guitar into the air and brought it crashing down into an amplifier, annihilating it, it was absolutely thrilling.

Pete Townshend: Yeah. I smashed the one on the Letterman show even though I didn't really want to. They asked me to do it and I told them I would if they sold the guitar for charity. They gave me a fabulous guitar – a Gibson J-200 blond, an Elvis Presley-type guitar.

20. Townshend plays at a private party for the *Tommy* cast, in the China Club, New York.

July 1993

2. The Crystal Room, Mayfair Hotel, London.

An acoustic premier of *Psychoderelict*, including the "English Boy" video, is performed in front of 100 or so press representatives, by Pete Townshend and the actors John Labanowski, Linal Haft and Jan Ravens.

Pete Townshend: I had written a bunch of songs, but I thought, "What the fuck am I doing making records, anyway? What's the point? I don't belong here any more. I'm not willing to do what is necessary." But still, I was about to deliver the songs because they were done. Then I had a bike accident and fucked up my hand. It took a year to heal, so I had all that time to think. And I decided, "Fuck it, I'm not going to put the record out. It doesn't mean anything." Before the accident I would have delivered the record. I think it would have got some interest. I would have carried on about what it was supposed to be about, and people would have thought, "Fine. The guy's getting old." Then I would have announced to the record label that I really didn't want to deliver the last couple of albums in my deal. And that would be it. But I had a year to sit there, recovering, and I thought about why I was so bored and realized that it was because I forgot why I do this for a living. Then I worked on the *Tommy* play and again became inspired about the form. I went back and listened to the new songs and asked what I was really writing about. I remembered that when I wrote the songs I was thinking about my son and thinking I wanted an honest vision of his future. That's what the songs were about.

It is a slightly comic-booky kind of story, but it contains a lot of what I wanted to say. It's what I know about. The effect of fame. Loss of family. Redemption. Regaining ideals. But then the record comes out and much of the meaning is missed, of course. A song such as "Outlive The Dinosaur" comes out and people think I'm writing about how it feels to be a dinosaur. But the song is actually about outrunning history. It's not a nod in the direction of *Jurassic Park* or The Rolling Stones. It's about trying to not become extinct, for heaven's sake.

3. Townshend's solo album *Psychoderelict* is released in the UK.

Roger Daltrey: *Psychoderelict* would have been a great Who album. *Psychoderelict* for me was fatally flawed because it was obviously autobiographical, even down to the woman, for fuck's sake, which is what's been going on. It's all out in the open now. It's been in the papers in England. It's fatally flawed because he didn't have the balls to act the character on the record, so then it becomes just pretentious.

If the Who had gotten hold of that it would have cut that pretence out and he would have written for me in the third person. It would have given it a different strength. It would have been a great Who album.

10. Townshend begins his first solo tour at Massey Hall, Toronto, Canada.

12-13. Beacon Theater, New York.

15. Tower Theater, Philadelphia, Pennsylvania.

17. Arie Crown Theatre, Chicago, Illinois.

29. When Townshend's solo tour plays at the Wiltern Theater, Los Angeles, his band is joined on stage by John Entwistle for "Magic Bus", "Let's See Action" and "Won't Get Fooled Again".

31. The original cast album of the soundtrack to the stage show of *Tommy* peaks at No. 114 on the US chart.

August 1993

2-3. Community Theater, Berkeley, California.

1994

February 1994

23-24. Roger Daltrey performs two nights of "Daltrey Sings Townshend" at Carnegie Hall, New York.

Roger Daltrey: Sheer terror the first night, mainly because we didn't have time to get a run-through of it. It was the first time we had put the whole show together. And believe me, it's a lot different playing with 70 musicians than with seven.

But the second night really did kick in. A lot of people said to me, "You've got to do this again. You've got to let other people hear this." Who music isn't like any other music. I can't sing those songs the same because I don't feel the same, but it doesn't make the way I sing them any less valid. When you're middle-aged you're no longer angry. It doesn't mean you're less passionate. It's just the anger becomes something else.

I think if you're still angry at 50 it's very unbecoming. Something's really fucking wrong.

25. Roger Daltrey performs "Substitute", backed by The Spin Doctors, on "The Late Show With David Letterman" on CBS-TV in the US.

March 1994

1. On his 50th birthday, Roger Daltrey learns in a letter that he has a daughter, Kim Binks, and a grandson, Liam, whom he has never met.

Roger Daltrey: I do remember her mother, Lydia, but only vaguely. You must realize that it was years ago and the sixties were a very wild time. It was a brief relationship but we were friends – it wasn't a one-night stand.

2. The original cast album of the soundtrack to the stage show of *Tommy* collects a Grammy, at Radio City Music Hall, New York.

April 1994

5. Kurt Cobain of Nirvana commits suicide in Seattle.

Pete Townshend: The people that have learned the lesson of Kurt Cobain's death are really just a handful of people that are very close to him. His wife, his poor little kid who's going to grow up in the spotlight without a father, and the other guys in the band. Look at my generation. How did that work? Jimi Hendrix. Brian Jones. Janis Joplin. Keith Moon. The list is fucking endless. They're dead people. My life is full of dead people. My friends are dead. My friends. They might be your fucking icons. They're my fucking friends. They're dead. Dead people in my life. Lots of them. People that I knew, fucked, loved, played with, grew up with. Now, we have Generation X which is responding to this big significant moment, which is Kurt Cobain committing suicide, and I just think this shouldn't happen again. It will happen again, but it shouldn'., In the sixties, we really thought that we were changing the world and we didn't. When we got college degrees and jobs and became lawyers and politicians, then we started to change the world. If you want to change the world, you have to get out there and change it. Music is not going to change it. Music changes the way you live in the world. It changes the way you see it. But it doesn't change the world itself.

July 1994

16. The boxed four-CD retrospective *30 Years of Maximum R&B* enters the UK album chart at its peak position, No. 48.

John Entwistle: I like some of the box. I don't like other bits of it. I prefer the video that came out at the same time. I think it's a much better item. Parts of the boxed set are interesting because it's stuff that hasn't been heard before or stuff that hasn't been heard before off of bootlegs.

23. *30 Years of Maximum R&B* reaches No. 170 in the US.

September 1994

11. Roger Daltrey's show "A Celebration: The Music Of Pete Townshend And The Who" plays at the Mann Music Center, Philadelphia, Pennsylvania.

1995

March 1995

4. A remastered, extended version of the *Live At Leeds* album peaks at No. 59 in the UK on its week of entry.

November 1995

5. At Avery Fisher Hall, New York, Roger Daltrey plays the Tin Man in an all-star charity performance of *The Wizard Of Oz.*

1996

February 1996

19. At the Brit Awards in London, Townshend presents Oasis with the Best British Group Award.

29. Townshend's solo album Empty Glass is certified platinum in the US.

Roger Daltrey: A lot of Empty Glass would have been a great Who album. It could have been a great, great album. It was a great album by Pete but if you add the magic of The Who it would have been better.

March 1996

17. CD-ROM *Pete Townshend Presents Tommy – The Interactive Adventure* is released in the US.

April 1996

23. MasterCard announces that Eric Clapton, The Who, Bob Dylan and Alanis Morissette will headline "the biggest rock concert in London's Hyde Park for 20 years", a benefit for The Prince's Trust Fund. 150,000 tickets are sold in 48 hours.

Harvey Goldsmith (promoter): Pete Townshend and I presented the first ever Prince's Trust Rock Gala and he was always very sympathetic to the charity. During the previous summer he performed a show on Long Island as a fund-raiser for kids with Paul Simon and Annie Lennox. So I called Pete up and said, "Why don't you repeat the show for Hyde Park?" But it was really Paul Simon's gig and I didn't realize that Pete was a minor part of it. He called Paul but he was writing a musical [*The Capeman*] and couldn't really do it, and Annie didn't want to work.

But Pete was really keen to do something and we talked it through. He said, "I've got this idea. Tommy's doing well, what do you think about Quadrophenia?" When Bill Curbishley [Who manager] returned from a tour abroad, we all met up and started to put the whole idea together. Pete then asked Roger Daltrey and John Entwistle to get involved. Having a premiere of sorts at Hyde Park adds a kind of poignancy to the whole show.

Pete Townshend: We went straight to Mastercard – cut out all the people in-between – got $400,000 and put the thing up. It's a strange place to be to realize that . . . all I have to do is stroll into a room with a few old guys and say, "I fancy doing *Quadrophenia* as a dramatic work," and they say "Hey, we'll give you money." That may sound cynical, but the fact is I can do it, and I trust myself to do it well.

I've never got on me knees to anyone, ever . . . but I actually said to Roger, "I really want to do *Quadrophenia* in Hyde Park and I really don't think I can do it without you." He said, "I don't really want to do it." And I said, "Well, please will you consider it and help me put it together?" And he said, "Well, what's gonna be different? You're just a [expletive] dictator." And I said, "Well, listen, you know, I'm not, I am different, I have grown up and I've learned a lot from working in music theatre, give it a crack." And he was willing to give it a crack . . . He found it very confusing at first dealing with a Pete Townshend that listened.

I asked Roger to help me stage the thing. I couldn't do it on my own. And no one could sing the stuff like he can. When he agreed, it became natural to bring John in, partly to capitalize on the feeling that this is a Who project and to make sure that we sold tickets, but partly to get the karma in. Roger didn't simply show up to be the vox. Roger and I creatively collaborated on the script. It's the first thing we've ever creatively collaborated on in our lives.

With Zak Starkey on drums and my brother on guitar we've managed to spin some karma into the piece, which makes it feel very comfortable for me.

But what Zak has is a lot of karmic Keith Moon about him, which is wonderful. It's easy to make too much of that – he really is his own drummer. He has his own style. But he's very intelligent. What he did was adapt his own style as an imitator of Keith Moon – he does a garage band imitation of Keith Moon which is probably unbeatable – but he's modified that, moderated it, in a very intelligent and musical way so that he won't be directly compared. He won't evoke uncomfortable memories for the audience.

May 1996

28. Roger Daltrey appears in the BBC Radio 4 programme "Fly Fishing By R.H. Daltrey".

June 1996

28. During rehearsals for the next day's performance of *Quadrophenia*, Roger Daltrey is accidentally hit in the eye by Gary Glitter.

29. The Who play live in Hyde Park, London. The event is a live performance of parts of *Quadrophenia*, and guests include Dave Gilmour of Pink Floyd and Gary Glitter.

Pete Townshend: I'd decided to do it solo; me, an acoustic guitar and a movie screen. Then the promoter, Harvey Goldsmith, told me half a million people were coming and I said, "I'm scared, I don't think I can do it."

John Entwistle: I had a lot of trouble at the beginning. Someone had put one of my rack units into utility mode which actually locked it. When I walked on stage it was on program 66 which is my solo program, very loud and very sustained. When I pushed the button it didn't change so during the first three songs I was in solo mode and I couldn't control the volume of the sound. I didn't realize it because the video lights in the front of the stage were shining on my equipment, on the fascia. It wasn't until the lights had dimmed a bit did I realize I was stuck in the mode. By the time I looked back from the lights to the amplifiers and back again I had a huge green blob in front of my eyes, from the lights, so I couldn't even see the fingerboard, especially at the top of the neck.

So I was messing up a lot in my high intros. I told my road manager Andy to get the lights turned off and he came back and told me they can't. So I told him to tell them I can. I was just about to go and kick the damn thing off the front of the stage. It's like having flash bulbs go off in your face. When I closed my eyes, I had nine images of video light I could see. I basically couldn't see what I was playing.

We were trying to get the whole general stage volume of the band down on stage since there were so many open mikes on stage. We try to cut them down and screen them off so you can cut the overall volume down. There was that long ramp in front of my rig and all these people kept coming down on stage in front of my equipment so I couldn't actually stand in front of the equipment. I was getting a false impression of how loud it was and I was playing a lot harder to compensate for it.

July 1996

6. During a brief return to the UK album chart, *Quadrophenia* peaks at No. 47.
16-22. *Quadrophenia* is staged at Madison Square Garden, New York, with Gary Glitter and Billy Idol in the leading roles.

Pete Townshend: You know what's really weird? In '96 and '97 we were just playing *Quadrophenia*, and one day there were a couple of girls out in the audience with leather jackets and blonde hair. And they were kind of shouting, "The Who," and I thought, "A couple of rock-chick Who fans, just like the old days. It's great that they've turned out for something as intellectual as *Quadrophenia*." Then I realized that they were actually shouting, "Be The Who! Be The Who! Be The Who!" And I thought, "That's weird. We are The Who." What they meant was, "Pretend to be The Who. Pretend to be who you used to be."
27. "My Generation" returns yet again to the UK singles chart, peaking at No. 31.

August 1996

24. The compilation *My Generation – The Very Best Of The Who* peaks at No. 11 in the UK.

October 1996

13. *Quadrophenia* goes on tour in the US, starting at the Rose Garden, Portland, Oregon.

November 1996

16. *Live At The Isle Of Wight Festival 1970* peaks at No. 194 on the US album chart.
19. The *Quadrophenia* tour ends at the Continental Airlines Arena, East Rutherford, New Jersey.

December 1996

6. *Quadrophenia* is performed at Earl's Court, London.

1997

January 1997

15. Earl's Court, London.

Sylvie Simmons (reviewer, *Rolling Stone*):

The evening is rounded off with the ultimate badge of grown-up rock, an unplugged set. It's this, not the tribulations-of-a-young-mod film, that brings on the waves of nostalgia. Your eyes see Townshend with the acoustic guitar he's worn most of the evening, then your ears hear, "pick up my guitar and play, just like yesterday" and your heart begs for no more reunions, no more rewritten history.

July 1997

19. Another US tour of *Quadrophenia* begins at Riverport Amphitheater, Maryland Heights, Missouri.

September 1997

14. Townshend unveils an English Heritage plaque, marking the house Jimi Hendrix had lived in, at 23 Brook Street, London.

November 1997

4. The Who collect a Lifetime Achievement Award at the Q Awards in the Park Lane Hotel, London.

December 1997

13. John Entwistle's parents share a lottery jackpot of £4m as part of a syndicate of 30 friends in their village, Rhiwderin, Newport, Wales.

1998

February 1998

27. Emma Townshend releases her debut album, *Winterland.*

Emma Townshend: I feel sorry for my dad in a way, because he's never not been famous. He's never done an ordinary job in an ordinary office and been treated as an ordinary person. That's quite a loss. He can't just go into a shop and listen to other people's conversations. He's never had a private glimpse into other people's worlds because he's been a rock star since he was 18.

June 1998

9. Townshend delivers an address at the memorial service for Linda McCartney, in the church of St Martin-in-the-Fields, London.

Pete Townshend: I did hold Paul McCartney in high esteem because of the way that he conducted his relationship. I have those kind of old-fashioned family values. And that has infuriated, to the point of hysteria, certain American rock critics and musicians, who think that once you've thrown a TV through a hotel-room window, that's you for life and you don't actually have a home to go to – you just grow a long beard like ZZ Top and live in a fucking Greyhound bus or something.

August 1998

14. Townshend participates in a three-day event, A Day In The Garden, held on the site of the original Woodstock Festival, in Bethel, New York.

Pete Townshend: When I appear as a solo performer, even the staunchest Who fans know that I'm going to do what I want to do and that it might be quite mischievous. So that gives me great freedom.

November 1998

27. Roger Daltrey opens as Scrooge in a Broadway staging of Charles Dickens's *A Christmas Carol.*

Roger Daltrey: I loved that. But 15 shows a week, that's fuckin' hard work, I'll tell you – it was harder than a Who tour or any tour I've ever done. Fucking exhausting.

1999

October 1999

29. US tour begins at MGM Grand Garden, Las Vegas, Nevada, where The Who earn $2m for a live on-line concert.

November 1999

13. US tour ends at The House Of Blues, Chicago, Illinois.
21. An interview with Townshend appears in the *Sunday Times*.

Pete Townshend: The Who was always a band that had a strange will. I speak to Roger now and he still thinks of The Who as a band that didn't really fail – we got a few things wrong, he'd say, but if we picked everything up from where we were before, we could go on and everything would be great.

For me, what's interesting about the latter stages of The Who was not just that we failed, it was that we failed and I was really trying hard.
29. Townshend reveals that he has left Karen, his wife of 31 years, and set up home in Richmond Hill. The break followed a four-year affair with New York fashion writer Lisa Marsh, 21 years his junior, which had ended in 1997.

Pete Townshend: The end of the marriage was not to do with the affair which I admit happened, and which Karen knows about. The affair was the symptom of our marriage being on the rocks, it was not the cause of the troubles. It's down to the fact that you change as you get older. I'm a good dad, but a bad husband.

December 1999

5. Pete Townshend's *Lifehouse* project finally gets its premiere, on BBC Radio 3 in the UK.

Pete Townshend: The bit I've always really liked about *Lifehouse* is the concert at the end, which appeals to my Philip Glass pretensions, my experimental composer pretensions, which have always been there. The ripply noises at the back of "Baba O'Riley" or the funny noises behind "Won't Get Fooled Again". I love The Who sounds but I always wanted to be a little bit arty, orchestral, cooler in a way.

6. *The Lifehouse Chronicles*, a six-CD set, is released by Townshend's Eel Pie Productions.

Pete Townshend: I've been working on *Lifehouse* for 30 years on and off (mainly off). *Lifehouse Chronicles* took about a year. The time span has not helped me, but it has helped the audience to grasp some of the ideas contained in it.

I would like to see a film made of *Lifehouse.* I have dozens of ideas. In fact I'm about to break a long-held rule and going to start making my own films. I think most film directors are a little strange, so I will have to be careful.

22-23. Two shows at the Empire, Shepherd's Bush, London mark the final concerts of the old millennium for The Who.

Pete Townshend: I enjoyed the shows. I enjoyed the fact that Roger and I have a more honest relationship now, although there's always been a lot of love between us and he's a great ally.

But it's been very – the psychological word is "co-dependent", I suppose. I've needed to have him at arm's length in order to feel that I've had any control over my life, and he's needed to feel frustrated that I won't do what he wants me to do. Another thing is the Who are so loud I worry about going deaf – John uses hearing aids in both ears now.

2000

Live album, *Blues To The Bush.*

John Entwistle: This live album is basically where we are now, after four days of rehearsals. We played a lot smoother on *Live At Leeds*, but I know damn well that I'm playing a lot better than I did on *Live At Leeds.* So you've got the better musicianship to balance it off. But it's a lot more raggedy. We could have gone in and overdubbed like crazy and made it sound wonderful, but we didn't want that. We wanted people to know bloody where we were even down to our mistakes. We did do a couple of repairs.

May 2000

28. Townshend explains his current state of mind in the *Los Angeles Times.*

Pete Townshend: What's happened to me recently is not that I've had any revelations or discovered who I am, I've just had a long period of acceptance, which is partly to do with giving up booze and finally realizing that I used to drink because it fixed something that was wrong with me – which was a feeling of being unable to fit in, unable to value myself.

So now, instead of avoiding specifics – you know, let's keep it fuckin' abstract! – I tend to be writing songs about whether I love life, or whether I love God, or whether I love my girlfriend, or whether I love me, or whether I love anybody at all.

June 2000

25. The Who begin a new 20-date US tour in Chicago, Illinois, along with Jimmy Page and The Black Crowes.

Roger Daltrey: It's Pete this time who really wants to go out and do it. And I can't believe it's happening! To be really honest, this is something that's grown out of those benefit shows last year, and I'm just taking it a day at a time. And of course, I love being with the band – to be on a stage, and even though we're playing songs that are old, they're our songs . . .

Pete Townshend: Roger and I had a little five-minute squabble during the rehearsal for the Chicago charity show, and I think we both loved it, really, in a sick kind of way. It was a misunderstanding over something, and it was meaningless, but it kind of exploded into something and we realized what we were doing was playing out old roles that had nothing to do with the way we feel today. And it was quite amusing. Most of all, I think there's an acceptance of the fact that these things happened, and they must have happened for a reason.

John Entwistle: The last couple of times, there were so many people on stage doing my job, there weren't hardly any holes for me to fit in and do my little bass bit. Now there are a lot more holes, and I can play a lot better. Pete and myself have gotten eye contact back again, so we're playing like we used to, not letting someone else play all the melody lines, which didn't allow us to improvise – which is what I always loved about The Who, and I think a lot of our fans missed that. They'd come and see *Quadrophenia* two nights in a row and it'd be almost exactly the same show. Now all the shows are different.

The John Entwistle Band is a lot harder work. Playing with The Who after that is like a holiday. I don't have to save my voice because I'm not singing, I'm not having to go to the mic to make announcements, trying to keep the whole thing going while somebody's changing a fucking string. It's a lot harder work, and touring with The John Entwistle Band is a lot more Spartan. We travel by bus, and The Who by private plane with big hotel suites. I'm lucky to get a hotel room with my band over $60. It's a cheapo, cheapo production. So The Who is a vacation compared to that.

Roger Daltrey: I think he [Townshend] is a genius. Well, let's put it this way – he was a genius. I don't know whether he is now. There's a difference between talent and genius. Talent you possess, which is what he's still got, but genius is when you are possessed, which is what he was.

I think when he wrote the songs, there was no doubt that he was a genius. And he's still got potential to become obsessive again and get back to there, but when you are like that, far too often you're surrounded by people who just tell you that everything you do is wonderful. And it's death to an artist – fucking death. Because of course a lot of what you do is wonderful, but nobody – nobody – can do everything wonderfully. We all need that person to say, "Buddy, don't be a prat — that's crap!"

Pete Townshend: The unfinished business of The Who is the friendship. I know that sounds a bit cheesy, but it's true. We did such a lot of great work together and we should have enjoyed our friendship more, and we didn't. And now we do. I think that we're finishing that, and what may come out of that might be very profound, I think.

THANKS AND ACKNOWLEDGEMENTS

Very special thanks and a big hug to Sylvie Simmons for allowing me access to unpublished material from her interviews with Roger Daltrey. Also to Dennis Locorriere for his patience.

MY OWN INTERVIEWS:

Roger Daltrey, John Entwistle, Ken Russell, Simon Napier-Bell, Barry Gibb, Ray Davies, Shel Talmy, Phil May, Keith Altham, Richard Barnes, John Steele (The Animals), Chris Downing, Chris Welch, John Einarson, John Burgoyne, John Francis, Steve Davies, George McManus, Malcolm Cook. Special thanks to Richard Barnes, author of *The Who – Maximum R'N'B* (Plexus).

BOOKS

The Who Concert File (Joe McMichael and "Irish" Jack Lyons, Omnibus, 1997)
Dear Boy: The Life Of Keith Moon (Tony Fletcher, Omnibus, 1998)
Behind Blue Eyes (Geoffrey Giuliano, Coronet, 1996)
The Who (John Swenson, Star Books, 1981)
The Who – The Illustrated Biography (Chris Charlesworth, Omnibus Books)
The Who In Sweden (compiled by Olle Lundin, Squeeze Box, 1995)
A Fortnight Of Furore – The Who And The Small Faces Down Under (Andrew Neill, Muttley Press, 1998)
The Record Producers (John Tobler and Stuart Grundy, 1982)
London Live (Tony Bacon, Balafon, 1999)
The Fillmore East (Richard Kostelanetz, Schirmer Books, 1995)
Days In The Life (Jonathon Green, Minerva, 1989)
The Who In Their Own Words (Steve Clarke, Omnibus, 1979)
Randy Bachman: Takin' Care of Business (John Einarson and Randy Bachman, McArthur & Co., 2000)
Dark Star – An Oral Biography Of Jerry Garcia (Robert Greenfield, Plexus, 1996)
Bill Graham Presents (Bill Graham and Robert Greenfield, Delta, 1992)
Quite Naturally – The Small Faces (Keith Badman and Terry Rawlings, Complete Music Publications, 1997)
Woodstock – The Oral History (Joel Makower, Sidgwick & Jackson)
The Ossie Clark Diaries (Bloomsbury, 1998)
Clapton – The Authorized Biography (Ray Coleman, Sidgwick & Jackson, 1994)

No More Sad Refrains – The Life And Times Of Sandy Denny (Clinton Heylin, Helter Skelter, 2000)
Live And Kicking – The Rock Concert Industry In The Nineties (Mark Cunningham, Sanctuary, 1999)

WEBSITES

http://www.wdkeller.com/pta.htm
http//www.geocities.com/SouthBeach/Terrace/4475/index.html

PERIODICALS

Mojo, Q, Rolling Stone, NME, Melody Maker, Generations, Record Collector, Observer, Sunday Times, Independent, Photoplay, Playboy, Daily Mail, Creem, Crawdaddy, Goldmine, International Musician, Musician, In Music We Trust, Oui, Guitarist, Guitar 1.

PEOPLE

Rob Chapman, Nina Antonia, Tony Bacon, Eddy Hailwood, Graham Seaman, David Wells, Anne Nightingale, Mike Kaufman, Nicholas Barber, Mat Snow, Phil Sutcliffe, Eamon Percival, Richie Unterberger, Alex Steininger, Sera McGovern.